Beloved of God and Called to Be Saints

What People Are Saying About *Beloved of God and Called to Be Saints*

In this book, Scott Postma strikes the fine balance of being practical without being polemical and devotional without being doctrinaire. These "crumbs" will nourish readers and encourage a deeper appreciation for the feast of Holy Scripture.

—Dr. Gregory Soderberg, Teaching Fellow in Historical Theology (The Alexandrian Institute)

Rather than offering a traditional commentary, Scott distills the riches of Romans into clear, digestible insights that reward both careful study and devotional reading.

Especially noteworthy is his treatment of Romans 9 and Romans 11. These chapters, often misunderstood or avoided, are handled with scholarly rigor and biblical faithfulness consistent with the historic Reformed tradition. Scott neither softens nor sensationalizes the doctrines found there, but allows Scripture to speak with clarity and authority.

This book is equally at home in a pastor's study, a small group setting, or around the family table during worship. The structure makes it remarkably versatile and accessible.

These "crumbs" are anything but small—they are rich, sustaining portions drawn from one of the most theologically profound letters in the New Testament.

—Brian Primer, Pastor, UpRiver Bible Church, Fernwood, Idaho

In his uniquely structured commentary on Romans, Dr. Postma writes with the soul of a Christian humanist, blending contemporary scholarship with a historical conversation spanning from Augustine to Calvin. By weaving in diverse voices like C.S. Lewis and Bob Dylan, he creates a bridge to Paul's letter for those feeling like "strangers in a strange land." Postma approaches the text with a rare mix of reverence and intellectual rigor. Even where readers disagree, they will be instructed and heartened by a guide who walks closely with the Lord and warmly invites us to do the same.

—Dr. Robert M. Woods, Director of Humanities Graduate Studies, Faulkner University

Beloved of God and Called to Be Saints combines two rare things: an orthodox understanding of Christian theology with the Christian humanist's practice of close reading. Scott Postma brings together "the whole counsel of God" to exegete Romans and reads Paul's epistle in light of the Great Tradition. The result is a clear, articulate, enjoyable day-by-day, verse-by-verse commentary on Romans. This study would be great for small groups and churches to go through together.

—Dr. Josh Herring, Founder, Logres Institute for Classical Liberal Studies

FROM THE *CRUMBS FROM OUR MASTER'S TABLE* SERIES

Beloved of God and Called to Be Saints

CRUMBS FROM PAUL'S LETTER TO THE ROMANS

SCOTT POSTMA

EPISTOLAE
PRESS

FERNWOOD, IDAHO

Published by
Epistolae Press
Fernwood, Idaho
epistolaepress.com

Cover design, interior layout, and ebook conversion by Valerie Anne Bost.
Cover image: Salomon Corrodi (1810–1892), *View of Rome with the Colosseum and the Roman Forum,* watercolor on thin cardboard, public domain.

ISBN: 978-0-9977589-0-0

Version: 20260717print

Contents

To mom, who first shared the gospel with me

and

to all those who love the gospel,

especially the unnamed Canaanite woman

whose great faith has continued to strengthen my own.

Foreword

IN *BELOVED OF GOD AND CALLED TO BE SAINTS*, SCOTT POSTMA offers not a mere commentary, but a table set with nourishing portions drawn carefully from the riches of Holy Scripture. These are, as he fittingly calls them, "crumbs from our Master's table," yet they are anything but meager. Each reflection is a theological morsel, rich with clarity, reverence, and pastoral warmth, inviting the reader not only to understand Paul's letter but to dwell within it.

Postma writes with the steady hand of one who refuses both novelty and triviality. He neither strains for originality nor retreats into abstraction, but instead allows the text to speak with a plainness that is both refreshing and deeply instructive. His work stands comfortably within the Great Tradition, echoing voices from Augustine to Calvin, while remaining accessible to the modern reader who longs for substance in an age of superficiality.

What is particularly compelling is the devotional rhythm of the work. These "crumbs" are not substitutes for the feast of Word and Sacrament, but they do what good crumbs always do: they sustain, they awaken hunger, and they remind us that even the smallest portion from the Master's table carries the wisdom, mercy, and power of God.

This volume will serve pastors, families, and congregations alike. It is well-suited for the study, the table, and the quiet morning hour. And perhaps most importantly, it trains the reader to approach Scripture not as a text to be mastered, but as a feast to be received.

REV. DR. URIESOU T. BRITO
Senior Pastor, Providence Church, Pensacola, Florida, and
Founder, Kuyperian Commentary

Introduction to *Crumbs From Our Master's Table*

WITH THE INVENTION OF THE SMARTPHONE AND THE emergence of social media, the selfie has become a social phenomenon. You've likely snapped a few of your own. And if you're a pro, you probably even have a selfie stick. What are we to make of this selfie phenomenon, anyway? According to Dr. Mariann Hardey, a lecturer in marketing at Durham University, it's all about the obsession we have with "presenting [ourselves] in the best way."[1]

This shouldn't surprise us. Presenting ourselves in the best possible light is innate to the human condition. It's one of the reasons we tend to lie. It's also why Botox, face lifts, and breast augmentations are ubiquitous in modern society. It is why photographers touch up wedding photos and school pictures. And it's why we take that one last look in the mirror before opening the door for our guests.

We give a lot of attention to how we present ourselves to the world around us, often with very little thought to the fact that it is such a natural part of our social behavior. In many cases such preparation is normal and expected. Of course we are expected to prepare for the big job interview and practice or memorize our scripts before speaking in front of an audience. It is appropriate to dress up nice to go on a date. It's responsible to put our best foot forward when we present a business plan to a group of investors. These are just a few examples where it serves the greater good to present our best selves.

1. Professor Mariann Hardey (www.durham.ac.uk/business/our-people/mariann-hardey) quoted in *The Guardian* mg.co.za/article/2013-07-26-how-selfies-became-a-global-phenomenon.

However, there are other occasions where it would be considered inappropriate and vain to present ourselves in the best way, if by "best way" we mean our most aesthetically pleasing self. For example, it would be appalling to see emergency personnel checking their hair in the mirror before performing CPR when someone's life is hanging in the balance. It would be vain for someone to wear designer clothes to a job that required coveralls or protective gear. It would be dangerous for a soldier to be concerned with the polish on his boots in the middle of combat with bullets flying over his head. In these latter cases, presenting ourselves in the best way would mean presenting our best gifts and abilities to the situation at hand and not worrying how well we aligned ourselves to popular social aesthetic conventions.

More importantly, there is a condition in which "presenting ourselves in the best way" would be eternally damning. God knows the true and particular condition of each and every person's soul, and yet there are those who would attempt to present themselves to God in the best way possible. The author of the Proverbs reminds us "Most men will proclaim every one his own goodness: But a faithful man who can find?" (Proverbs 20:6). It is common to present ourselves as good, faithful, steadfast, and loving, but like so many social media profiles, people are usually a lot better in presentation than they are in person. It seems natural for us to minimize our vices and exalt our virtues, but that's the problem. A natural man looks in the spiritual mirror, sees his flaws, and hurries past them, quickly forgetting what he really looks like (James 1:23–24).

Sometimes, however, someone comes along who surprises us. When a particular Canaanite woman came out to meet Jesus as he made his way through the district of Tyre and Sidon, the idea of "presenting herself in the best way" completely escaped her. Had she been living in modernity, one might imagine her with a smartphone trying to get a selfie with Jesus so she could post it on her feed. No doubt, uploading a picture with Jesus would have earned her a lot of "likes." Who knows, her selfie may have gone viral, and A&E would have hooked her up with her own reality TV show. (They might call it *Jesus Feeds the Dogs.*) Instead, this Gentile woman took an approach that was different than the "natural man." She debased herself in the most humiliating way: she agreed with Jesus and identified as a dog. Matthew records the account in his gospel:

> And Jesus went away from there and withdrew to the district of Tyre and Sidon. And behold, a Canaanite woman from that region came out and was crying, "Have mercy on me, O Lord, Son of David; my daughter is severely oppressed by a demon." But he did not answer her a word. And his disciples came and begged him, saying, "Send her away, for she is crying out after us." He answered, "I was sent only to the lost sheep of the house of Israel." But she came and knelt before him, saying, "Lord, help me." And he answered, "It is not right to take the children's bread and throw it to the dogs." She said, "Yes, Lord, yet even the dogs eat the crumbs that fall from their masters' table." Then Jesus answered her, "O woman, great is your faith! Be it done for you as you desire." And her daughter was healed instantly. (Matthew 15:21–28)

Typically, the dogs in Jesus' day weren't the cute household companions we think of today: pets with vaccinations, grooming, and special toys and treats. Dogs were, more often than not, mangy scavengers fit for the garbage dumps and destined to die in the streets. That's why the Jews used the term dog as a pejorative idiom to describe the Gentiles who were the pagan enemies of God. Like the four-legged scavengers of the streets and dumps, the Gentiles were appallingly unclean (Ezra 9:1–3). Jesus framed his response to the Canaanite woman by creating a word picture of a common Hebrew family eating at the dinner table and enjoying the blessings of God. These were the Israelites. Then he explained that it would be inappropriate to give the children's food to the dogs, the scavengers who were possibly laying under the table or by the front door. These were the Canaanite woman and her daughter. Jesus's insinuation is as offensive as the image is appalling.

In the 1937 Disney classic *Snow White,* the evil Queen looks into a magic mirror and asks, "Magic mirror on the wall, who is the fairest one of all?" In her vanity, she seeks the affirmation of the magic mirror to tell her what she desires to hear—that she is the fairest in the land. Her value and self-worth depend on a good report from the magic mirror. But when she learns Snow

White is the fairest in the land, she makes three brash attempts to kill her. The Queen's value and identity is completely wrapped up in a favorable report of her *self*, and her obsession with this "best" view of herself drives the plot of the fairy tale. But what are faerie stories for anyway?

According to J. R. R. Tolkien, author of *The Hobbit* and *The Lord of the Rings* trilogy, fairy tales are effective in helping us regain "a clear view" of real life. Tales like "Snow White" take us out of the familiar and place us in a realm where we are arrested by the unfamiliar, a place where we see reality more clearly. In this story, the mirror reveals the Queen is evil because the question is at the root of her heart. Not the other way around. Asking the question doesn't turn her into an evil witch; asking the question reveals that *she is an evil witch already*. Both her question and her response to the answer reveal this about her heart. She doesn't ask who is the fairest in the land to give honor where honor is due. She asks to make sure she still maintains the status of "fairest of all." Otherwise, she would not have been horrified by the answer when she learned Snow White had taken her place.

This same experience is true of us. What we see when we look in the mirror of truth and reality reveals the true condition of our hearts. And how we respond to what we see only serves to affirm what has already been revealed. According to Jesus, the one who sees herself as deserving and entitled to a fair status is blind still. He told the religious right of his day, "If you were blind, you would have no guilt; but now that you say, 'We see,' your guilt remains" (John 9:41).

Unlike Snow White's evil queen, the Canaanite woman in Matthew's gospel was not blind; she could see clearly. She could see that she did not belong at the table of the Master. She could see that, spiritually speaking, she was indeed a dog. Spiritually speaking, she was no more than a mangy scavenger whose destiny was to scrounge the garbage dumps until she finally died in the miserable streets of this damned world. Seeing her situation was desperate, she laid aside any vanity she might hope to muster, and begged for scraps, even a crumb of mercy: "Have mercy on me, O Lord, Son of David; my daughter is severely oppressed by a demon."

It would have been bad enough to have been oppressed herself, but her own oppression came vicariously through watching her daughter suffer severely. She would have readily traded places with her, but reality would not allow it. Her child was in the throes of evil, and she was helpless to change the matter. So she humbly accepted her reality and pleaded for mercy. It was not simply the kind of desperation that stirred a mother to go out of her way or suffer some minor inconvenience to cure the situation. It was the kind of desperation that moved a Canaanite, a Syrophoenician to be exact, to kneel before a Jew and ask for his help. It was the kind of desperation that moved an enemy of God to cry out to Him for mercy.

Mercy is not what the blind ask for. The blind, when they suffer hardship or evil, demand justice, or at least what they believe they deserve. The blind become distraught—and enraged—when they cannot see the reality they envision should be theirs. The blind blame the darlings for their pain and trick them into eating poisoned apples, and send hunters to pierce the heart of the "fairest in the land." Filled with bitterness, the blind spend eternity gnashing their teeth and summoning the powers of hell to give them their way. But they will never get it. And they will never, ever, see reality. They will only go on in their blindness, blindly pretending, blindly believing they are getting closer to justice, but wandering deeper and deeper in the blackness of their dark blindness. It's the helpless and undeserving, the dogs, who see; and because they see, they cry desperately for the crumbs that fall from the Master's table.

> Then Jesus answered her, "O woman, great is your faith! Be it done for you as you desire." And her daughter was healed instantly. (Matthew 15:28)

In a humorous magazine article, a pet-owning couple rushed home from work to prepare for guests they had invited to dinner, only to discover their dog had been sick and left his stomach contents—along with its putrid odor—throughout the entire house. The article recounted the rollicking antics of the couple's unfortunate discoveries and hilarious attempts to rectify their situation. Eventually, they determined one of them had left packages of thawing steaks, intended for their guests, low enough for the dog to get a hold of them. The moral of the story was captured in the title of the article: "Raise the Steaks!"

One of the great things about the gospel is its accessibility. Jesus didn't "raise the steaks" as it were. He put the gospel down on the bottom shelf where everyone—including the dogs—could get to it (Galatians 3:28–29). The Canaanite woman's desperate situation opened her eyes to the severity and hopelessness of her spiritual condition. When she humbled herself and acknowledged that Jesus's assessment of her condition was true, the gospel, having always been well within reach, was now visible to her once blind eyes.

Notably, during this period of history, the Gentiles of the Tyre region were constantly robbing the poor Jews of earthly bread. By acknowledging Jesus as Lord, i.e., Son of David (v. 22), the Jews as the children of the Lord (cf. Mark 7:27–28), and herself as a dog, the Canaanite woman was doing more than acknowledging her humble station as a sinner alien to the commonwealth of Israel (Ephesians 2:12). She was also making a spiritual observation about this ongoing conflict between the Jews and the Canaanites of the region. In a word, she was acknowledging the priority of Israel in God's plan to provide spiritual bread to the Gentiles through the Jews; and in an expression of faith, she thought it not stealing to eat the crumbs that fell from the Master's table. Again, Matthew's gospel records the event:

Jesus said to her, "O woman, great is your faith!" By resisting her initial request, but without heeding his disciples' plea to send her away, Jesus tried her faith, revealing *a mere crumb of the great wisdom of God.*

"Be it done for you as you desire," Jesus said. By answering her petition, he gave her *a mere crumb of mercy*, a foretaste of the healing all his elect would experience when the fullness of his kingdom is realized (Revelation 21:4).

Scripture further tells us, "And her daughter was healed instantly." By healing the woman's daughter, Jesus revealed *a mere crumb of the power of God.* Not many days later, He would unleash the full power of the Godhead by dying on a cross and then raising to life again (Romans 1:16, cf. 2 Corinthians 13:4).

This same wisdom, mercy, and power of God is available to every dog who desires the crumbs that fall from our Master's table (John 6:37).

When I was a kid, my mom would make oversized, sweet rolls, thick with rich cinnamon-sugar and plump raisins smeared between every layer. The outer layers were sweet and flaky, slightly crunchy. They were perfect for dipping in milk or coffee. But my brother's and I loved the center of the cinnamon roll, where all the sweet, buttery goodness was absorbed into the dough and kept the pastry soft and gooey. If there wasn't milk to dip the crunchy outer layers in, we might pass these "crumbs" to the dog so we could focus on the rich gooey center. One might say we were cinnamon roll snobs. Crumbs are mere morsels, beggar's food. They are not what the deserving eat; they are niblets for the desperate and humble. Snobs abhor crumbs. They do not suffer paupers' vittles. Their palates crave rich, moist cuisine. They won't tolerate the crumbs. But those who are truly hungry, beggars, happily find satisfaction in the crumbs that Jesus drops for us.

When the Canaanite woman said, "Yes, Lord, yet even the dogs eat the crumbs that fall from their masters' table," she wasn't asking for the center of the cinnamon roll as it were. She was content with the discarded crusty edges because they were more than she deserved, more than enough to meet her needs, and more delicious and satisfying than any of the delicacies the world had to offer. The world's meat left her spiritually desperate, but mere crumbs changed her life, because they were crumbs from the Master's table.

Typically, crumbs will not sustain a person long term. To grow strong and live healthy, one must have milk and meat and bread and wine. But crumbs can offer sustenance for the in-between times. Even though crumbs are often just scraps, leftovers from the children's plates or food prep in the kitchen, there is nourishment in every morsel when they come from the Master's table. In fact, crumbs are not a substitute for the weekly meal of Word and Sacraments dished generously from the Lord's table on the Sabbath, but they are good for daily food; and they're great with a cup of coffee in the morning.

The *Crumbs from Our Master's Table* series is a daily morsel of theological soul food—not a sermon mind you—just a crumb of nourishment from Scripture, usually one or two verses at a time. These crumbs were originally emailed each morning to subscribers at *Books and Letters* (scottpostma.net). They are collected here in a single volume to be read devotionally or as a simple commentary on a book of the Bible.

Introduction to Paul's Letter to the Romans

THIS VOLUME TREATS PAUL'S LETTER TO THE CHURCH AT Rome, written around AD 57. Letters such as this are called *occasional* letters, epistles written to a particular communion of Christians for a particular occasion. This means Paul's letters are not theological treatises or systematic theologies, per se; rather, they are letters written to address immediate and specific concerns. Because these letters are not written to us directly, they function as *literature* in the most fundamental sense of the word. Of course, they are, without a doubt, divinely inspired literature; so even though they are not written *to* us, we must read them as having been written and preserved *for* us. Thus, the instructions, exhortations, corrections, and encouragements must be applied to our own lives in principle. In other words, to read them properly, we must consider the occasion under which Paul wrote a specific letter to understand how he intended the letter to be understood by the original audience; only then can we lift those theological principles from the context of Paul's writing and apply them to our own situation. I have attempted to do that in my own comments.

The occasion for this specific letter is Paul's desire for those in first-century Rome who are "beloved of God and called to be saints" to support his missionary work to Spain. Because he is interested in laying out before them his vision for Christian ministry so they can be assured he is worthy of their support, his letter is subsequently packed with theology. As a matter of fact, Paul's letter to the Church at Rome is his longest and most sustained theological explanation of the gospel. Thus, we can say the theme of this letter is the gospel's power to save the unrighteous and establish a flourishing humanity in the new age of Spirit-led liberty, a humanity that is united in and by Jesus Christ for the glory of God the Father.

In my comments on Paul's letter, I have not sought to be original; neither have I sought to appease any particular theological tradition, denomination, or ideology. I write as a Christian humanist, one who, with Irenaeus, believes the glory of God is a living man, and with Erasmus, that Christ is more interested in personal piety than our straining pedantically over the finer points of dogma, and with J. I. Packer and Jens Zimmerman, that Christianity is the ultimate humanism since it is deeply concerned with texts, human flourishing, and society's common good.

My approach is to simply exposit the text as plainly as possible, verse by verse as much as Paul's intended thought allows. On occasion, I draw on insights from other commentaries or expound on the original language, especially where I believe others' words express the meaning best, and where a treatment of the original language provides some weighty or significant insight. Taking a cue from C. S. Lewis, who noted the best devotional reading was chewing on some rich theology, this work can serve as both commentary and devotional. Yet, as I mentioned in the series introduction, these readings are mere crumbs, crumbs from our Master's table, to be sure; but they are just theological morsels meant to foster your appetite for the whole meal of Scripture; they are no substitute for Word and Sacrament.

Notwithstanding, it is my prayer that daily ruminating on Paul's thoughts about the gospel will help you better follow the One to whom our apostle and man of letters, in his great liberty, found himself endearingly enslaved.

SCOTT POSTMA
Advent 2025

Crumbs from Paul's Letter to the Romans

1. The Revelation of a Personal Introduction

Paul, a servant of Christ Jesus, called to be an apostle, set apart for the gospel of God . . . —*Romans 1:1*

HOW A PERSON INTRODUCES HIMSELF IS REVEALING. RECALL how you introduce yourself at various gatherings: at a work-related cocktail party or a church potluck, to a new neighbor, to a stranger you sit next to on an airplane.

Since the apostle Paul had not yet been to Rome, the letter he was writing to the church organized there required a proper introduction. The way he introduced himself needed to give them some idea of his person and ministry.

To this end, Paul identifies himself as a *doulos* (a bond servant) of Jesus Christ. *Doulos* can also be translated as *slave.* Either way, the description implies he is under the complete and utter control of Christ.

Next, he acknowledges that he is *called to* the office of an apostle. A couple of observations are noteworthy. To be called is to be *officially* invited. And such invitations, while voluntary, are not optional. In medieval times, the expression, *Durante bene placito regis* (meaning "during the good pleasure of the king"), was used to convey the essential idea that someone was holding their official position at the King's will. On the flip side, they also recognized they could be removed from that office at any time without explanation. Today, we often hear the expression, "I serve at the pleasure of the President." This is the idea that Paul has in mind.

In its most generic sense, an apostle in the early church often denoted anyone who proclaimed the gospel and was not strictly limited. However, more formally, it was a designation given to one who had been sent by Christ, a title that was applied to highly honored believers who had been recognized by the church to have a special function as God's envoys.

Finally, Paul is *set apart* for the gospel of God. That is, he has been consecrated to do a specific work, the work of preaching and ministering to Gentiles. Thus, his use most likely falls into the latter, more formal designation.

Taking this altogether, the language Paul uses seems to indicate that he had, at least proverbially, identified with the OT slaves who affirmed their allegiance to their masters even after their obligations were up, because the circumstances on his Master's estate were clearly blessed of God and better for his family:

> Now these are the judgments which thou shalt set before them. If thou buy an Hebrew servant, six years he shall serve: and in the seventh he shall go out free for nothing. If he came in by himself, he shall go out by himself: if he were married, then his wife shall go out with him. If his master have given him a wife, and she have born him sons or daughters; the wife and her children shall be her master's, and he shall go out by himself. And if the servant shall plainly say, I love my master, my wife, and my children; I will not go out free: Then his master shall bring him unto the judges; he shall also bring him to the door, or unto the door post; and his master shall bore his ear through with an aul; and he shall serve him for ever. (Exodus 21:1–6)

In essence, like the slave, Paul could honestly say, "I love my master . . . I will not go out free."

2. A Promise Kept

. . . which he promised beforehand through his prophets in the holy Scriptures . . .
—Romans 1:2

IN THE INTRODUCTION OF HIS LETTER TO THE CHRISTIANS IN Rome, Paul establishes his office as one who has been entrusted with the gospel, the good news for which the children of Israel had been waiting. And it was not just for them, but for the whole world.

The gospel is the good news that what had been promised by God's prophets in the holy Scriptures (i.e., Old Testament) concerning Messiah had now been realized in the person of Jesus Christ, as he will demonstrate in the verses following.

Paul preaches a similar message in Antioch of Pisidia when he says, "And we bring you the good news that what God promised to the fathers, this he has fulfilled to us their children by raising Jesus, as also it is written in the second Psalm, "'You are my Son, today I have begotten you'" (Acts 13:32–33).

At the close of this letter to the Romans, Paul will exhort his readers with an application of what he said here at the opening of the letter, namely that what was promised in ages past is being fulfilled now in his time.

> Now to him who is able to strengthen you according to my gospel and the preaching of Jesus Christ, according to the revelation of the mystery that was kept secret for long ages but has now been disclosed and through the prophetic writings has been made known to all nations, according to the command of the eternal God, to bring about the obedience of faith—to the only wise God be glory forevermore through Jesus Christ! Amen. (Romans 16:25–27)

What Paul establishes here is that God keeps his promises and can be trusted. Moreover, what has been manifested in Christ Jesus, this fulfillment of the promise, is the most significant turning point in human history so far—the redemption of the cosmos and the creation of a new humanity has begun.

From this time forth, nothing will ever be the same.

3. Creeds: A Faithful Witness

. . . concerning his Son, who was descended from David according to the flesh and was declared to be the Son of God in power according to the Spirit of holiness by his resurrection from the dead, Jesus Christ our Lord . . . —Romans 1:3–4

IT IS WELL ARGUED AND PROBABLY ACCURATE THAT PAUL IS using an early church creed in his explanation of the gospel to the church at Rome. Doing so not only lends him credibility with the Roman church that doesn't yet know him, personally, but it also accurately articulates orthodox Christian belief held by the apostles that had been with Jesus in his earthly ministry.

In the first place, the creed contrasts and connects the two natures of Jesus (hypostatic union): his human nature as part of the lineage of David and his divine nature (declared to be the Son of God) according to the spirit of holiness (not to be confused with the Holy Spirit or Holy Ghost who is the third person of the Godhead), the proof of which was demonstrated by his resurrection from the dead.

This Son of God is, in fact, Jesus, the Christ (Messiah), our Lord (*Kyrios*). It is by him all things were created and through him that all things consist (Colossians 1:16, 20)—including Paul's own ministry.

In addition to learning from his theology, one important takeaway from Paul's example is his use of creeds. We would be helped to know that less than thirty years after the resurrection of Christ, there were already creeds in circulation amongst Christians summarizing orthodox faith. While Scripture is premiere, we would be wise not to dismiss—as some modern traditions have unfortunately done—the trustworthy summaries of Christian faith that the Church has produced over its long history.

They are as helpful today for the edification of believers as they were in the early church.

4. Gifts and Callings

... through whom we have received grace and apostleship to bring about the obedience of faith for the sake of his name among all the nations ... —Romans 1:5

ANOTHER WAY TO SAY THIS IS, THROUGH [CHRIST] (VV. 3–4), we received grace and apostleship to call all the Gentiles to the obedience that comes from faith for his name's sake.[1]

The obedience of faith refers to the obedient act of believing the gospel of Christ.

> But thanks be to God, that you who were once slaves of sin have become obedient from the heart to the standard of teaching to which you were committed ... But they have not all obeyed the gospel. For Isaiah says, "Lord, who has believed what he has heard from us?" (Romans 10:16, 6:17).

In sum, the apostle Paul was sent to the Gentiles to preach the gospel to them that they might believe (i.e., obedience that comes from faith) for Christ's namesake. (See Acts 9:15, cf. Romans 11:13, Ephesians 3:8).

It is through Christ that Paul, on the road to Damascus, received grace and apostleship (Acts 9: 1–16). And, this is true of all believers. It is through Christ that each of us receive our particular gifts and callings.

> There is one body and one Spirit—just as you were called to the one hope that belongs to your call— one Lord, one faith, one baptism, one God and Father of all, who is over all and through all and in all. But grace was given to each one of us according to the measure of Christ's gift ... And he gave the apostles, the prophets, the evangelists, the shepherds and teachers, to equip the saints for the work of ministry, for building up the body of Christ, until we all attain to the unity of the

1. Colin G. Kruse, *Paul's Letter to the Romans*, ed. D. A. Carson, The Pillar New Testament Commentary *(Grand Rapids, MI: Eerdmans, 2012)*, 49.

> faith and of the knowledge of the Son of God, to mature manhood, to the measure of the stature of the fullness of Christ, so that we may no longer be children, tossed to and fro by the waves and carried about by every wind of doctrine, by human cunning, by craftiness in deceitful schemes. (Ephesians 4:4–7, 11–14)

While the passage under consideration is not directly prescriptive, it should invoke a question in each of us: If God's gifts and callings to all believers are irrevocable (Romans 11:29), how well are we stewarding those gifts we have received for the purpose for which they were given—to bring about the obedience that comes from faith (i.e., the salvation of the nations) for his namesake?

5. We Are All His Subjects

. . . including you who are called to belong to Jesus Christ, To all those in Rome who are loved by God and called to be saints:

Grace to you and peace from God our Father and the Lord Jesus Christ . . .
—Romans 1:6–7

RIGHT OUT OF THE GATE, IN PAUL'S INTRODUCTION AND greeting, readers are met with a pair of curious expressions: "you who are *called* to belong to Jesus Christ" and "all those in Rome who are *loved by God* and *called* to be saints."

The word *called* is the Greek word, *κλητός (kletos),* and means God's summons or appointment. Note its presence as the root word for church, *ἐκκλησία* (*ekklesia* = called-out assembly).

In some limited uses *κλητός* can merely mean *invited* as when Jesus said, "For many are *called,* but few are chosen" (Matthew 22:14), but of the eleven times the word is used in the New Testament, it is only used this way once, as noted here.

Paul is telling the Roman believers that their salvation (*their obedience of faith for the sake of Christ's name among all nations*; v. 5) came from the Lord who "set them apart" as *saints.* (*Saints* = *ἅγιος* = set apart, holy, sanctified.) In this scenario, God is the actor in salvation and the Roman believers are the receptors.

Finally, grace and peace are extended to them (all those in Rome who are loved by God). Note again that they are the objects of God's love and God's is the one who loves cf. "We love because he first loved us" (1 John 4:19).

One of the most important aspects of our walk with Christ is not so much understanding that "Christianity is a relationship rather than a religion" (as we so often hear), but understanding the orientation of that relationship. If we don't get that right, we'll miss everything else of significance.

And if we do get it right, the first thing we're likely to become aware of is the fact that God is *not* democratic. As we will soon discover, he is a faithful and just monarch; and we are all his subjects.

6. All The World Knows About You

First, I thank my God through Jesus Christ for all of you, because your faith is proclaimed in all the world. —Romans 1:8

THE USE OF THE WORD *FIRST* IS SORT OF A TRADEMARK OF THE apostle's writing. It's possible he means that *before* he addresses anything else, he wants to start with thanksgiving.

But given he dictates most of his letters using a scribe, scholars suggest his letters can appear to be more in the form of "streams of consciousness" (i.e., a first without a second) than a formally outlined letter. That said, this letter to the Romans is quite well structured, so my conclusion is the former explanation is more weighty.

I further suggest the following chiastic structure of chapters best informs us of Paul's ultimate purpose in writing to the Romans.

1:1–17 Introduction
- 1:18–3:30 Chaos (Devolution of Humanity)
  - 4–5 Faith Saves
    - 6–7 Two Regimes
      - 8 The Glory of the Gospel
    - 9–11 Two Branches
  - 12–13 Faith Works
- 14–15 Cosmos (Evolution of Humanity)

16 Farewell

Paul thanks God for all of them *through Jesus Christ* because without Christ, we have no access to the throne room of God (Ephesians 2:18, 3:12, cf. Romans 5:2 and Hebrews 4:16).

He is thankful *to* God *for* them because they possess the same faith he is preaching, and they are in Rome, the epicenter of the known world. Additionally, their faith is not obscure, but has a good reputation throughout the known world of that day.

7. The Gospel of His Son

For God is my witness, whom I serve with my spirit in the gospel of his Son, that without ceasing I mention you always in my prayers, asking that somehow by God's will I may now at last succeed in coming to you. —Romans 1:9–10

PAUL HERE MAKES A SOLEMN AFFIRMATION OF THE TRUTH, literally an oath, of two things to which only God has knowledge. The first being that he prays for them consistently and the second being that he desires—if it be God's will—that he can go to Rome to see them.

One particularly noteworthy consideration is that Paul sees the gospel of God's son (Jesus) as central to his service to God. The gospel is defined by Paul in verses 2–4 as relating to the fulfillment of God's Messianic promise through the line of David and confirmed by the power demonstrated in resurrection.

The resurrection of Jesus is the chief event regarding the gospel of God—the good news that the Kingdom of God has come in the person of Jesus Christ. In other words, for Paul, everything depends on the resurrection. He further confirms and expounds on this precept in his letter to the Corinthians (1 Corinthians 15:1–58 is worth reading at length).

If the resurrection of Christ is true, there is nothing else more worthy of living for. If it's not, then we who proclaim Christ are of all men most miserable.

8. Mutually Encouraged

For I long to see you, that I may impart to you some spiritual gift to strengthen you— that is, that we may be mutually encouraged by each other's faith, both yours and mine. —Romans 1:11–12

PAUL HERE IS INDICATING THAT ONE OF THE REASONS HE longs to go to Rome and see the believers there is for mutual encouragement. First, he wants to impart some spiritual gift to strengthen them; and, second, he wants to be encouraged by their faith as they will be encouraged by his.

Spiritual gift (πνευματικὸν χάρισμα *pnuematikon charisma*) is used in a general sense, meaning anything that builds up their spiritual life. But as we shall see, one specific gift Paul hopes to receive is the Church's support for his ministry to Spain.

Spiritual gifts are mentioned again in his letters to the Corinthians (12:1–11) and to the Ephesians (4:7–16). Peter also instructs his readers in spiritual gifts (1 Peter 4:7–11)

While there has been much debate in the modern church as to what the spiritual gifts consist of, it's clear in the context of Paul's other letters that in contrast to being worshippers of dead idols, the living Holy Spirit of God issues gifts to Christ's followers as he pleases and when he wills in order to support the advancement of the gospel and the common good of humanity.

Paul is not suggesting he had the power to impart these gifts but that through his ministry, the Spirit would work (ἐνεργῶν *energon* cf. 1 Corinthians 12:6) to strengthen the faith of the Roman Christians as well as his own through their ministry to him. His coming would be for their mutual benefit.

This is one of the primary reasons why it is essential for believers to live in covenantal community with one another—*that we may be mutually encouraged by each other's faith* via our unique spiritual gifts.

9. Not Our Schedule; Not our Agenda

I do not want you to be unaware, brothers, that I have often intended to come to you (but thus far have been prevented), in order that I may reap some harvest among you as well as among the rest of the Gentiles. —Romans 1:13

PAUL HAD OFTEN INTENDED TO GO TO ROME TO BE WITH THE church there. The word *often* seems to mean he had made *frequent* attempts but had been providentially hindered from going to Rome on those occasions (i.e., prevented is translated from *κωλύω* [koluō] meaning to keep something from happening, hinder, prevent, forbid).[2]

Since Paul is writing this letter in about AD 57, near the end of his third missionary journey, one of those occasions was perhaps Claudias' expelling of all Jews from the city of Rome (c. AD 41–53). Suetonius suggests that around AD 49 Claudius exiled the Jews from Rome because they were raising havoc over one named *Chrestus*. Could this be a variation of Christos (*χριστος*)?

In Acts 18:2 we learn Aquila and Pricilla were exiled from Rome by Claudius because they were Jews. By the time Paul writes this letter to the church at Rome, however, he sends them a greeting; therefore, it is assumed they have returned.

This is also likely why the church at Rome is predominantly Gentile by this point—many Jews had left the region—and Paul hopes to reap some harvest among them—as well as among the rest of the Gentiles.

Being providentially hindered from going before is not a setback in Paul's estimation because he serves at the pleasure of the Lord, not his own schedule or agenda.

2. William Arndt et al., A Greek-English Lexicon of the New Testament and Other Early Christian Literature (Chicago: University of Chicago Press, 2000), 580.

10. The Weight of the Debt of the Gospel

I am under obligation both to Greeks and to barbarians, both to the wise and to the foolish. So I am eager to preach the gospel to you also who are in Rome.
—Romans 1:14–15

AS THEOLOGIANS ARE OFTEN DIVIDED ABOUT NUANCES OF meaning in words and the construction of language, various theories abound about the meaning of Paul's obligation to these various categories of Gentiles.

Some scholars suggest the Gentiles had contributed to his understanding of the meaning of life. He was first educated at Tarsus (Roman education; his father was a Roman citizen) and then later at the feet of Gamaliel (Jewish education).

Others have suggested that he had "harvested fruit" (see vs 13) among the various nations and was thus indebted to all of them. This is why he now hoped to gather fruit among the Romans as well; thus, depending on how one views the expression, Paul wanted to either incur a debt with them in Rome as well or discharge his debt to all Gentiles by preaching to them at Rome.

While there may be some measure of truth to each of these theories, it is more likely Paul Minear's explanation best expresses Paul's meaning: "To the extent that Paul was indebted to God for this call, to that very extent he was indebted to those Gentiles for whose sake God had called him."[3]

Understanding his meaning this way has a universal application in that believers should see the gospel as imposing a debt on all of us who receive it, a debt for which the only repayment consists of passing on the good news of Jesus Christ to someone else.[4]

Jesus paid the sin debt of the world (1 John 2:2). Some have, by the grace of God, realized the significance of that payment and trusted in Christ's mercy; others are still lost in their sins, groping for the truth. Perhaps, Paul's *eagerness to preach the gospel* to the Romans reveals the degree to which he realized the weight of the debt of the gospel.

3. Paul S. Minear: *The Obedience of Faith* (London, 1971) quoted by Leon Morris, *The Epistle to the Romans*, The Pillar New Testament Commentary (Grand Rapids, MI: W.B. Eerdmans, 1988), 63.
4. Morris, *The Epistle to the Romans*, 63.

11. Not Ashamed of the Gospel

For I am not ashamed of the gospel, for it is the power of God for salvation to everyone who believes, to the Jew first and also to the Greek. For in it the righteousness of God is revealed from faith for faith, as it is written, "The righteous shall live by faith." —Romans 1:16–17

AND HERE, BY WAY OF INTRODUCTION, IS PAUL'S ENTIRE MISsion for living and the point of his letter wrapped up in a simple aphorism. He states emphatically, that he is *not ashamed* of the gospel (cf. Mark 8:38), then explains why.

In the first place, ashamed (ἐπαισχύνομαι *epaischynomai*) means to experience a painful feeling or sense of loss of status because of some particular event or activity.[5] For Paul, who had quite the resume amongst the Jewish rulers and community, believing and preaching the good news of Jesus Christ's death, burial and resurrection was no loss of status, and it was certainly worth suffering for. Actually, it was worth more than anything else in this world (cf. Philippians 3:4–11).

The reason *why* is that he understood the value, the scope, and the efficacy of the gospel he preached. It was the power of God unto salvation (cf. 1 Corinthians 1:18). It was for everyone who believes—Jew and Greek alike (cf. Galatians 3:28 and Romans 10:12). It revealed God's righteousness—both God's attributes as revealed in the person of Jesus Christ and our standing as possessing the righteousness of God imputed in the person of Jesus Christ—from faith to/for faith.

That is, the gospel is based on faith through and through. God's faithfulness sends Christ (cf. Romans 3:21–22). Our faith is a gift from God (Ephesians 2:8–10) that enables us to grasp Christ. We demonstrate that faith in God's promise by growing up into faithful men and women of God (Ephesians 4:13–15).

5. William Arndt et al., *A Greek-English Lexicon of the New Testament and Other Early Christian Literature* (Chicago: University of Chicago Press, 2000), 357.

12. All the Way to Their Bitter End

For the wrath of God is revealed from heaven against all ungodliness and unrighteousness of men, who by their unrighteousness suppress the truth. —Romans 1:18

HAVING INTRODUCED HIMSELF AND HIS PURPOSE FOR WRITing this letter—it's all about the gospel of Jesus—Paul immediately turns to show man's need of God's righteousness before showing what it is and how it works in the human experience.

Why does mankind need the righteousness of God? Because every last one is under the "wrath of God," who is "implacably and vigorously opposed to every evil." God does not overlook one single sin. He is not passive concerning the transgression of his law; and therefore every single one of us must give an account of himself to God one day (cf. Romans 14:12 and Hebrews 4:13).

And how is the wrath of God revealed? In some ways, we can see it in the suffering and pain that are the inherent consequence of sin. Ironically, the refusal to see this dynamic by much of the secular world is a sad consequence of secularism itself. Modern man now fails to equate much of the world's pain and suffering—even much of our own individual pain and suffering—as being a consequence of our sin, as being the wrath of God revealed from heaven. For many to make such a connection would be absurd, or would make God a monster in their eyes.

But, it is more likely that Paul means here *the cross of Christ.* Calvary is the revelation of the wrath of God, the just dying for the unjust because the wages of sin is death in a moral universe.

And this wrath is not the arbitrary and capricious feelings of God. Rather, is the objective outpouring of justice on the ungodliness and uprightness of men, men who in and by way of their unrighteousness, suppress the truth. Man is not ignorant of his responsibilities to God which is why atheists often tend to be angry at someone they claim not to believe exists.

Atheists, agnostics, and idolators are all unrighteous men who know the truth but choose to suppress it by embracing and promoting their unrighteousness all the way to their bitter end.

13. It's So Plain They Are Without Excuse

For what can be known about God is plain to them, because God has shown it to them. For his invisible attributes, namely, his eternal power and divine nature, have been clearly perceived, ever since the creation of the world, in the things that have been made. So they are without excuse. —Romans 1:19–20

NO ONE CAN HONESTLY SAY THERE IS NOT A GOD, OR THAT God does not see, or does not care. Everything about him that can be known, including his invisible attributes like eternal power and divine nature, have not only been revealed but revealed in such a way as to have been clearly perceived throughout the natural order ever since the creation of the world.

This is what theologians refer to as general revelation. Though nature does not tell us about our need for salvation or how to attain it, nature does tell us there is a Creator and Sustainer of the cosmos to whom we are accountable in some way. This is also what Galileo called *the first book* of God; the second being the Holy Scriptures.

Mankind is, therefore, without excuse for suppressing the truth in rejecting, denying, and rebelling against God because he has literally shown himself to all of creation in a way that can easily be perceived.

Verses 18–20 lay the foundation for the devolution of man; that is, his declining trajectory as a result of the fall. While Paul gives us this picture in a historical sense, the pattern can be witnessed in individuals as well as societies and generations of people.

God reveals himself in creation to such a degree that his eternal power and Godhead are so apparent that no man could deny it. In response, man suppresses the truth—he lies to himself and to others—and as it is yet to be demonstrated, he subsequently refuses to honor God or be grateful to him (v. 21).

14. The Darkness of a Foolish Heart

For although they knew God, they did not honor him as God or give thanks to him, but they became futile in their thinking, and their foolish hearts were darkened. —Romans 1:21

THE WORD *FOR* REMINDS US THAT PAUL IS LAYING OUT HIS argument logically. That is, one thing follows another. One choice has consequences which produces another choice with consequences, and so on.

Since mankind (humanity) possessed real knowledge of God and chose to suppress the truth, they refused to give him the honor or glory due to him as God. This is not a circumstance of ignorance. It's deliberate. There are enough of God's attributes revealed in creation to warrant certain honor and certain thanksgiving; yet, they refused.

Because they refused, they became futile, or vain, empty, in their thinking. In other words, the thoughts of humanity were pointless and vainglorious; they chose their own way—man-constructed religion instead of God-given revelation. Thus, their foolish hearts were darkened (cf. Psalm 14:1 and 53:1). Because they rejected the light (said in their hearts there is no God), they were left in darkness (without light). It was their choice.

One common metaphor is that denying God this way is akin to trying to hold a beach ball underwater all the while denying the existence of beach balls. One can't sustain such a posture for long before there are real consequences (i.e., beach ball will shoot up eventually).

The idolatry of mankind (worship a god of one's own making) is a denial of reality that can only logically lead to darker and darker delusions: there is no God and man is the maker of himself. He is "the master of [his] fate . . . the captain of [his] soul."[6] The gods he creates for himself tell him he can worship as he pleases, indulge as he pleases, have sex with whom he pleases, be whatever he pleases.

6. William Ernest Henly, "Invictus," 1875.

Thus, the "woke," trans-delusional society we are witnessing in the 21st century is the only possible result of a society that first really knew God, but refused to honor him as God or give him thanks.

15. An Ignominious Exchange

Claiming to be wise, they became fools, and exchanged the glory of the immortal God for images resembling mortal man and birds and animals and creeping things. —Romans 1:22–23

THE RESULT OF THEIR FUTILE THINKING IS A TRAGIC IRONY. They gave up the glory of the immortal God, not just for images (idols) resembling mortal man, but also for lower idols resembling birds, animals, and insects. This is the outcome of rejecting God. What else could a darkened foolish heart, contrive.

In one way, the arrogant, foolish thinking Paul has in mind is reminiscent of what scholars have assumed was Gaucus's hubris and stupidity when he and Diomedes exchanged armor on the battlefield of Troy:

> For Diomed's brass arms, of mean device,
> For which nine oxen paid, (a vulgar price,)
> He gave his own, of gold divinely wrought,
> A hundred beeves the shining purchase bought.[7]

Having lost his mind, he traded armor of gold worth 100 beef cows for armor of brass that cost just nine oxen. Something like, "I'll give you my new Rolls Royce for that 1970s Ford Pinto." Or in C. S. Lewis's estimation, it's like a child giving up a holiday at the beach to make mud pies in the backyard.

Likely Paul had in mind Psalm 106:20 "They exchanged the glory of God for the image of an ox that eats grass," which references the incident in Exodus 32:1–34 where the children of Israel abandoned their covenant with God to make golden calves to worship.

One other possible incident could be the Adamic fall in which Adam and Eve, seeking to be wise, only became foolish by partaking of the fruit (Genesis 3:1–7).

7. Homer, *Pope's The Iliad of Homer*, trans. Alexander Pope, ed. Paul Shorey (Boston: D. C. Heath & Co., 1899), book VI, lines 292–295.

In any case, this seems to be the red thread through human history. Man rejects God in order to be his own god; but having rejected the light, his foolish, darkened heart is self-deceptive and he believes the idols he fashions with his own hands (and its pseudo-divinity in which he imparts to it with his futile mind) are the true gods, the true religion of man.

16. God Gave Them Up to Dishonor

Therefore God gave them up in the lusts of their hearts to impurity, to the dishonoring of their bodies among themselves, because they exchanged the truth about God for a lie and worshiped and served the creature rather than the Creator, who is blessed forever! Amen. —Romans 1:24–25

AT THIS STAGE OF PAUL'S ARGUMENT, HE PURPOSES TO MAKE clear that God is active in the process by which the consequences of sin follow the committing of sin. It's true, we live in a moral universe which holds intrinsic consequences for sin but that does not mean God is strictly passive as the Deists suppose. Rather, when they consciously gave God up for idols, he gave them up in the lust of their hearts.

God said there would be certain consequences for sin, and yet he providentially governs the natural course of those things he decrees.

He says, "So I gave them over to their stubborn hearts, to follow their own counsels" (Psalm 81:12).

> And they made a calf in those days, and offered a sacrifice to the idol and were rejoicing in the works of their hands. But God turned away and gave them over to worship the host of heaven, as it is written in the book of the prophets: "Did you bring to me slain beasts and sacrifices, during the forty years in the wilderness, O house of Israel? You took up the tent of Moloch and the star of your god Rephan, the images that you made to worship; and I will send you into exile beyond Babylon." (Acts 7:41–43)

That is not to say, he is capricious, malicious, or vindictive. Rather, he allows them to have what they demand; and in having it, they also get the consequence. The consequence of their lustful desire is impurity. And as is the case with sin, it costs more than the sinner bargains for.

Because they exchanged the truth about God for a lie and worshipped and served idols, their foolish hearts were darkened, which led to a passionate desire for forbidden pleasure. God, giving them up to their lustful pleasures, allowed them to suffer a particular impurity, the dishonoring of their bodies among themselves.

As Franz Leenhart notes, "Man has mocked the honour of God by deifying the bodies of creatures erected into idols; God therefore abandons man to passions which dishonour his own body."[8]

8. Franz J. Leenhardt: *The Epistle to the Romans* (London, 1961).

17. The Tyrannical Other Ruler

For this reason God gave them up to dishonorable passions. For their women exchanged natural relations for those that are contrary to nature; and the men likewise gave up natural relations with women and were consumed with passion for one another, men committing shameless acts with men and receiving in themselves the due penalty for their error. —Romans 1:26–27

PAUL CONTINUES HIS LOGICAL ARGUMENT BY EXPLAINING more clearly, giving deeper insight, into the effects of their idolatry: Their "giving up God," and God's resultant "giving them up."

It's difficult to expound more eloquently than the early church father, Chrysostom, who said of this passage,

> But when God abandons a person to his own devices, then everything is turned upside down. Thus not only was their doctrine satanic, but their life was too. . . . How disgraceful it is when even the women sought after these things, when they ought to have a greater sense of shame than men have.[9]

Paul starts with the women, likely because female homosexuality, though present in Greek and Roman culture, was not nearly as common as male homosexuality. Rhetorically, the unnaturalness of female perversion would be more striking to his audience and thus give clarity to his argument.

The men, likewise, says Paul, gave up (i.e., abandoned) natural relations with women and were consumed with passion (i.e., inflamed with an insatiable longing) for other men. Paul calls these acts they committed with one another, shameless (ἀσχημοσύνη *aschēmosynē*). The Greek word means "behavior that elects disgrace, is unbecoming and abnormal."[10]

9. Gerald Bray, ed., Romans (Revised), Ancient Christian Commentary on Scripture (Downers Grove, IL: InterVarsity Press, 1998), 45.

10. William Arndt et al., A Greek-English Lexicon of the New Testament and Other Early Christian Literature (Chicago: University of Chicago Press, 2000), 147.

And what do they receive for it? An intrinsic punishment. God literally turned them over to another ruler, their passions. He allowed them to suffer under the tyranny of their sinful acts and the subsequent outworking of those acts in the menacing and malevolent effects upon all who were involved in such relationships.

As Bob Dylan would sing, “You’ve got to serve somebody.”[11] If mankind rejects their benevolent Creator, they will be abandoned to the tyrannical despot of their fallen and perverse natures.

But let us not forget, there is hope in Jesus Christ, even for those abandoned to unnatural desires.

> Or do you not know that the unrighteous will not inherit the kingdom of God? Do not be deceived: neither the sexually immoral, nor idolaters, nor adulterers, nor men who practice homosexuality, nor thieves, nor the greedy, nor drunkards, nor revilers, nor swindlers will inherit the kingdom of God. And such were some of you. But you were washed, you were sanctified, you were justified in the name of the Lord Jesus Christ and by the Spirit of our God. (1 Corinthians 6:9–11)

11. BobDylan, “Gotta Serve Somebody,” Slow Train Coming, Columbia, 1979.

18. What Ought Not to Be Done

And since they did not see fit to acknowledge God, God gave them up to a debased mind to do what ought not to be done. —Romans 1:28

FOR THE THIRD TIME, PAUL EXPLAINS THAT "GOD GAVE THEM up" but this is the finale. Colin Kruse notes, "Paul makes a play on words here. He says that since people did not think it *worthwhile* to acknowledge God, he gave them over into the tyranny of a mind that was *not worthwhile/depraved.*"[12]

In other words, because they rejected the knowledge of God that he made available to them through creation (cf. 1:21–24, 24–27), God gave them up to the kind of mind that would allow them to go further than a moral conscious could have thought possible, *to do things that ought not to be done.* The things that ought not to be done, Paul lists in verses 29–31.

But before unpacking the nature of the evil deeds, it is worth contemplating the fact that it is possible to reject God in this manner to the degree that one's conscience can no longer comprehend its transgressions. Like those rare people with nerve damage that don't allow them to feel the extreme heat from a stove burner, for example. They will smell their burnt flesh long before they are ever aware they are in danger.

Sin takes a man further than he bargains to go, costs him more than he bargains to pay, and leaves him to his devices longer than he bargained to stay.

12. Colin G. Kruse, *Paul's Letter to the Romans*, ed. D. A. Carson, *The Pillar New Testament Commentary* (Cambridge, U.K.; Nottingham, England; Grand Rapids, MI: William B. Eerdmans Publishing Company; Apollos, 2012), 105.

19. All Manner of Unrighteousness

They were filled with all manner of unrighteousness, evil, covetousness, malice. They are full of envy, murder, strife, deceit, maliciousness. They are gossips, slanderers, haters of God, insolent, haughty, boastful, inventors of evil, disobedient to parents, foolish, faithless, heartless, ruthless. —Romans 1:29–31

AS WE HAVE BEEN FOLLOWING PAUL'S LOGIC, GOD GAVE UP those who refused to acknowledge him as God and proceeded to darken their minds with idolatry to the lusts of their perverted hearts. As they embraced their immorality, he gave them up to the kind of mind that would allow them to go further than a moral conscience could have thought possible, *to do things that ought not to be done.*

What Paul is describing is similar to the way God dealt with Pharaoh when he said, "Who is the LORD, that I should obey his voice and let Israel go? I do not know the LORD, and moreover, I will not let Israel go" (Exodus 5:2). From that point, with each new exchange, God hardened the heart of Pharaoh by giving himself up to the tyranny of his own wicked heart (Exodus 8:32, cf. 10:20).

Another way of saying this is that God withdraws his sustaining grace, the common grace all humanity has received that prevents them from doing all their depraved hearts are capable of doing.

Ballor and Charles explain,

> After the fall into sin, it is on the one hand clear that humanity continues to exist, but that it does so not on the basis of any inherent merit or desert. God deigns to forbear, and his patience is an unmerited gift. It seems entirely appropriate to describe this divine preservation as *grace*. "In the day when Adam and his wife ate of the forbidden tree, they did not die, which would have happened if no grace had been granted them," concludes Kuyper. Likewise, this grace is not limited to a chosen few. It applies to everyone who lives, whether or not they will

> ultimately be saved or damned. It again seems entirely appropriate to identify the extension of such graciousness to everyone as *common*.[13]

So, here is what mankind with a measure of common grace withdrawn is filled with (for if it were completely withdrawn he would not live):

- *all manner of unrighteousness* (wickedness and injustice)
- *evil* (state or condition of a lack of moral or social values)
- *covetousness* (desiring to have more than one's due)
- *malice* (the state of wickedness that is the opposite of ἀρετή [virtue])
- *envy* (having an evil eye, desiring others lose what you don't have)
- *murder* (unwarranted killing)
- *strife* (rivalry, discord)
- *deceit* (taking advantage through craft and underhanded methods)
- *maliciousness* (hurtful to others, mean-spiritedness)

From the above described state of being follows consistent actions, behaviors that become characteristic of the individual. *They are:*

- *gossips* (rumormonger, tale-bearer)
- *slanderers* (speaking ill of others)
- *haters of God* (The Greek is one compound word, θεοστυγεῖς, from *theos*, meaning God and *stygetos*, meaning despicable. It is usually translated in the passive form, such as godforsaken or despised by God. Here the construction of the sentence puts it in the active form. Thus, these are godforsaken God-haters)
- *insolent* (violent disrespectfulness)

13. Jordan J. Ballor and J. Daryl Charles, "Editors' Introduction," in *Common Grace: God's Gifts for a Fallen World: The Doctrinal Section*, ed. Jordan J. Ballor, J. Daryl Charles, and Melvin Flikkema, trans. Nelson D. Kloosterman and Ed M. van der Maas, vol. 2, Abraham Kuyper Collected Works in Public Theology (Bellingham, WA: Lexham Press; Acton Institute, 2019), xxv.

- *haughty* (arrogant, proud)
- *boastful* (braggart)
- *inventors of evil* (one who forms strategies or tactics to effect what is morally reprehensible)
- *disobedient to parents* (unpersuadable, contumacious)
- *foolish* (void of understanding, senseless)
- *faithless* (one to renege on their word)
- *heartless* (without regard or feeling for others)
- *ruthless* (unmerciful)

In other words, they are filled with all manner of unrighteousness.

20. Practicing and Approving Sin

Though they know God's righteous decree that those who practice such things deserve to die, they not only do them but give approval to those who practice them. —Romans 1:32

WE HAVE BEEN FOLLOWING PAUL'S ARGUMENT THAT BY REFUSING to acknowledge God and glorify him as such, man's path is a downward spiral, accelerating faster and faster the further he goes down his moral black hole. There seems to be three stages or landings on the staircase to hell: worthless thinking, moral insensitivity, and religious stupidity.

This final stage of devolution in man's moral and spiritual descent ironically becomes his highest demonstration of culpability. Paul asserts "they know God's righteous decree." In the next chapter, speaking to and about the Jews, specifically, he says something remarkable related to this final stage in human culpability:

> For all who have sinned without the law will also perish without the law, and all who have sinned under the law will be judged by the law. For it is not the hearers of the law who are righteous before God, but the doers of the law who will be justified. For when Gentiles, who do not have the law, by nature do what the law requires, they are a law to themselves, even though they do not have the law. They show that the work of the law is written on their hearts, while their conscience also bears witness, and their conflicting thoughts accuse or even excuse them on that day when, according to my gospel, God judges the secrets of men by Christ Jesus. (Romans 2:12–16)

The law does not have to be written anywhere for human beings to know when they break God's law. It is written on their hearts. The proof is the fact that not only do our consciences bear witness against us (2:15–16), but also societies make laws outlawing murder, perjury, theft, etc.

Not only do they know God's righteous decree, they know that those who live in defiance of it deserve to die. Not only is the law written on man's heart, his just deserts for breaking them are too. Yet, filled with Knowledge of God—to the degree that they are without excuse—fallen man not only continues to practice his wickedness, but embraces and affirms others who do the same.

Is it any wonder, then, that God's law (including the Mosaic Law) is so despised while every kind of wickedness (i.e., abortion, homosexuality, etc.) has wealthy advocates who invest large amounts of time, money, and propaganda lobbying for its legalization and cultural embrace?

21. Every One of You Who Judges

Therefore you have no excuse, O man, every one of you who judges. For in passing judgment on another you condemn yourself, because you, the judge, practice the very same things. We know that the judgment of God rightly falls on those who practice such things. —Romans 2:1–2

CHAPTER 2 OPENS WITH PAUL TURNING HIS ATTENTION TO the religious hypocrites in general, and his own people, the Jews, in particular (v. 17) in order to demonstrate that none are in fact righteous before God.

Calvin describes this group of people as those "who dazzle the eyes of men by displays of outward sanctity, and even think themselves to be accepted before God, as though they had given him full satisfaction."[14]

In other words, Paul is speaking now to those who put on airs of righteousness outwardly by passing judgment on another. For in the privacy of their homes and the privacy of their hearts and minds (for that's where sin takes place cf. Matthew 5:19–22) they do the very same thing for which they are judging others.

Therefore, they too are ἀναπολόγητος (*anapoleoietos,* without excuse).

In verse two, Paul reminds them that God's judgment rightly falls on those who practice such things. By rightly, he means according to the righteous character of God and the truth of things regardless of who commits it.

There is no class of people who receive special privilege. There is no potential for God to make an error in judgment. And, there is not any way for the judge of all the earth to not do justly by overlooking even the smallest sin—even the sin of the heart.

All sin will be judged, even especially the sins of those who pass judgment.

14. John Calvin and John Owen, *Commentary on the Epistle of Paul the Apostle to the Romans* (Bellingham, WA: Logos Bible Software, 2010), 83–391.

22. Do You Suppose?

Do you suppose, O man—you who judge those who practice such things and yet do them yourself—that you will escape the judgment of God? —Romans 2:3

FROM VERSE ONE TO VERSE FIVE, PAUL IS PRESENTING A SINgle argument about the hypocrisy of those who believe they are safe from the judgment of God because of some unique position they hold. The reader quickly learns, if not intuitively then by direct address, Paul is ultimately speaking to the Jews (verses 9–11, cf. 17). Given the rhetorical nature of Paul's writing, there is a timelessness about the argument that could, in other circumstances, strike the heart of any religious hypocrite.

Speaking of rhetorical argument, there are notable shifts in Paul's perspective. In verse one, he writes in the second person perspective ("you have no excuse, O man"). In verse two, he shifts to first person plural to include his audience and make them a participant, rather than the object, of in his argument ("We know . . ."). By verse three, he has returned to second person ("Do you suppose, O man . . .").

In a court of law, or in a political argument, Paul's use of this accusative rhetorical device usually comes after the point has been clearly proven. The rebuke follows the conviction. But Paul is appealing to the reader's conscience, knowing that if they were willing to allow themselves to be scrutinized before God rather than men, a sharp rebuke of their "fictitious sanctity" is the only thing that will shake such a class of men who possess such astonishing security in themselves. Such trust in oneself is the hypocrisy of religion.

Acting as our own prosecutor (1 Corinthians 11:31), the question we can ask ourselves before God's tribunal of our consciences is whether we who judge those who practice such wickedness and yet do them ourselves will escape the judgment of God?

23. What God's Kindness Does

"Or do you presume on the riches of his kindness and forbearance and patience, not knowing that God's kindness is meant to lead you to repentance?" —Romans 2:4

NOT ONLY DO SELF-RIGHTEOUS HYPOCRITES SUPPOSE THEY will escape God's judgment because they perceive they are of a favored class, but their prosperity further deceives them.

Though God blesses them in this life that they might know a material symbol of his genuine paternal goodness, they suppose their success is on account of their own ingenious achievements.

Moses had already brought this fact to their attention: "You shall remember the Lord your God, for it is he who gives you power to get wealth, that he may confirm his covenant that he swore to your fathers, as it is this day" (Deuteronomy 8:18).

But they presumed on the riches of God's kindness, forbearance, and patience. What was designed to lead them to repentance becomes material evidence for their just damnation.

24. A Cursed Treasure

But because of your hard and impenitent heart you are storing up wrath for yourself on the day of wrath when God's righteous judgment will be revealed.
—Romans 2:5

THIS PASSAGE IS REMARKABLE IN THAT IT EMULATES THE SIMilar process of those in chapter one, where the outwardly unrighteous are continuously hardened by their further rejection of God.

While the outwardly wicked—having turned from God and are being given up by God continue the cycle by hardening themselves even more—are given over to the lusts of their minds until they are utterly destroyed, these outwardly religious, these self-righteous, these hypocrites are similarly accumulating to themselves the indignation of God, but in a unique manner.

In the same manner that he gives up the unrighteous to do what their depraved minds desire to do, he gives gifts upon gifts, blessings upon blessings, to the self-righteous, which they continually enjoy, not to their improvement as the gifts are intended, but to the increase of their condemnation.

The gifts of God only harden the hearts of the self-righteous in the same way the selfish desires of the unrighteous harden theirs. Both are literally storing up the evidence against themselves for the unspeakable day of judgment when the fullness of God's righteous judgment will be revealed.

> A day of wrath is that day, a day of distress and anguish, a day of ruin and devastation, a day of darkness and gloom, a day of clouds and thick darkness . . . . (Zephaniah 1:15)

> Woe to you who desire the day of the Lord! Why would you have the day of the Lord? It is darkness, and not light . . . . (Amos 5:18)

As John Calvin soberly noted, "Let us then take heed, lest by unlawful use of blessings we lay up for ourselves this cursed treasure."[15]

15. John Calvin and John Owen, *Commentary on the Epistle of Paul the Apostle to the Romans* (Bellingham, WA: Logos Bible Software, 2010), 88.

25. Each One According to His Works

He will render to each one according to his works: to those who by patience in well-doing seek for glory and honor and immortality, he will give eternal life; but for those who are self-seeking and do not obey the truth, but obey unrighteousness, there will be wrath and fury. There will be tribulation and distress for every human being who does evil, the Jew first and also the Greek, but glory and honor and peace for everyone who does good, the Jew first and also the Greek. For God shows no partiality. —Romans 2:6–11

PAUL ADDRESSES THE POINT OF THIS PASSAGE—THE EQUITY of God's judgment—using a chiastic structure. While the passage will need to be unpacked further, the simple meaning of his argument is contrasted poetically using the chiasm.

A God will judge everyone equitably (v. 6)
  B Those who do good will attain eternal life (v. 7)
    C Those who do evil will suffer wrath (v. 8)
    C′ Wrath for those who do evil (v. 9)
  B′ Glory for those who do good (v. 10)
A′ God judges impartially (v. 11)

In short, God will judge everyone equitably and impartially. Those who do good will receive glory and attain eternal life. Those who do evil will suffer God's wrath.

26. Either Christ or Self

He will render to each one according to his works: to those who by patience in well-doing seek for glory and honor and immortality, he will give eternal life; but for those who are self-seeking and do not obey the truth, but obey unrighteousness, there will be wrath and fury. There will be tribulation and distress for every human being who does evil, the Jew first and also the Greek, but glory and honor and peace for everyone who does good, the Jew first and also the Greek. For God shows no partiality. —Romans 2:6–11

WITH PAUL'S CHIASMUS IN MIND, WE CAN NOTE THAT HE CONTINUES to divide the two classes of individuals being judged.

First, there are "those who by patience in well-doing seek for glory and honor and immortality" (i.e., "everyone who does good, the Jew first and also the Greek"). To theses he promises to give "glory and honor and peace . . . eternal life."

"but," second, "for those who are self-seeking and do not obey the truth, but obey unrighteousness, there will be wrath and fury. There will be tribulation and distress for every human being who does evil, the Jew first and also the Greek."

In the first group, it is important to recognize—to not confuse the language as saying something it is not saying given the context—that Paul is not speaking of law works, or works righteousness. The first group is not "earning" their salvation by being "patience in well-doing" and "seek[ing] for glory and honor and immortality." This is not suggesting merit equals reward.

Those who patiently persevere are seeking that which is glorious, honorable, and eternal (immortality)—Christ (Colossians 3:1), by which they are demonstrating their *real* walk with God in Christ (cf. Matt. 24:13; Heb. 3:14). These can be assured of their reward.

The second group are those who seek the very opposite—*self*—for which their reward will be equally fitting: "wrath and fury . . . tribulation and distress."

27. No Partiality

He will render to each one according to his works: to those who by patience in well-doing seek for glory and honor and immortality, he will give eternal life; but for those who are self-seeking and do not obey the truth, but obey unrighteousness, there will be wrath and fury. There will be tribulation and distress for every human being who does evil, the Jew first and also the Greek, but glory and honor and peace for everyone who does good, the Jew first and also the Greek. For God shows no partiality. —Romans 2:6–11

WE HAVE SO FAR SEEN IN THIS PREGNANT-WITH-TRUTH PASSAGE that Paul has set up a contrast in judgment between two classes of individuals: those who *seek God* and those who *seek self*. For the first, glory, honor, peace, and eternal life is the reward. For the second, there will be hell to pay.

A final notable truth Paul emphasizes keeps us connected to the larger context: "*God shows no partiality.*" The Jew and Greek alike will be judged "each one according to his works," not according to his social class, ethnic class, or his religious class, per se.

The Jewish expectation was that Gentiles would be judged for their sins while the Jew, being chosen by God, would be spared. But this runs counter to what the prophets of the OT proclaimed (cf. Jer. 25:29; Amos 3:2). In fact, it will be God's priestly nation who will be judged first.

Additionally, just as the expression, Heaven and Earth, is meant to encompass all of creation, so the expression, Jew and Greek, are meant to encompass all of mankind.

Thus, Paul is arguing no one, neither the cultured class (Greek), nor the religious class (Jew), will escape the judgment of God because God doesn't play favorites.

28. With or Without the Law

For all who have sinned without the law will also perish without the law, and all who have sinned under the law will be judged by the law. —Romans 2:12

HERE PAUL CLEARLY AFFIRMS THAT THE JUST CONDEMNATION of a sinner does not require a written law. Since God is impartial when he judges, he will judge "those without the law" by the revelation they have received, both in nature and in their consciences.

By these alone, they will be found guilty—without excuse—because they have not acted in accordance with the light they've been shown. And, as we've seen previously, some of that judgment is intrinsic, meaning it is realized in the consequences of their sin.

He further affirms that the Jews, having been given a written law through Moses, stand condemned by their law. Deuteronomy 27:26 says, " *'Cursed be anyone who does not confirm the words of this law by doing them.' And all the people shall say, 'Amen.'* "

In other words, being a Jew does not mean absolute security from judgment; rather, it means absolute clarity, absolute certainty, and absolute priority in judgment.

29. Hearing and Obeying Are Not the Same

For it is not the hearers of the law who are righteous before God, but the doers of the law who will be justified. For when Gentiles, who do not have the law, by nature do what the law requires, they are a law to themselves, even though they do not have the law. They show that the work of the law is written on their hearts, while their conscience also bears witness, and their conflicting thoughts accuse or even excuse them on that day when, according to my gospel, God judges the secrets of men by Christ Jesus. —Romans 2:13–16

IN RHETORIC, WE WOULD CALL THESE LINES THE *REFUTATIO*, a refutation of an anticipated argument against the former claim of verse 12: *"For all who have sinned without the law will also perish without the law, and all who have sinned under the law will be judged by the law."*

As taught in Deuteronomy, Paul reminds his anticipated objectors that hearing the law and knowing it is not enough. You must keep the law, obey the whole of it, to be justified. "And now, O Israel, listen to the statutes and the rules that I am teaching you, and do them, that you may live, and go in and take possession of the land that the Lord, the God of your fathers, is giving you" (Deuteronomy 4:1).

The Gentiles, remember, don't have a law in the same way the Jews have the law. The fact that they naturally hold similar values of justice and injustice is a law unto them. In other words, their own attitudes toward sacrilege, rebellion, murder, stealing, adultery, false witness, etc., reveal they have the law written on their hearts.

And the day is coming when God, by Jesus Christ, will judge the secrets of all men's hearts. And just as the Gentiles will be judged in that manner, so will the Jews be judged on that day, whose *conscience also bears witness, and their conflicting thoughts accuse or even excuse them.*

In other words, Paul is saying, all men, Jew and Gentile alike, those with the law and without the law alike, know better. They know they are sinners, rebels against God, and they know they are suppressing the truth; and, the truth they are suppressing will be revealed on Judgment Day.

30. With Great Vanity

But if you call yourself a Jew and rely on the law and boast in God and know his will and approve what is excellent, because you are instructed from the law; and if you are sure that you yourself are a guide to the blind, a light to those who are in darkness, an instructor of the foolish, a teacher of children, having in the law the embodiment of knowledge and truth— you then who teach others, do you not teach yourself? While you preach against stealing, do you steal? You who say that one must not commit adultery, do you commit adultery? You who abhor idols, do you rob temples? You who boast in the law dishonor God by breaking the law. For, as it is written, "The name of God is blasphemed among the Gentiles because of you." —Romans 2:17–24

NOTA BENE: *VERSES 17–24 ARE, TOGETHER, ONE COMPREHENSIVE argument; so, it is beneficial to read the passage repeatedly as a single passage while examining various parts of the whole over a few days.*

The name Jew was a later development as the distinction between the tribes began to dissolve into one another and into the nations to which they were taken captive. During and after the captivity, the name *Jew* for any of Israel's offspring became commonplace. See 2 Kings 16:6; Esther 4:3; Jeremiah 38:19; Daniel 3:8; Ezra 4:12; Nehemiah 2:16.

To *rely on the law and boast in God* does not mean they were attending to God's Law in obedience, as Paul notes in the following verses. Rather, they were boasting in their stewardship of God's Law.

As happens so often with all of God's gifts to humanity, the Jews inflated, with great vanity, their privileges as the priestly nation, and turned that which was to be a blessing to the nations into their own reproach.

31. The Jews' High Privilege

But if you call yourself a Jew and rely on the law and boast in God and know his will and approve what is excellent, because you are instructed from the law; and if you are sure that you yourself are a guide to the blind, a light to those who are in darkness, an instructor of the foolish, a teacher of children, having in the law the embodiment of knowledge and truth— you then who teach others, do you not teach yourself? While you preach against stealing, do you steal? You who say that one must not commit adultery, do you commit adultery? You who abhor idols, do you rob temples? You who boast in the law dishonor God by breaking the law. For, as it is written, "The name of God is blasphemed among the Gentiles because of you." —Romans 2:17–24

IN VERSES 17–18, PAUL LISTS FIVE PRIVILEGES THE JEWS claim to possess as their own. The Jew

- relies on the law,
- boasts in (about his relationship with) God,
- knows God's will,
- (is able to) approve what is excellent, and
- is instructed from the law.[16]

In verse 18, Paul speaks of the last three in the list: *know his (God's) will and approve what is excellent, because you are instructed from the law . . .*

The Jews' knowledge of God's will is not a specialized knowledge of his *inscrutable* will; they don't have secret knowledge about God's future plans for individuals or nations, for example. Rather, in contrast to the Pagan nations, they have been instructed by God's perfect law of liberty about what is excellent (virtuous) regarding ethics, justice, and morality. Consider Psalm 19:7–10 (cf. James 1:25):

16. Colin G. Kruse, *Paul's Letter to the Romans*, ed. D. A. Carson, The Pillar New Testament Commentary *(Grand Rapids, MI: Eerdmans, 2012)*, 145.

> The law of the LORD is perfect, reviving the soul; the testimony of the LORD is sure, making wise the simple; the precepts of the LORD are right, rejoicing the heart; the commandment of the LORD is pure, enlightening the eyes; the fear of the LORD is clean, enduring forever; the rules of the LORD are true, and righteous altogether. More to be desired are they than gold, even much fine gold; sweeter also than honey and drippings of the honeycomb. (Psalm 19:7–10)

> But the one who looks into the perfect law, the law of liberty, and perseveres, being no hearer who forgets but a doer who acts, he will be blessed in his doing. (James 1:25)

In other words, they have been privileged to know, more than any other nation has, how God desires people to live. As the Psalmist proclaims, "Your word is a lamp to my feet and a light to my path" (Psalm 119:105).

This is the Jew's high privilege; it is also his bitter condemnation when he fails to obey.

32. The Light to Those in Darkness

But if you call yourself a Jew and rely on the law and boast in God and know his will and approve what is excellent, because you are instructed from the law; and if you are sure that you yourself are a guide to the blind, a light to those who are in darkness, an instructor of the foolish, a teacher of children, having in the law the embodiment of knowledge and truth— you then who teach others, do you not teach yourself? While you preach against stealing, do you steal? You who say that one must not commit adultery, do you commit adultery? You who abhor idols, do you rob temples? You who boast in the law dishonor God by breaking the law. For, as it is written, "The name of God is blasphemed among the Gentiles because of you." —Romans 2:17–24

IN VERSES 19–20, HAVING ADDRESSED THEIR PRIVILEGES AS Jews, Paul addresses their *perspective* about their privileges. The imaginary Jewish interlocutors Paul is addressing are "sure" that their place in the world is to be a guide to the blind, a light to those in darkness, an instructor of the foolish, and a teacher of children. In fact, there is a sense in which they are not wrong.

> I am the Lord; I have called you in righteousness; I will take you by the hand and keep you; I will give you as a covenant for the people, a light for the nations, to open the eyes that are blind, to bring out the prisoners from the dungeon, from the prison those who sit in darkness. (Isaiah 42:6–7)
>
> And nations shall come to your light, and kings to the brightness of your rising. (Isaiah 60:3)

God had given the Jewish nation the revelation that was to be distributed to all nations, the revelation of the law, which is *the embodiment of knowledge and truth*. Their privilege wasn't to be an end in itself; their "chosen" status was like that of the apostles, for the purpose of teaching all mankind about God. (See John 6:1–14 for a beautiful picture of the Jews' purpose to this end.)

Their condemnation, Paul is about to point out, is that these who taught others failed to teach themselves.

33. You Who Boast in the Law

But if you call yourself a Jew and rely on the law and boast in God and know his will and approve what is excellent, because you are instructed from the law; and if you are sure that you yourself are a guide to the blind, a light to those who are in darkness, an instructor of the foolish, a teacher of children, having in the law the embodiment of knowledge and truth— you then who teach others, do you not teach yourself? While you preach against stealing, do you steal? You who say that one must not commit adultery, do you commit adultery? You who abhor idols, do you rob temples? You who boast in the law dishonor God by breaking the law. For, as it is written, "The name of God is blasphemed among the Gentiles because of you." —Romans 2:17–24

FROM VERSES 21–23, PAUL BEGINS TO DETAIL THE KINDS OF hypocrisy for which the Jews were guilty. He appears to be quoting loosely from Psalm 50:18: "If you see a thief, you are pleased with him, and you keep company with adulterers."

He may also be drawing from our Lord's Sermon on the Mount (Matt. 5:21–48), at least in form:

> And he said to them, "You have a fine way of rejecting the commandment of God in order to establish your tradition! For Moses said, 'Honor your father and your mother'; and, 'Whoever reviles father or mother must surely die.' But you say, 'If a man tells his father or his mother, "Whatever you would have gained from me is Corban" (that is, given to God)—then you no longer permit him to do anything for his father or mother, thus making void the word of God by your tradition that you have handed down. And many such things you do." (Mark 7:9–13)

> "You have heard that it was said, 'You shall not commit adultery.' But I say to you that everyone who looks at a woman with lustful intent has already committed adultery with her in his heart." (Matthew 5:27–28)

> And Jesus entered the temple and drove out all who sold and bought in the temple, and he overturned the tables of the money-changers and the seats of those who sold pigeons. He said to them, "It is written, 'My house shall be called a house of prayer,' but you make it a den of robbers.'" (Matthew 21:12–13) (The Talmud also documents Jews who would profit by facilitating the sale of idols to Gentiles though they would not worship the idols themselves.)

> "Woe to you, scribes and Pharisees, hypocrites! For you are like whitewashed tombs, which outwardly appear beautiful, but within are full of dead people's bones and all uncleanness. So you also outwardly appear righteous to others, but within you are full of hypocrisy and lawlessness." (Matthew 23:27–28)

Those same Jews who were reveling in their privilege (i.e., boasting in the law) were dishonoring God by breaking that same law. Like white-washed sepulchers, they were washed on the outside while the hypocrisy ran deep on the inside.

34. The Name of God Blasphemed

For, as it is written, "The name of God is blasphemed among the Gentiles because of you." —Romans 2:24

PAUL SEEMS TO HAVE PARAPHRASED THIS CONCLUDING STATEMENT about his Jewish interlocutor's hypocrisy from either Ezekiel 36:20 or Isaiah 52:5. Both have merit to their arguments.

> "But when they came to the nations, wherever they came, they profaned my holy name, in that people said of them, 'These are the people of the Lord, and yet they had to go out of his land.'" (Ezekiel 36:20)
>
> "Now therefore what have I here," declares the Lord, "seeing that my people are taken away for nothing? Their rulers wail," declares the Lord, "and continually all the day my name is despised." (Isaiah 52:5)

Both verses highlight the fact that because of the Jews, God's name has been blasphemed among the Gentiles. That is, the name of God has been reviled and defamed because those to whom his character and reputation had been entrusted were themselves untrustworthy. Such defamation of God's good name is no small sin. Consider the following passages of Scripture which demonstrate just how much God values his good name. It is even a virtuous pursuit he extends to us.

> For the LORD will not forsake his people, for his great name's sake, because it has pleased the LORD to make you a people for himself. (1 Samuel 12:22)
>
> He restores my soul. He leads me in paths of righteousness for his name's sake. (Psalm 23:3)
>
> "Therefore say to the house of Israel, 'Thus says the Lord GOD: It is not for your sake, O house of Israel, that I am about to act, but for the sake of my holy name, which you have profaned among the nations to

which you came. And I will vindicate the holiness of my great name, which has been profaned among the nations, and which you have profaned among them. And the nations will know that I am the LORD, declares the Lord GOD, when through you I vindicate my holiness before their eyes.'" (Ezekiel 36:22–23)

"For my name's sake I defer my anger; for the sake of my praise I restrain it for you, that I may not cut you off. Behold, I have refined you, but not as silver; I have tried you in the furnace of affliction. For my own sake, for my own sake, I do it, for how should my name be profaned? My glory I will not give to another." (Isaiah 48:9–11)

A good name is to be chosen rather than great riches, and favor is better than silver or gold. (Proverbs 22:1)

A good name is better than precious ointment . . . . (Ecclesiastes 7:1)

35. When Circumcision Becomes Uncircumcision

"For circumcision indeed is of value if you obey the law, but if you break the law, your circumcision becomes uncircumcision." —Romans 2:25

THE JEWS GLORIED IN CIRCUMCISION AND REGARDED IT AS being most important. They believed it unthinkable that anyone who possessed this physical covenant sign could lose his salvation. But Paul dashes this erroneous concept onto the rocks of reality.

Paul knew that circumcision was *the sign of admission* to the covenant (Gen. 17:9–14), but it was *not*, itself, the covenant (i.e., 1 Cor. 7:19; Gal. 5:3). The covenant was an inward reality marked by a physical one. The sign (circumcision) is the seal of the thing it signifies (covenant redemption). Circumcision, therefore, was a sign of one's commitment to whole-heartedly keep the Law of God. Without perfect obedience to the law, circumcision would be nothing more than empty pretense.

John Calvin states, "it always happens, that those who dare to set up their own merits against the righteousness of God, glory more in outward observances than in real goodness; for no one, who is seriously touched and moved by the fear of God, will ever dare to raise up his eyes to heaven, since the more he strives after true righteousness, the clearer he sees how far he is from it. But as to the Pharisees, who were satisfied with imitating holiness by an outward disguise, it is no wonder that they so easily deluded themselves."[17]

Covenant baptism is the same for Christians today. It is of no avail unless one, from the heart, lives faithfully as a member of the covenant people of God who trust in and follow Christ.

17. John Calvin and John Owen, *Commentary on the Epistle of Paul the Apostle to the Romans* (Bellingham, WA: Logos Bible Software, 2010), 109–110.

36. When Uncircumcision Is Regarded as Circumcision

"So, if a man who is uncircumcised keeps the precepts of the law, will not his uncircumcision be regarded as circumcision?" —Romans 2:26

IN THIS AND THE FOLLOWING VERSES, PAUL UNPACKS THE logic for his case. We should not suppose there is a particular occasion Paul has in mind but a theoretical case in which he demonstrates the value of keeping the Law with the value of the physical sign all by itself. We also should not suppose Paul has in mind a scenario of salvation by works righteousness.

Rather, the simple point of Paul's argument is that the honest keeping of the Law is superior to the act of circumcision, which is an outward sign of this inward commitment; it is, therefore, subordinate to the Law. Circumcision was made to be a sign for those who were committed to the keeping of the Law, not the other way around. The Law was not for the keeping of circumcision.

Therefore, hypothetically, if there happened to be found a Gentile who had never been circumcised (not out of conscience rejection of the rite but for some unwitting reason Paul leaves to the imagination) but he faithfully kept the Law of God, his keeping of the Law would be of more value in the sight of God than the Jew's circumcision who ignored the Law or only kept it as outward show (i.e., vainglory).

Perhaps Paul has in mind a situation much like Peter discovered in Cornelius: "At Caesarea there was a man named Cornelius, a centurion of what was known as the Italian Cohort, a devout man who feared God with all his household, gave alms generously to the people, and prayed continually to God" (Acts 10:1–2).

37. A Comparative Case of Condemnation

Then he who is physically uncircumcised but keeps the law will condemn you who have the written code and circumcision but break the law. —Romans 2:27

WHAT THEN BECOMES OF THESE TWO COMPARATIVE CASES IF laid out before the courts of Heaven? The Gentile who actually keeps the Law will be a testimony against the Jew who is a transgressor of the Law, even though it is he who carries the sign of the covenant in his body.

This kind of comparative case is not Paul's line of argument alone. This was the position of Jesus himself:

> "The queen of the South will rise up at the judgment with this generation and condemn it, for she came from the ends of the earth to hear the wisdom of Solomon, and behold, something greater than Solomon is here." (Matthew 12:42)

> "The men of Nineveh will rise up at the judgment with this generation and condemn it, for they repented at the preaching of Jonah, and behold, something greater than Jonah is here." (Luke 11:32)

NOTA BENE: Speaking of carrying the sign of the covenant in his body, it might be helpful here to clarify a common misconception. Circumcision was not a guarantee or promise of salvation, per se. It was the sign that sealed God's promise that righteousness would be granted on the basis of one's faith (See Genesis 15 & 17).

The circumcision of Abraham's foreskin as the sign drew attention to the promise of a seed (Genesis 17:1–8), and, in some sense, foreshadows the Deuteronomic covenant where God promises to remove the uncleanness of their flesh if the Israelites keep the covenant (Deuteronomy 30:6) and cut off from the people God those who break it (Deuteronomy 30:17–20). In short, it was a visible reminder to every head of household regarding the promise of God: He would bless faith in his promises and punish apostasy.

38. A Matter of the Heart

For no one is a Jew who is merely one outwardly, nor is circumcision outward and physical. But a Jew is one inwardly, and circumcision is a matter of the heart, by the Spirit, not by the letter. His praise is not from man but from God. —Romans 2:28–29

THIS PASSAGE CONCLUDES PAUL'S LARGER ARGUMENT THAT began in verse 17, and it emphasizes the reality of internalized faith. It's true that real internalized belief will manifest outward fruit, but outward activity is not a true indicator of one's faith if it is divorced from a believing heart. This is a repeated theme in Scripture.

> "For this is the covenant that I will make with the house of Israel after those days," declares the Lord: "I will put my law within them, and I will write it on their hearts. And I will be their God, and they shall be my people." (Jeremiah 31:33)

> Who has made us sufficient to be ministers of a new covenant, not of the letter but of the Spirit. For the letter kills, but the Spirit gives life. (2 Corinthians 3:6)

> Therefore, while the promise of entering his rest still stands, let us fear lest any of you should seem to have failed to reach it. For good news came to us just as to them, but the message they heard did not benefit them, because they were not united by faith with those who listened. (Hebrews 4:1–2)

Physical circumcision is the cutting off of the foreskin, not as representing the corruption of one part of the body, but similar to synecdoche (a part that represents the whole), it serves as a symbol of the corruption of the whole nature. Therefore, circumcision is really "a matter of the heart," symbolizing the mortification of the flesh, the mortification of the whole Adamic nature.

To be a Jew, was to be the people of God, inwardly. The Spirit refers to the spiritual nature of the rite, whereas the letter refers to the outward rite alone—as that which lacks the necessary inward piety.

The true Jew seeks the praise and affirmation of God, who alone sees the inward, and not the praise of man, who is limited to only seeing the outward. "But the Lord said to Samuel, 'Do not look on his appearance or on the height of his stature, because I have rejected him. For the Lord sees not as man sees: man looks on the outward appearance, but the Lord looks on the heart'" (1 Samuel 16:7).

39. Much in Every Way

"Then what advantage has the Jew? Or what is the value of circumcision? Much in every way. To begin with, the Jews were entrusted with the oracles of God." —Romans 3:1–2

SINCE PAUL HAS NOW SUFFICIENTLY PROVED THAT CIRCUMCISION did not make the Jews superior to the Gentiles, he must address the natural implications of his argument. Then what's the point of being a Jew?

Though circumcision itself did not add merit to their personal standing before the holiness of God, there must be some advantage or benefit of being a Jew. Since such a separation from the Gentiles was God's design, what value does circumcision have?

Paul's response is "Much in every way." Then he enumerates the Jew's advantage, beginning with the chief benefit. The Jews were entrusted with revelation. They were given the oracles of God. Or to put it in the words of John Calvin, "God had deposited with them the treasure of celestial wisdom."[18]

By the grace and mercy of God, he chose the Jew and set him apart for his priestly purposes. "'And you shall be to me a kingdom of priests and a holy nation.' These are the words that you shall speak to the people of Israel" (Exodus 19:6).

While this position did not by itself automatically warrant the Jew's salvation or absolve him of his sins, it did put him in a privileged position among men—a position which would, by its virtue alone, *add* to his responsibility, not *alleviate* him of it.

18. John Calvin and John Owen, *Commentary on the Epistle of Paul the Apostle to the Romans* (Bellingham, WA: Logos Bible Software, 2010), 114.

40. God Alone Is True

What if some were unfaithful? Does their faithlessness nullify the faithfulness of God? By no means! Let God be true though every one were a liar, as it is written,

> *"That you may be justified in your words,*
> *and prevail when you are judged."*

—*Romans 3:3–4*

PAUL ANTICIPATES THE LIKELY RESPONSE OF HIS IMAGINED interlocutor and uses the answer to set up the next *confirmatio*: God alone is righteous and faithful.

The question is, since you've now proved the Jews—privileged as they were to receive the oracles of God—were unfaithful, does that mean their faith*less*ness has nullified the faith*ful*ness of God?

Paul's answer is that the faithfulness of God is so far from being hindered "by the perfidy and apostasy of men,"[19] that its opposite is actually established.

Quoting from Psalms 116:11 and 51:4—"I said in my alarm, 'All mankind are liars' and 'Against you, you only, have I sinned and done what is evil in your sight, so that you may be justified in your words and blameless in your judgment'"—Paul establishes that while all men are inclined to falsehood and deceit, that they are always shunning the truth and running after lies, God, on the contrary, will always stand by his promises because whatever God declares, he fulfills, despite the falseness of mankind.

This should be a great consolation to us. Whatever God commands will become a reality no matter what men do. God's faithfulness to his word does not depend on man's faithfulness to his.

19. John Calvin and John Owen, *Commentary on the Epistle of Paul the Apostle to the Romans* (Bellingham, WA: Logos Bible Software, 2010), 116.

41. Emphatic Repudiation

But if our unrighteousness serves to show the righteousness of God, what shall we say? That God is unrighteous to inflict wrath on us? (I speak in a human way.) By no means! For then how could God judge the world? —Romans 3:5–6

PAUL, SPEAKING ON BEHALF OF HIS INTERLOCUTOR, RAISES the objection that if the main result of man's sin is that it advances God's purpose in the world, then doesn't it seem that God is unjust for punishing sin? Sin is simply giving God the opportunity to display his righteousness. Therefore it is unjust to punish sinners who are simply advancing his agenda.

Cue the emphatic repudiation: *By no means!*

It is not the sin that gives God the opportunity to reveal his righteousness. It's God's providential way of dealing with sin that provides the opportunity for his righteousness to be revealed.

Otherwise, how could he judge the world justly—and be just himself—if he simply let the sinner go free?

Imagine an earthly judge who let criminals go free because, as he might reason, their crimes gave him job security?

42. Etched in High Relief

But if through my lie God's truth abounds to his glory, why am I still being condemned as a sinner? And why not do evil that good may come?—as some people slanderously charge us with saying. Their condemnation is just. —*Romans 3:7–8*

WHILE PAUL MIGHT SEEM TO BE UNNECESSARILY REPEATING his previous argument in verses 5–6, he is actually advancing his argument by answering a similar question a different way.

It seems to me, these two closely-related arguments with different kinds of answers act as a rhetorical parallelism—like those seen in Hebrew poetry. On one hand, Paul is strengthening his point by presenting the same point twice. On the other hand, he is talking about two different (but closely related) ideas that can each provide its own answer.

In the first argument, he etches in high relief the righteousness of God by comparing it to the (un)righteousness of men. In the second argument, he similarly etches the truthfulness of God by comparing it to the (un)truthfulness of men.

And, instead of an emphatic repudiation, he uses it as an opportunity to defend his true position against the slanderers (untruthful men) who have apparently made Paul notorious by saying he teaches that men should do evil that good may come. He will denounce this same accusation again in chapter six.

He concludes by saying their condemnation (God's judgment against them) is just because they are willfully speaking untruthfully about him and the message they are actually preaching. In any event, just because God is able to make good come out of men's evil doesn't mean he approves of evil. The providential work of our sovereign God does not make him complicit with men's sin, but it does etch in high relief the majesty and power of God by comparing it to the character of men (slanderers).

43. Are the Jews Any Better Off?

What then? Are we Jews any better off? No, not at all. For we have already charged that all, both Jews and Greeks, are under sin, as it is written:

> *"None is righteous, no, not one;*
> *no one understands;*
> *no one seeks for God.*
> *All have turned aside; together they have become worthless;*
> *no one does good, not even one."*
> *"Their throat is an open grave;*
> *they use their tongues to deceive."*
> *"The venom of asps is under their lips."*
> *"Their mouth is full of curses and bitterness."*
> *"Their feet are swift to shed blood;*
> *in their paths are ruin and misery,*
> *and the way of peace they have not known."*
> *"There is no fear of God before their eyes."*

—Romans 3:9–18

VERSES 9–20 IN OUR ENGLISH BIBLE ARE A SINGLE PERICOPE, so it is difficult to break this longer passage down without the possibility of doing damage to the integrity of the argument. Thus, we'll focus on the first part of the argument here; next, we'll consider the passage as a whole while focusing on the second part of the argument.

Here Paul is offering a *refutatio* to counter the claim made by some Jews that they are "any better off." There is some question about the voice of the verb (προεχόμεθα *proechometha*) which is translated "Are (we any) better off." It's not used this way anywhere else in Scripture. Depending on how it is rendered, it could be referring to Paul protecting an advantage for himself against accusations regarding his argument. Or, it could be referring to the Jews as a people having an advantage for being Jews. Given its place in the context of the argument, the end result of the meaning of the passage when taken as a whole is the same regardless of which voice scholars believe Paul's verb takes.

The question, *"What then? Are we Jews any better off?,"* receives another emphatic repudiation: *"No, not at all."* This time it is followed by an explanation and a list of authoritative testimony from the Old Testament, namely the Psalms, the Proverbs, and the Prophets (i.e., Isaiah and Jeremiah).

The Jews are not better off, spiritually, because he has *"already charged that all, both Jews and Greeks, are under sin."* Those without the law sinned against the law written on their hearts and those with the law sinned against the law written on tablets.

The collection of passages Paul gathers from the Hebrew Scriptures is damning. Not one person—Jew or Gentile—is righteous, understands, or seeks after God. Every last Jew and every last Gentile alike has turned aside from the truth, lied, deceived, and even murdered—at least in his heart. Neither Jew nor Gentile has feared God the way his character, power, and majesty demands.

44. Every Mouth Stopped

Now we know that whatever the law says it speaks to those who are under the law, so that every mouth may be stopped, and the whole world may be held accountable to God. For by works of the law no human being will be justified in his sight, since through the law comes knowledge of sin. —Romans 3:19–20

PAUL USES THE WORD "LAW" HERE IN THE WIDEST SENSE POSsible, the Hebrew Scriptures, to include the prophets and the books of wisdom. As a matter of fact, of all the passages he quoted above (vs 10–18), none were actually from the Pentateuch.

Paul has removed any claim the Jewish people might make in saying they are more righteous than the Gentiles. By condemning the Jews with their own law which only highlighted their glaring failures, Paul silences all claims by his imaginary Jewish interlocutor to be in any way morally superior to Gentiles.

He has, in essence, stopped their mouths. Since the Jewish people are no better than Gentiles, then the whole world stands condemned before God.

He concludes with an application drawn from Psalm 143:2: "Enter not into judgment with your servant, for no one living is righteous before you."

Now that it is clear that all are condemned, then the deeper purpose of the Law becomes even more clear. It cannot justify anyone because no one can keep it. It can only condemn because it highlights our moral failures by making our sin known.

45. The Mercy of God Alone

But now the righteousness of God has been manifested apart from the law, although the Law and the Prophets bear witness to it. —*Romans 3:21*

SO NOW THAT IT HAS BEEN ESTABLISHED THAT THE THE works of the law can justify no one—Jew or Gentile—and it can only reveal our sin to us, we are left without any kind of righteousness of our own by which to justify ourselves before God. This is an utterly hopeless condition in which we find ourselves.

Paul says, "but now," which signifies an adversative position rather than strictly signifying a place in time. In other words, we are not left without hope. There is something else God had in mind, something to which (the teachings of) the Law and the Prophets both testified—the righteousness of God is manifest (made known or revealed) apart from (the works of) the law.

Therefore, it follows that if justification (a righteous standing before God) depends neither on the law itself nor on our own works, then it must depend on something else—the mercy of God alone!

46. Righteousness apart from the Law

But now the righteousness of God has been manifested apart from the law, although the Law and the Prophets bear witness to it— the righteousness of God through faith in Jesus Christ for all who believe. For there is no distinction . . .
—Romans 3:21–22

SINCE THE LAW REQUIRES PERFECT AND ABSOLUTE OBEDIENCE, and not one has been found to have been so obedient as to have attained the required perfect measure of holiness, then it follows all have fallen short—Gentile and Jew alike. There is no distinction between the two on these grounds.

The righteousness that God requires of all men must then issue from himself and be manifest to us in the Son, Jesus Christ, who is alone just. Through the instrument of faith (which is also a gift God gives to us, cf. Ephesians 2:8–10), this righteousness is transferred to those of us who believe.

John Calvin notes, "Ut ergo justificemur, causa efficiens est misericordia Dei, Christus materia, verbum cum fide instrumentum." [When therefore we are justified, the efficient cause is the mercy of God, the meritorious is Christ, the instrumental is the word in connection with faith.][20]

This is why the Reformers would say we are justified by faith alone (*Sola Fide*). They didn't mean by faith exclusively, as to exclude Christ alone, etc. Neither did they mean mere mental assent. They meant faith alone is the instrument by which we receive Christ, in whom righteousness is conveyed to us. It's not our works according to the Law that merits our salvation; yet, our faith as an instrument for receiving grace does have a component of activity as the apostle James so manifestly clarifies (i.e., it's a faith that works):

> So also faith by itself, if it does not have works, is dead. But someone will say, "You have faith and I have works." Show me your faith apart from your works, and I will show you my faith by my works. You believe that God is one; you do well. Even the demons believe—and

20. John Calvin and John Owen, *Commentary on the Epistle of Paul the Apostle to the Romans* (Bellingham, WA: Logos Bible Software, 2010), 138.

shudder! Do you want to be shown, you foolish person, that faith apart from works is useless? Was not Abraham our father justified by works when he offered up his son Isaac on the altar? You see that faith was active along with his works, and faith was completed by his works; and the Scripture was fulfilled that says, "Abraham believed God, and it was counted to him as righteousness"—and he was called a friend of God. You see that a person is justified by works and not by faith alone. And in the same way was not also Rahab the prostitute justified by works when she received the messengers and sent them out by another way? For as the body apart from the spirit is dead, so also faith apart from works is dead. (James 2:17–26)

47. Exceedingly Short

For there is no distinction: for all have sinned and fall short of the glory of God . . . —*Romans 3:22–23*

HERE, PAUL REITERATES AND SUMMARIZES IN THE FORM OF A maxim what he has been arguing thus far. It is necessary for all men—Jew and Gentile alike—to seek by faith the righteousness of God which is in Christ because without exception all are sinners before the throne of God.

Because all have sinned, there is not one single person of any race or tribe who has anything in which he might glory before God.

Like Adam, who hid himself from God in the garden, we are all "confounded and lost" under the burden of the shame of our sin so that none can even bear the presence of God, let alone stand in his presence as one who has merited his favor.

Woe to all of us! We have fallen exceedingly short of God's glory! Lord, have mercy!

48. A Propitiation by Blood

. . . for all have sinned and fall short of the glory of God, and are justified by his grace as a gift, through the redemption that is in Christ Jesus, whom God put forward as a propitiation by his blood, to be received by faith. This was to show God's righteousness, because in his divine forbearance he had passed over former sins. —*Romans 3:23–25*

THERE MAY NOT BE IN SCRIPTURE A MORE CONCISE YET THOROUGH explanation of God's redemptive work than Paul makes here. He lays out the efficacy of God's righteousness (*to show God's righteousness*) in a slightly modified expression of Aristotelian "causes."

The efficient cause is God's mercy (*are justified by his grace as a gift . . . in his divine forbearance he had passed over former sins*). The meritorious cause is Christ Jesus (*put forward as a propitiation by his blood*). The formal cause is the instrument of faith (*to be received by faith*). The final cause is the glory of God (*to show God's righteousness*), particularly his justice, goodness, and righteousness. The material cause is (*all [who] have sinned and fall[en] short of the glory of God*).

Another notable point is Paul's use of propitiation. The English word used here is a translation of the Greek word, ἱλαστήριον (*hilasterion*) which can mean either propitiation or expiation.

Propitiation means the turning away of anger by the offering of a gift. The word was often used by the pagans in antiquity, for they thought of their gods as unpredictable beings, liable to become angry with their worshipers for any trifle. When disaster struck it was often thought that a god was angry and was therefore punishing his worshipers. The remedy was to offer a sacrifice without delay. A well-chosen offering would appease the god and put him in a good mood again. This process was called propitiation.[21]

Expiation means atonement, purification, or removal of sin or its guilt. Expiation speaks fundamentally of a solution for sin, and the most common

21. Walter A. Elwell and Barry J. Beitzel, "Propitiation," *Baker Encyclopedia of the Bible* (Grand Rapids, MI: Baker Book House, 1988), 1784.

association is with the idea of atonement. It has to do with the blot of sin, and hence the term is related to such words as "forgive," "purge," "cleanse," or "atone." All New Testament references to expiation have to do with the sacrifice of Christ for human sin.

In the Bible, both expiation and propitiation are part of God's atoning work. Christ's sacrifice both propitiates (turns away) the wrath of God and expiates (covers) human sin.[22]

22. Walter A. Elwell and Barry J. Beitzel, "Expiation," *Baker Encyclopedia of the Bible* (Grand Rapids, MI: Baker Book House, 1988), 746.

49. Just and Justifier

It was to show his righteousness at the present time, so that he might be just and the justifier of the one who has faith in Jesus. —Romans 3:26

"AT THE PRESENT TIME" SHOULD BE UNDERSTOOD IN RELATION to "passed over former sins" in the previous verse. ". . . This was to show God's righteousness, because in his divine forbearance he had passed over former sins" (Romans 3:25).

It has now been established by Paul's argument that the whole human race is condemned for their injustice, and God alone has the honor of being just.

Though God is merciful in delaying judgment on sins past, he is not merely merciful; he is also gracious because he does not hold back the riches of his righteousness.

In addition to being merciful toward us for our past sins, he further demonstrates the fullness of his righteousness now (at Christ's revelation) by extending forth and imputing his righteousness to all who have faith in Jesus.

And in being the "justifier of the one who has faith in Jesus," he, in no way, compromises his own integrity to do it. That is, he remains just because he has executed his divine wrath, which was due compensation for those "former sins," upon Jesus.

The German Reformer, Martin Luther, called this "the Great Exchange."

50. All Boasting Is Shut Out!

Then what becomes of our boasting? It is excluded. By what kind of law? By a law of works? No, but by the law of faith. —Romans 3:27

PAUL HAS ALREADY PROVEN IN VERSES 17–24 THAT BECAUSE the Jews disobeyed the Law and thus dishonored God, causing his name to be blasphemed among the Gentiles, there is nothing for them to boast about regarding their own righteousness.

But here he takes a slightly different approach to drive the final nail in the coffin. There are legitimate things for which the Jews may boast (Romans 9:4–5), but the law of works is not one of them. Boasting is excluded because righteousness is obtained by the law of faith in Christ—apart from the works of the Law.

To say it another way, the Jews may boast in their heritage and special anointing of God to be priests to the world (and all the privileges that come with that) but they do not obtain righteousness any other way than through faith in the true Israel, Jesus Christ—just as the Gentiles do (See also Galatians 3:16, 24–29).

In regards to righteousness, the only boasting that is allowed is boasting in the cross of Christ (which he is about to unpack in chapter 4).

NOTA BENE: The Greek reads: *Ποῦ οὖν ἡ καύχησις; ἐξεκλείσθη. διὰ ποίου νόμου; τῶν ἔργων; οὐχί, ἀλλὰ διὰ νόμου πίστεως (pou oun e kauxēsis? exekleisthe! dia poiou nomou? ton ergon? ouxi, alla dia nomou pisteos).*

- Law (*νόμου = nomou*) in this instance is being used more generally than specifically referring to Tora. It's more like *principle* (I.e., law of gravity, law of supply and demand, etc.).
- Literal translation
    - *Ποῦ οὖν ἡ καύχησις (pou oun e kauxēsis?)* = Where is the boasting?
    - *ἐξεκλείσθη (exekleisthe) = It is shut out! [often rendered, "it is excluded!"]* (it is the aorist passive indicative third person singular

verb form of κλείω, which means "to shut") See its use in Galatians 4:17: "*They make much of you, but for no good purpose. They want to shut you out, that you may make much of them.*"

- *διὰ ποίου νόμου (dia poiou nomou?)* = by which law?
- *τῶν ἔργων (ton ergon?)* = of works?
- *οὐχί (ouxi)* = negated adverb (i.e., no, not)
- *ἀλλὰ διὰ νόμου πίστεως (alla dia nomou pisteos)* = but by (a, the) law of faith.

51. Justification by a Faith That Works

For we hold that one is justified by faith apart from works of the law. —Romans 3:28

THIS IS THE APOSTLE'S MAIN PROPOSITION CLEARLY AND concisely stated. His conclusion is incontrovertible, indisputable, irrefutable, incontestable, and undeniable. Paul is saying there are no two ways about it! This is our position: one is justified (before God) by faith apart from works of the law. The end.

But there have been some who have taken issue with the apostle Paul, claiming that James, the brother of the Lord, preached otherwise. For, as was explained previously (Romans 3:21–22), James says in his letter to the church:

> What good is it, my brothers, if someone says he has faith but does not have works? Can that faith save him? (James 2:14)
>
> Do you want to be shown, you foolish person, that faith apart from works is useless? (James 2:20)
>
> You see that a person is justified by works and not by faith alone. (James 2:24)

It must be affirmed and clarified again that there is not a contradiction in the thinking and writing of these two apostles. Their arguments simply have *different objects in view*.

For Paul, the object of his argument is to show that the righteousness of God can be received no other way than through faith in Christ alone. It cannot be obtained by works, by keeping the law.

For James, the object of his argument is to show that the righteousness of God received by faith actually works. It works itself out in the actions of the one who has genuine faith in Christ. A believer is justified before God by faith in Christ, but he is justified before men by the works his faith produces.

To paraphrase Martin Luther, we are saved by faith and not by works, but the faith that saves us is a faith that works. And, the apostle Paul would agree with both James and Luther. For he writes to the Philippians, "Therefore, my beloved, as you have always obeyed, so now, not only as in my presence but much more in my absence, work out your own salvation with fear and trembling, for it is God who works in you, both to will and to work for his good pleasure" (Philippians 2:12–13).

52. By and Through Faith

Or is God the God of Jews only? Is he not the God of Gentiles also? Yes, of Gentiles also, since God is one—who will justify the circumcised by faith and the uncircumcised through faith. —Romans 3:29–30

THE PERSON OF CHRIST WAS THE PLAN OF GOD FOR THE WHOLE world from the beginning of time. Peter states this clearly in his first epistle:

> but with the precious blood of Christ, like that of a lamb without blemish or spot. He was foreknown before the foundation of the world but was made manifest in the last times for the sake of you who through him are believers in God, who raised him from the dead and gave him glory, so that your faith and hope are in God" (1 Peter 1:19–21).

Therefore, God is not the God of the Jews only, but the God of the Gentiles also. Paul has already treated the privilege of being a Jew and clarified that theirs was a special inheritance as priests to the world but that righteousness is obtained by all the same way, by faith alone in Christ alone. Paul applies this very truth in response to the racial conflicts in the church at Ephesus:

> For he himself is our peace, who has made us both one and has broken down in his flesh the dividing wall of hostility by abolishing the law of commandments expressed in ordinances, that he might create in himself one new man in place of the two, so making peace, and might reconcile us both to God in one body through the cross, thereby killing the hostility. (Ephesians 2:14–16)

Paul's last statement in verse thirty of Romans 3 has been the subject of some debate, namely what is meant that God, who is one, will justify the circumcised (the Jew) *by* faith and the uncircumcised (the Gentile) *through* faith? He is saying essentially the same thing. There is nothing in the syntax that suggests a difference in how justification is obtained. *By* and *through* seem to mean the same thing in this context.

There are two potential explanations, however. One is that Paul is conscientiously varying his word choice for literary purposes (so his writing doesn't sound awkward). Although that is probable, I'm not convinced of this argument.

The other is that Paul is accommodating the Jewish position to explain how they obtain justification *by* faith, meaning more directly, because of their privileged proximity to God as a priestly nation; and, the Gentiles obtained justification *through* faith, that is indirectly, through the priestly work of the Jewish people (they are the physical, human source of Jesus the Christ). And by stating this way, he is only reaffirming more precisely what he has previously argued via syllogism.

Regardless, at the end of the day, the expressions mean essentially the exact same thing: justification is by/through faith in Christ for all who believe.

53. Faith in Christ Upholds the Law

Do we then overthrow the law by this faith? By no means! On the contrary, we uphold the law. —Romans 3:31

IT IS THE SAME OLD STORY. THE SAME ACCUSATIONS LEVELED against Paul were also made against Jesus—that he was trying to abolish the law. Jesus said to the Jews, "Do not think that I have come to abolish the Law or the Prophets; I have not come to abolish them but to fulfill them" (Matthew 5:17).

NOTA BENE: The word *overthrow* is the word the ESV translators used for the Greek word Paul uses, καταργοῦμεν (*katargoumen*), which means *to abolish; set aside; wipe out.* The verb is conjugated from καταργέω (*katargeo)*, which means to lose its power or effectiveness, invalidate, make powerless. The KJV and NKJV translators chose the expression "make void." The translators of the NIV and EOB used "nullify."

Righteousness by faith in Christ does not overthrow, make void, or nullify the efficacy of the law. It must be remembered that the law was never meant to produce righteousness by works. Effectually, it revealed the moral character of God and the immoral character of fallen man.

What then? In reality, the law is confirmed and established through faith in Christ, inasmuch as it was given to the Jews for this reason. The law, by showing man his own iniquity, in turn, points men to Christ. As Paul says later in this very letter, "*. . . if it had not been for the law, I would not have known sin. For I would not have known what it is to covet if the law had not said, "You shall not covet"*" (Romans 7:7).

It would be like complaining that the salted oats did not quench your horse's thirst. They were never meant to. The oats were salted to make the horse drink the water. Though this is not a perfect analogy—for the law wasn't meant to make us sin but to show us our sinfulness—it gives us a better understanding of its purpose.

Perhaps the mirror is a better example. The mirror only reveals the broccoli stuck in our teeth, it can't remove it. But now having seen how gross the broccoli looks stuck in our teeth, we reach for our toothbrush. The Law is the mirror and the toothbrush is Christ.

Paul's later explanation continues this way:

> . . . I would not have known what it is to covet if the law had not said, "You shall not covet." But sin, seizing an opportunity through the commandment, produced in me all kinds of covetousness. For apart from the law, sin lies dead. I was once alive apart from the law, but when the commandment came, sin came alive and I died. The very commandment that promised life proved to be death to me. For sin, seizing an opportunity through the commandment, deceived me and through it killed me. So the law is holy, and the commandment is holy and righteous and good. (Romans 7:8–12)

54. Father Abraham

What then shall we say was gained by Abraham, our forefather according to the flesh? —Romans 4:1

PAUL NOW MOVES FROM COGENT ARGUMENTS IN CHAPTERS 1–3 to "confirmation by example" in chapter 4. This is also a good time to recall that the chapters and verses we use today were helpfully added later in church history—around AD 1277 by Stephen Langton, who was the Archbishop of Canterbury—and what the Romans who received the epistle would have read was a single cogent letter. The point being, we don't want to get distracted by the divisions of chapters and verses and miss the continuity of Paul's thought.

Moving from the theological framework to the specific example of the Father of Israel, Abraham, would be the most natural way to progress. How does the way God dealt with Abraham teach us about God's plan for today?

And this is a key point too often dismissed in modern Christianity. Christianity is an inheritance of the Jews and Jews have their inheritance in Abraham. Thus, Abraham is our forefather. There is a continuity to our faith. We have a heritage and that heritage has purchase on our worship and works.

It is important for us to remember the Christian tradition was not manifest in a vacuum. It wasn't developed in the philosophical schools of Greece or Egypt (albeit the Hellenistic Greco-Romans world certainly influenced the language and thought of Christianity expressed). Nor was it thought up by a rag-tag group of dissenting Jews.

It has its roots in Abraham, whom God called out of Ur of the Chaldeans (the metropolitan hub of ancient Paganism) and gave him a new name. "You are the Lord, the God who chose Abram and brought him out of Ur of the Chaldeans and gave him the name Abraham" (Nehemiah 9:7, cf. Genesis 11:28–12:5).

St. Ambrose, writing in the fourth century, emphasized the continuity of this inheritance, when he noted that Christians are the heirs of Abraham's faith. He wrote, "I do not demand a reason from Christ. If I am convinced by reason, I deny faith. Abraham believed God. Let us also believe, so that we who are the heirs of his race may likewise be heirs of his faith."[23]

23. Gerald Bray, ed., Romans (Revised), *Ancient Christian Commentary on Scripture* (Downers Grove, IL: InterVarsity Press, 1998), 107.

55. A Better Sacrifice

For if Abraham was justified by works, he has something to boast about, but not before God. For what does the Scripture say? "Abraham believed God, and it was counted to him as righteousness." —Romans 4:2–3

IN VERSE 2, PAUL OFFERS SOMETHING LIKE AN *ENTHYMEME*—an argument with an implied premise (because it should be obvious based on what has already been established by Paul's argument)—to set up his next train of arguments: that Abraham's example proves righteousness is obtained by faith.

If the enthymeme in verse 2 were expanded into a complete syllogism, it could be understood to say:

Premise 1: If Abraham was justified by works, he would have something to boast about (or glory in) before the throne of God.

Premise 2: But he does not have any works to bring before God which would merit his own righteousness

Conclusion: therefore, he was not justified by works.

With this, Paul immediately moves to his real point. By testimony of the Scripture, he demonstrates that Abraham was justified by faith. Here he quotes from Genesis 15:6: "*And he [Abraham] believed the Lord, and he counted it to him as righteousness.*"

God's righteousness was imputed to Abraham because he simply believed what God promised him. Some contend that Paul stretches the use of this scenario to apply it to eternal salvation by faith in Christ. But it's no stretch. God's promise to Abraham was a covenant of grace, like ours: "And behold, the word of the Lord came to him: 'This man shall not be your heir; your very own son shall be your heir.' And he brought him outside and said, 'Look toward heaven, and number the stars, if you are able to number them.' Then he said to him, 'So shall your offspring be'" (Genesis 15:4–5).

Whereby having taken possession of the covenant by faith, it was counted (added to his income ledger as it were) to Abraham as righteousness, which is the same thing as saying he was counted justified before the throne of God.

Commenting on this verse, John Calvin says, "Abraham, by believing, embraced nothing but the favour offered to him, being persuaded that it would not be void. Since this was imputed to him for righteousness, it follows, that he was not otherwise just, than as one trusting in God's goodness, and venturing to hope for all things from him."[24]

Like Abraham, we today who are under the new covenant (really, the same covenant of faith but with a better sacrifice cf. Hebrews 6:13–8:13) are also not justified by our own works. (If Abraham couldn't be, we certainly couldn't be.) Rather, the promise of the gospel is brought to us—that is the good news of Christ's work on our behalf—and we can only take possession of the promise by the instrument of faith.

If we believe God about the ministry of Jesus, it is counted to us as righteousness before the throne of God.

24. John Calvin and John Owen, *Commentary on the Epistle of Paul the Apostle to the Romans* (Bellingham, WA: Logos Bible Software, 2010), 156.

56. Wages Are Not a Gift

Now to the one who works, his wages are not counted as a gift but as his due. And to the one who does not work but believes in him who justifies the ungodly, his faith is counted as righteousness . . . —Romans 4:4–5

IT'S A GOOD TIME TO REMEMBER THAT PAUL IS NOT TALKING here about how to live our lives as Christians. That will come later, in chapters 12–16. He is talking here about how to be saved, how the ungodly can be justified and counted righteous.

He argues from the understanding that the one who works is called a worker. Workers are given wages, earnings for what they have done. And as Paul has already demonstrated, we cannot earn merits with God by our works of the law because, as he will eventually demonstrate, "*. . . the wages of sin is death, but the free gift of God is eternal life in Christ Jesus our Lord*" (Romans 6:23).

Additionally, if it were to be called a wage, it couldn't be called a gift because a wage signifies something is owed; and that makes men mercenaries and God beholden to them. Instead God counts our belief as righteousness imputed to us. Our belief, or faith, is not meritorious. Faith is simply the instrument given to us by God that is used so that righteousness can be imputed.

St. Augustine's manner of distinguishing between the gift of grace and works is insightful. He wrote,

> Paul was speaking here of the way wages are given. But God gave by grace, because he gave to sinners so that by faith they might live justly, that is, do good works. Thus the good works which we do after we have received grace are not to be attributed to us but rather to him who has justified us by his grace. For if God had wanted to give us our due reward, he would have given us the punishment due to sinners.[25]

Martin Bucer summarizes the whole of the passage this way:

25. Gerald Bray, ed., Romans (Revised), Ancient Christian Commentary on Scripture (Downers Grove, IL: InterVarsity Press, 1998), 107–108.

> If one merits any thing by his work, what is merited is not freely imputed to him, but rendered to him as his due. Faith is counted for righteousness, not that it procures any merit for us, but because it lays hold on the goodness of God: hence righteousness is not due to us, but freely bestowed.[26]

Charles Spurgeon summarized the difference between grace and works by explaining that faith is merely the hands of the undeserving beggar used to take hold of the alms offered by the one with something to give.

26. John Calvin and John Owen, *Commentary on the Epistle of Paul the Apostle to the Romans* (Bellingham, WA: Logos Bible Software, 2010), 158.

57. Privileged Recipient of Divine Favor

. . .just as David also speaks of the blessing of the one to whom God counts righteousness apart from works:

> *"Blessed are those whose lawless deeds are forgiven,*
> *and whose sins are covered;*
> *blessed is the man against whom the Lord will not count his sin."*

—Romans 4:6–8

PAUL INTRODUCES ANOTHER TESTIMONY FROM SCRIPTURE and another way of thinking about God's imputing righteousness to men, David's negative clause from Psalm 32:1–2: "Blessed is the one whose transgression is forgiven, whose sin is covered. Blessed is the man against whom the Lord counts no iniquity, and in whose spirit there is no deceit."

God justifies men by *not* imputing his sin to his account. Instead he *forgives* his lawless deeds by covering them.

The word *forgiven* is the Greek work, ἀφίημι (*apheimi*), which means to release from legal or moral obligation or consequence. The word *covered* is the Greek word, ἐπικαλύπτω (*epikalypto*), which means to put out of sight.

Righteousness then is the remission of sins, something not earned by works but given gratuitously by God.

This is what it means to be blessed μακάριος (*makarios*), meaning *privileged recipient of divine favor.*[27]

27. William Arndt et al., *A Greek-English Lexicon of the New Testament and Other Early Christian Literature* (Chicago: University of Chicago Press, 2000), 611.

58. The Blessing Is for Both

Is this blessing then only for the circumcised, or also for the uncircumcised? For we say that faith was counted to Abraham as righteousness. —*Romans 4:9*

FOR THE JEWS OF PAUL'S DAY, CIRCUMCISION WAS CONSIDered to be the first work of the law toward righteousness. All other works needed to be established by that work first.

But Paul will show otherwise—that righteousness comes graciously from God alone and that no ceremony is able to produce the righteousness of God for our salvation.

Verses 9–17 make up the next stage of Paul's argument. But here he initiates the next stage by raising the question to whom belongs the blessing to which David refers (vss. 7–8)?

Is this forgiveness of sins for the circumcised only? Is it reserved for those, like David, who were under the covenant blessing? Or does the blessing apply to the uncircumcised also?

As it shall be seen, Paul will argue that it is for both since God made the covenant with Abraham 14 years before he was circumcised, while he was still an uncircumcised Gentile.

59. The Father of Uncircumcised Believers

How then was it counted to him? Was it before or after he had been circumcised? It was not after, but before he was circumcised. He received the sign of circumcision as a seal of the righteousness that he had by faith while he was still uncircumcised. The purpose was to make him the father of all who believe without being circumcised, so that righteousness would be counted to them as well . . .
—Romans 4:10–11

BY ARGUMENT OF CAUSE AND EFFECT, PAUL MAKES THE POINT, then gives the purpose for the point.

Paul reasons that if it was counted to Abraham as righteousness (the remission of sins) before he was circumcised, then it corresponds that righteousness was possessed by Abraham before he had been circumcised. Circumcision, then, was a sign of the righteousness he received by faith (when he was still an uncircumcised Gentile).

Why did God order the events this way? It was so Abraham would be the father of all who have faith and not only the father of all them who are circumcised. By being the father of all who have faith, it can be shown that it is by faith that one attains righteousness, not by circumcision.

Although it is not argued here, it was previously mentioned that James' letter has caused some consternation because it appears to some that he is contradicting Paul.

But, it is clear from Paul's reasoning that if one were to ask him hypothetically whether some offspring of Abraham who rejected circumcision and refused the rite but claimed he had faith were righteous (had received the remission of sins), Paul would say with James that "*faith by itself, if it does not have works, is dead*" (James 2:17).

In other words, righteousness is received through faith; but faith, if it is real, will result in works (i.e., circumcision).

60. "Faith in Christ" Is the Rule

He received the sign of circumcision as a seal of the righteousness that he had by faith while he was still uncircumcised. The purpose was to make him the father of all who believe without being circumcised, so that righteousness would be counted to them as well, and to make him the father of the circumcised who are not merely circumcised but who also walk in the footsteps of the faith that our father Abraham had before he was circumcised. —Romans 4:11–12

GOD ORDERED THE EVENTS THIS WAY NOT ONLY SO ABRAHAM would be the father of all who have faith while still uncircumcised (Gentiles), but also so he would be the father of all them *who are not merely circumcised but who also walk in the footsteps of the faith (True Israel).* "For not all who are descended from Israel belong to Israel" (Romans 9:6).

Who then among the Israelites are the true Israel? "For good news came to us (True Israel) just as to them (Ethnic Israel), but the message they heard did not benefit them, because they were not united by faith with those who listened" (Hebrews 4:2).

And "For neither circumcision counts for anything, nor uncircumcision, but a new creation. And as for all who walk by this rule, peace and mercy be upon them, and upon the Israel of God" (Galatians 6:15–16).

When Paul refers to "all who walk by this rule," he is referring to those who by faith are "a new creation [in Christ]." See Romans 6:4: "We were buried therefore with him by baptism into death, in order that, just as Christ was raised from the dead by the glory of the Father, we too might walk in newness of life."

Those who received the Word of God (about Christ's death, burial, and resurrection) by faith the way Abraham received the Word of God (about the promise) by faith, are new creations. This is the rule (faith in Christ) the true Israel walks by, not circumcision and uncircumcision minus faith.

This leads us to an important conclusion, one that Paul will qualify and expound on going forward: Abraham's faith and subsequent receipt of a promise prior to being circumcised shows that the covenant God made with him was real but a shadow of something better to come. In that sense it was temporary, as is the period of the Mosaic Law.

It was an inadequate, although preparatory, substitute for the ultimate and complete covenant that would be confirmed in the Incarnation and work of the Second Person of the Godhead himself, Jesus Christ.

61. Heirs of the World

For the promise to Abraham and his offspring that he would be heir of the world did not come through the law but through the righteousness of faith. —Romans 4:13

PAUL FINALLY SITUATES LAW AND FAITH IN DIRECT OPPOSItion. The promise of heirship was not made to Abraham because he earned favor with God by keeping the law. It had not yet been given. Abraham received it as a direct result of the mercy of God, through the righteousness of faith.

God's promise to give Canaan to Abraham and his heirs was a type (a foreshadowing) of the ultimate promise to give Christ not only the world he first created and later redeemed but also all those in it who believe.

While the ungodly attempt to gather to themselves the riches of this world, none of it belongs to them. The redeemed world belongs to the heirs of Abraham—and ultimately to Christ—that is, to all those who believe. Therefore, it is the *meek* who shall inherit the earth.

> For the evildoers shall be cut off, but those who wait *[hope in faith]* for the Lord shall inherit the land. In just a little while, the wicked will be no more; though you look carefully at his place, he will not be there. But the meek *[the bowed]* shall inherit the land and delight themselves in abundant peace. (Psalm 37:9–11)

> Blessed are the meek, for they shall inherit the earth. (Matthew 5:5)

Consider a smattering of additional testimony from Scripture affirming the true heirs of the world are those who follow Abraham's example by believing God's promise and receiving the righteousness of faith:

> I will tell of the decree: The Lord said to me, "You are my Son; today I have begotten you. Ask of me, and I will make the nations your heritage, and the ends of the earth your possession. You shall break

them with a rod of iron and dash them in pieces like a potter's vessel" . . . . Kiss the Son, lest he be angry, and you perish in the way, for his wrath is quickly kindled. Blessed are all who take refuge in him. (Psalm 2:7–9, 12)

For we know that the whole creation has been groaning together in the pains of childbirth until now. (Romans 8:22, cf. Hebrews 1:2: "But in these last days he has spoken to us by his Son, whom he appointed the heir of all things, through whom also he created the world.")

For God so loved the world (cosmos), that he gave his only Son, that whoever believes in him should not perish but have eternal life. For God did not send his Son into the world (cosmos) to condemn the world (cosmos), but in order that the world (cosmos) might be saved through him. (John 3:16–17)

62. Faith is Null and the Promise is Void

For if it is the adherents of the law who are to be the heirs, faith is null and the promise is void. —Romans 4:14

RAISING A HYPOTHETICAL SITUATION IN ORDER TO SHOW ITS ineffectiveness, Paul will conclude that faith is dead which rests in keeping the law instead of the goodness of God. And, if there is no faith—if it is in effect null and void—then there would be no way to claim the promise of heirship because faith is the instrument by which the promise is claimed.

John Calvin's note on this passage is, though incomplete, nevertheless instructive. He writes,

> who is there so conscious of so much perfection that he can feel assured that the inheritance is due to him through the righteousness of the law? Void then would faith be made; for an impossible condition would not only hold the minds of men in suspense and anxiety, but fill them also with fear and trembling: and thus the fulfilment of the promises would be rendered void; for they avail nothing but when received by faith.[28]

A consciousness so robust as to be in tune with perfection in terms of keeping the law would be required in order for it to be effective; therefore, trusting in God's goodness is the necessary choice, not the insufficient ability to keep the law perfectly. Although Calvin draws this hypothetical option, he affirms elsewhere that faith is a gift of God, an instrument by which the promise can be received rather than a scaling merit system.

What Paul is setting out to prove is that faith and adhering to the Law are mutually exclusive. As verse 15 will demonstrate, the law brings wrath, while Abraham's faith was in a gift freely given. The former directs faith toward the self's attempt at righteousness while the latter directs faith toward God's

28. John Calvin and John Owen, *Commentary on the Epistle of Paul the Apostle to the Romans* (Bellingham, WA: Logos Bible Software, 2010), 170.

righteousness. Only faith in God's righteousness can apprehend the promise because faith in our own righteousness (our ability to keep the law) is null making the promise void.

63. The Law Brings Wrath

For the law brings wrath, but where there is no law there is no transgression.
—Romans 4:15

PAUL IS HERE CONFIRMING WHAT HE WAS PREVIOUSLY explaining (verses 13–14), but now in terms of the contrary effect the law has on fallen man.

The ultimate end of the law for fallen man is wrath, not grace. When the law is not present, Paul does not mean man stops sinning or that man's sin doesn't offend God, but that his sin is not as apparent and therefore not always blatant.

The Greek word παράβασις (*parabasis*) translated *transgression* means *to violate an established boundary or norm, overstepping, transgression.*[29] When the law is present it teaches man what pleases and displeases God. And once he knows the boundaries eternally fixed by God and yet willfully and knowingly sins still, he stirs up the wrath of God—the true and just judgment of the holy Creator.

To illustrate, it's the difference between a hunter who is hot on the trail of his game and accidentally wanders on to private property and harvests his animal versus the hunter who also hot on the trail of his game, enters the private property at place where a 'no trespassing sign' has been posted and harvests his animal. The former who transgressed ignorantly may still be cited for his violation (and had he known it was private property may still have chosen to cross; but since there was nothing posted it cannot be known) but the latter who knew he was about to violate the law and then did so knowingly and willfully will be held to a higher account for his crime.

29. William Arndt et al., *A Greek-English Lexicon of the New Testament and Other Early Christian Literature* (Chicago: University of Chicago Press, 2000), 758.

64. Guaranteed to All His Offspring

That is why it depends on faith, in order that the promise may rest on grace and be guaranteed to all his offspring—not only to the adherent of the law but also to the one who shares the faith of Abraham, who is the father of us all . . .
—Romans 4:16

PAUL IS WRAPPING UP HIS ARGUMENT NOW. HE SUMMARIZES that if the promise is to be guaranteed to all of Abraham's offspring, then it must rest on grace; therefore, to that end, God has determined that the fulfillment of the promise should come through faith.

That is, the promise only stands firm when it depends on grace. John Calvin notes, "for by this expression Paul confirms this truth, that as long as men depend on works, they are harassed with doubts; for they deprive themselves of what the promises contain."[30]

In the next verse (vs 17), Paul will supply scriptural support for his argument's conclusion.

30. John Calvin and John Owen, *Commentary on the Epistle of Paul the Apostle to the Romans* (Bellingham, WA: Logos Bible Software, 2010), 173.

65. Fecundity *Ex Nihilo*

That is why it depends on faith, in order that the promise may rest on grace and be guaranteed to all his offspring—not only to the adherent of the law but also to the one who shares the faith of Abraham, who is the father of us all, as it is written, "I have made you the father of many nations"—in the presence of the God in whom he believed, who gives life to the dead and calls into existence the things that do not exist. —Romans 4:16–17

HERE IN VERSE 17, PAUL SUPPLIES SCRIPTURAL SUPPORT FOR the argument he is wrapping up in verse 16. In doing so, he recounts the covenant God made with Abraham: "No longer shall your name be called Abram, but your name shall be Abraham, for I have made you the father of a multitude of nations" (Genesis 17:5).

Abraham is the father of us all, Paul argues, because God established the covenant with Abraham by faith which made him the father of not only the Jews (those who would receive the Law some four hundred years later) but also of the Gentiles who share in the faith of Abraham.

In the final clause, Paul highlights the content (and the character of the content) of Abraham's faith—God.

Abraham neither trusted in his own merits, nor in the gods of the Chaldeans, but in the God who gives life to the dead and calls into existence things that do not exist.

This way of describing God obviously refers to the content of the promise God made to Abraham in Genesis 17, namely that Sarah who was 90 (far beyond childbearing age) would conceive and give them a son who would make Abraham the father of many nations. To do that, God would have to call into existence things that do not exist—fecundity, *ex nihilo*.

66. The Kind of Faith That Saves All Men

In hope he believed against hope, that he should become the father of many nations, as he had been told, "So shall your offspring be." —Romans 4:18

AND NOW, PAUL HIGHLIGHTS ABRAHAM'S ROBUST FAITH. Abraham believed God's promise when all things material were contrary to human reason. He was himself a hundred years old and Sarah, ninety. They were both beyond childbearing years; but what did that matter?

God told Abraham that he should become the father of many nations and he believed God rather than that which his reason, or his eyes, or his experience told him. As the author of the letter to the Hebrews notes, Abraham's was exemplary of the very definition of faith:

> Now faith is the assurance of things hoped for, the conviction of things not seen. (Hebrews 11:1)
>
> By faith Abraham obeyed when he was called to go out to a place that he was to receive as an inheritance. And he went out, not knowing where he was going. By faith he went to live in the land of promise, as in a foreign land, living in tents with Isaac and Jacob, heirs with him of the same promise. For he was looking forward to the city that has foundations, whose designer and builder is God. By faith Sarah herself received power to conceive, even when she was past the age, since she considered him faithful who had promised. Therefore from one man, and him as good as dead, were born descendants as many as the stars of heaven and as many as the innumerable grains of sand by the seashore. (Hebrews 11:8–12)

Ultimately, Paul is demonstrating that Abraham's faith—faith that believes what God says regardless of what man can prove—is the kind of faith that saves all men, Jew and Gentile alike.

67. Kind Versus Degree

He did not weaken in faith when he considered his own body, which was as good as dead (since he was about a hundred years old), or when he considered the barrenness of Sarah's womb. No unbelief made him waver concerning the promise of God, but he grew strong in his faith as he gave glory to God, fully convinced that God was able to do what he had promised. That is why his faith was "counted to him as righteousness." —Romans 4:19–22

THIS SHORT NARRATIVE IS A RECAP OF ABRAHAM'S FAITH IN preparation for Paul to return to his broader argument, namely that Abraham is the father of those who received righteousness by faith. Paul will return to the present application of faith under the New Covenant.

But here Paul tells us *how* Abraham believed. Instead of weakening in faith when he saw his circumstances, his faith in God was established as he gave God glory. He did not waver because looking to God instead of his circumstances he was fully convinced that God was able to do what he promised. There is something profound here. Paul explains that what happened between God and Abraham is the very reason why his faith was counted to him as righteousness.

This is not the place to debate the technicalities of synergism vs monergism (God and man working together versus God working on behalf of both parties)—and we do know that the Genesis narrative to which Paul is referring here shows that God put Abraham to sleep and performed the Covenant sacrifice on behalf of both parties—but Paul is clearly pointing to Abraham's faith in this passage.

Origin's comments on this passage are insightful and encouraging:

> As always, when the apostle Paul talks about faith, he adds hope as well, and rightly so, for hope and faith are inseparable. . . . Just as Abraham believed against hope, so all believers do the same, for we all believe in the resurrection of the dead and the inheritance of the kingdom of heaven. These appear to go against hope as far as human

> nature is concerned, but when we take the power of God into consideration, there is no problem.[31]

Abraham didn't believe his circumstances; he believed his God. That is the kind of faith God counts. It is a matter of *kind* and not *degree*. In other words, Abraham didn't muster enough faith in order to reach a threshold that satisfied God, who in turn, counted it to him for righteousness.

Rather, Abraham possessed the kind of faith that sees his truly impossible circumstances and simultaneously sees the glory and power of God and is convinced that God is able to do what he promises. Possessing the right kind, not the degree, of faith, God counted it to him as righteousness.

31. Gerald Bray, ed., *Romans (Revised)*, Ancient Christian Commentary on Scripture (Downers Grove, IL: InterVarsity Press, 1998), 118.

68. Written for Our Sakes

But the words "it was counted to him" were not written for his sake alone, but for ours also. It will be counted to us who believe in him who raised from the dead Jesus our Lord, who was delivered up for our trespasses and raised for our justification. —Romans 4:23–25

FINALLY, PAUL APPLIES HIS ILLUSTRATION OF ABRAHAM'S faith to his current point. The fact that Scripture records Abraham's faith as being counted to him for righteousness was not written merely to honor Abraham. If it was written to honor anyone, it was written to honor God's faithfulness to be merciful to sinners, to honor his righteousness.

But Paul tells us it was recorded for our sakes also!

Faith is counted as righteousness to Paul's readers also—if they believe the promises God gave to them. Here is a key. Abraham believed God about the promise made him. Though God's promise, long-range, included Christ, what was immediately promised was to give Abraham a son in his old age that would make him the father of many nations.

Abraham believed God. Though he may not have fully understood that the way God would accomplish the promise would be to crucify and resurrect a distant son of Isaac's, Abraham believed God's ability was greater than his own understanding.

This is true also for Paul's readers, and by extension, true for us reading Paul's letter today. God delivered up Jesus our Lord to pay for our trespasses, then he raised him up from the dead to vindicate Jesus (as one who was sinless, he did not deserve death; but he died for us) and for (on account of completing) our justification (Jesus is the first fruits of the resurrection, cf. 1 Corinthians 15:23).

In other words, Jesus's resurrection was the proof that God accepted Jesus' sacrifice (cf. "and was declared to be the Son of God in power according to the Spirit of holiness by his resurrection from the dead, Jesus Christ our Lord . . ." (Romans 1:4).

And now, every person who responds to the promise by faith (in kind with Abraham), it is counted to him for righteousness as well.

69. We Have Peace With God

Therefore, since we have been justified by faith, we have peace with God through our Lord Jesus Christ. —Romans 5:1

WHENEVER WE SEE A *WHEREFORE* OR A *THEREFORE* IN SCRIPTURE, it's a clue for us to go back and see what it's there for.

In our case, we have been following very closely with the developments of Paul's argument. He has demonstrated, by appealing to the Covenant promise God made to Abraham which was imputed to him by faith, that justification is by faith and not works of the Law.

Now that we have established, says Paul, that justification is by faith in God and that our faith has secured the same for us that it did for Abraham, we can be sure that we have *peace with God through our Lord Jesus Christ.*

The English word *peace* is translated from the Greek word εἰρήνη *(eirene)* which means to be in harmony, in a state of concord, and not in a state of war. This is worth meditating and reflecting on. We who were at enmity with God because of our sins, are no longer; we're at peace with him and counted as sons.

As the substance of God's promise to Abraham was heirship (peace as a son) through the seed of a once dead and now resurrected son (of which Isaac is a type: first as being dead in Abraham's loins and second as being resurrected on Mt. Moriah—which would later become the temple site where sacrifices were made), so is the substance of God's promise to us who have been justified by faith—peace as sons through God's resurrected Son (i.e., Mount Calvary).

Cross reference this with what Paul later writes in Romans 8:14–17:

> For all who are led by the Spirit of God are sons of God. For you did not receive the spirit of slavery to fall back into fear, but you have received the Spirit of adoption as sons, by whom we cry, "Abba! Father!" The Spirit himself bears witness with our spirit that we are children of God, and if children, then heirs—heirs of God and fellow heirs with Christ, provided we suffer with him in order that we may also be glorified with him.

70. We Rejoice in Hope

Through him we have also obtained access by faith into this grace in which we stand, and we rejoice in hope of the glory of God. —Romans 5:2

THROUGH HIM: HIM BEING JESUS CHRIST, WHO WAS MENtioned in the previous verse. Everything about our salvation depends on Jesus Christ. By signifying clearly to his readers upon whom their faith must rest, he dismisses altogether any possible alternative hope, like the merits of their works in the keeping of the Law of Moses.

Also, remarkable are the three movements of salvation in Pauline thought. Through faith in Jesus Christ we obtain *access* to grace, we *stand* in grace, and we *rejoice* in hope, specifically hope of the glory of God.

The word *access* here is quite significant. From the Greek word προσαγωγή (*prosagōgē*), it is used in both sacred and pagan literature to refer to that one place (a gate or a port) where entry can be made on ground or shoreline that offers no access to enemy forces.[32] Think of the gate of a fortress or the port of entry to a country.

So it is by no other than Jesus Christ that we can enter into the grace in which once we enter, we now *stand*. The Greek word ἵστημι (*histemi*) translated *stand* in English has a wide spectrum of meaning (like the English word "cool") so we must rely on the context to discern the specific meaning. Here it means *a condition or state of being*.[33]

Once we have obtained access to God's grace through faith in Jesus Christ, we now stand in this grace. This standing refers to our spiritual condition, literally, our standing before God. This condition, by virtue of the *kind* of faith that saves (not the degree), is immutable. It does not shift or change with our feelings or our failings because the object of faith is one who is immutable, the second person of the Godhead, Jesus Christ.

32. William Arndt et al., *A Greek-English Lexicon of the New Testament and Other Early Christian Literature* (Chicago: University of Chicago Press, 2000), 876.

33. William Arndt et al., *A Greek-English Lexicon of the New Testament and Other Early Christian Literature* (Chicago: University of Chicago Press, 2000), 483.

Once we have obtained access into the fortress of God's grace through the only gate—faith in Jesus Christ—we now stand righteous before God (remember our faith is imputed to us for righteousness); and, we rejoice—not in our own goodness or merits—but in *hope* of the glory of God.

Hope refers to the confidence we have in God's promise. "*Now faith is the assurance of things hoped for, the conviction of things not seen*" (Hebrews 11:1).

We enter, we stand, and we rejoice in this hope!

71. We Rejoice in Our Sufferings Too

Not only that, but we rejoice in our sufferings, knowing that suffering produces endurance, and endurance produces character, and character produces hope, and hope does not put us to shame, because God's love has been poured into our hearts through the Holy Spirit who has been given to us.
—Romans 5:3–5

WHILE BELIEVERS ARE AT PEACE WITH GOD, THE EVIDENCE of our personal experience shows that the world is not at peace with us. So Paul now uses the opportunity to speak to the sufferings of the believers and how it does not diminish but strengthen a true believer's assurance of salvation.

We not only rejoice in the hope of the glory of God but we also rejoice in our sufferings. This is not a sadistic kind of rejoicing but an extension of that foundational rejoicing in the hope of the glory of God. This could be said that we also rejoice in the hope of the providence of God. As a believer, Paul says, we know our suffering produces something good because we have entered and now stand in his grace.

Suffering produces endurance, which means the capacity to hold out or bear up in the face of difficulty.

Endurance produces character. The word translated character means the genuineness of something proved by testing. It's the idea of being without alloy; that is, metal purified by fire which has separated out the dross.

Character produces hope, which means confident expectation; or, having a reason for confidence respecting a promise's fulfillment.

And hope will never produce shame. This is a reference to Isaiah 28:16: "Therefore thus says the Lord God, "Behold, I am the one who has laid as a foundation in Zion, a stone, a tested stone, a precious cornerstone, of a sure foundation: 'Whoever believes will not be in haste.'"

And, the context is that the hope we have been given, will surely not disappoint us because it has been made sure by the manifestation of God's love through the Spirit (Acts 2:17–18, cf. Joel 2:28–29).

In his letter to the Ephesians, Paul calls it the "guarantee of our inheritance" (note how similar the language Paul uses here is to the way he writes in Ephesians 1:11–14).

In sum, we rejoice in our hope while we simultaneously rejoice in our suffering because while we have not yet seen the fulfillment of that hope and we still suffer, we have a confidence that the promise will be fulfilled and the suffering will yield good fruit because God gave us an earnest payment on his promise when he poured out to us the Holy Spirit.

72. At the Right Time

For while we were still weak, at the right time Christ died for the ungodly.
—Romans 5:6

HERE PAUL BEGINS A NEW ARGUMENT FOUNDED ON THE PREvious assertion regarding the love of God being poured out to us. He will argue from the greater to the lesser. That is, he will show that if God is willing to die for the ungodly (greater sinners), how much more will he keep those whom he has made righteous (lesser sinners).

But let us focus on this part of the argument, today. He says, *while we were still weak*. The Greek word for *weak* is ἀσθενής (*asthenēs*) and means *helpless* in a moral sense.

Recall Paul's earlier explanation: "Now we know that whatever the law says it speaks to those who are under the law, so that every mouth may be stopped, and the whole world may be held accountable to God. For by works of the law no human being will be justified in his sight, since through the law comes knowledge of sin" (Romans 3:19–20).

And here in 5:6, the context further reveals this fact in that weak corresponds with ungodly. While we were weak (morally destitute), Christ died for the ungodly (Gr. *ἀσεβής, asebēs*)—those who violate norms for a proper relation to deity, i.e., the impious.

But what is meant by *at the right time*? Paul explains this more fully in his letter to the Galatians: "But when the fullness of time had come, God sent forth his Son, born of woman, born under the law, to redeem those who were under the law, so that we might receive adoption as sons. And because you are sons, God has sent the Spirit of his Son into our hearts, crying, 'Abba! Father!'" (Galatians 4:4–6).

What Paul is demonstrating is that redemption is the master-plan of God, orchestrated in history *by* him *for* us, and each aspect has unfolded at its appropriate time. And at the writing of his letter to the Romans, the right time for the incarnation, death, burial, resurrection, and ascension of the Christ had come upon them, in the person of Jesus.

73. While We Were Still Sinners

For one will scarcely die for a righteous person—though perhaps for a good person one would dare even to die—but God shows his love for us in that while we were still sinners, Christ died for us. —Romans 5:7–8

TO ILLUSTRATE THE EXTENT OF GOD'S LOVE, PAUL APPEALS to the unexpected and shows how "the cross is the means by which God demonstrates his love."[34]

A righteous man in this case is in reference to other men, not toward God necessarily. He uses the word δίκαιος (*dikaios*), which is translated *righteous* here and means to be in accordance with high standards of rectitude: upright, just, fair.[35]

Paul is describing what men would say of someone who did what society expected of him (i.e., took care of his family, paid his bills on time, was lawful, and was a man who overall acted in accordance with one who was a good neighbor).

A good man here is used to surpass a merely righteous man in the worldly sense. The Greek word is ἀγαθός (*agathos*) and refers to one who is meeting a high standard of worth and merit.[36]

The good man is one who excels in his righteous behavior, one whom the community admires as above the status quo. He is not only lawful and kind but perhaps generous, maybe even heroic in some sense.

One would seldom find a person who would offer his life for a righteous person; perhaps you might find someone who would willingly lay down his life for one who was admired in the community. But God's love is greater. He died for the lawless ones whom no one would think to give their own precious lives for. That's you and me, says Paul.

Christ died for us who were not righteous or good, but sinners deserving of death.

34. Leon Morris, *The Epistle to the Romans,* The Pillar New Testament Commentary (Grand Rapids, MI: W.B. Eerdmans, 1988), 224.
35. William Arndt et al., A Greek-English Lexicon of the New Testament and Other Early Christian Literature (Chicago: University of Chicago Press, 2000), 246.
36. William Arndt et al., A Greek-English Lexicon of the New Testament and Other Early Christian Literature (Chicago: University of Chicago Press, 2000), 3.

74. Saved by His Life

Since, therefore, we have now been justified by his blood, much more shall we be saved by him from the wrath of God. 10 For if while we were enemies we were reconciled to God by the death of his Son, much more, now that we are reconciled, shall we be saved by his life. —Romans 5:9–10 (ESV)

USING *THEREFORE*, PAUL CONTINUES HIS ARGUMENT FROM the greater to the lesser, showing that salvation is all of God. That means if God is willing to die for the ungodly (greater sinners), how much more will he keep those whom he has made righteous (lesser sinners). Based on what has already been shown—that Christ died for sinners, not good or righteous men—*how much more* shall we be saved from the wrath of God?

The wrath of God is a judicious response to man's rebellion as described in chapter one, and it reveals God's pure hatred of sin. But we have been saved from it by the blood of Christ. Christ alone is our propitiation (1 John 2:2). He is our redeemer. Whatever the full expression of Hell entails, we have been saved from it.

Paul continues: even so, since God has reconciled us to himself by sacrificing his one and only Son for us while we were sinners, how much more will we be saved by the life of Christ now that we are his friends? Christ is now sitting at the right hand of the father making intercession for us.

> Who is to condemn? Christ Jesus is the one who died—more than that, who was raised—who is at the right hand of God, who indeed is interceding for us. (Romans 8:34)

> Consequently, he is able to save to the uttermost those who draw near to God through him, since he always lives to make intercession for them. (Hebrews 7:25)

> My little children, I am writing these things to you so that you may not sin. But if anyone does sin, we have an advocate with the Father, Jesus Christ the righteous. (1 John 2:1)

This is a case of being not only saved from our sins by Christ's ministry of death, but a case of being continually saved (i.e., persevering) by Christ's ministry of resurrection, ongoing intercession (i.e., saved by his life).

75. More Than That

More than that, we also rejoice in God through our Lord Jesus Christ, through whom we have now received reconciliation. —Romans 5:11

IN ADDITION TO REJOICING (BOASTING) IN THE HOPE OF THE glory of God as well as in our sufferings, we can also rejoice in God himself because Jesus Christ has completed our reconciliation. God is our lover and we are his beloved. God is our friend and we his befriended.

It is a wonder that the Christian has much to rejoice in because of Jesus Christ: we have hope in an eternal future with God, and even our sufferings are not meaningless or without hope. But even more than that, we can rejoice in our good standing and personal relationship with God. Our salvation is not merely forensic; it is personal!

As Colin Kruse points out in his commentary, Paul seems to closely link justification and reconciliation. Justification can be seen as the legal (forensic) aspect of our standing, whereas reconciliation speaks of our relational standing with God.[37]

The war between our rebellious hearts and God is over, so complete that he even paid the reparations due him on our behalf. Yet, there is more. We're not only no longer enemies; we are indeed reconciled friends, and allies with God.

37. Colin G. Kruse, *Paul's Letter to the Romans*, ed. D. A. Carson, The Pillar New Testament Commentary (Grand Rapids, MI: Eerdmans, 2012), 238–239.

76. Sin Came Into the World through One Man

Therefore, just as sin came into the world through one man, and death through sin, and so death spread to all men because all sinned—for sin indeed was in the world before the law was given, but sin is not counted where there is no law. Yet death reigned from Adam to Moses, even over those whose sinning was not like the transgression of Adam, who was a type of the one who was to come. —Romans 5:12–14

THIS MAY VERY WELL BE ONE OF THE MORE DIFFICULT PASsages of Paul's letter to understand due to the complicated analogy he is trying to create and the interruptions in his thought to explain elements of his argument as he goes.

The analogy is of two Adams—two federal heads. The federal head of the fallen human race of men and the federal head of the new redeemed race of men. But before he finishes his analogy, he breaks off to explain how the Law and sin worked together for his analogy and in the real experience of humanity.

The first Adam, the father of humanity created in Genesis, brought sin—and by it death—to the whole human race. Once Adam sinned, all of his offspring were considered sinners, first by virtue of being the son of sinners and second by virtue of their subsequent sinful actions.

For his analogy, he will show that Christ was righteous first by virtue of his being born of God and second by virtue of his faithfully keeping the law. But he must first explain that even though the Law would not come till Moses and would not be counted against man in the forensic sense of the law, in reality (eternal law) we know sin did in fact exist because people died between Adam and Moses.

Therefore those who lived between Adam and Moses sinned in reality because death is the wage for sinners, though they would not sin like Adam (a type of Christ in that he is a begotten son of God) who did not keep the law given to him (i.e., Don't eat from the tree of the knowledge of good and evil in the garden!).

In sum, all men living before Christ are in Adam; and all who are in Adam are condemned as sinners because they are his offspring.

77. The Free Gift Is Not Like the Trespass

But the free gift is not like the trespass. For if many died through one man's trespass, much more have the grace of God and the free gift by the grace of that one man Jesus Christ abounded for many. And the free gift is not like the result of that one man's sin. For the judgment following one trespass brought condemnation, but the free gift following many trespasses brought justification. For if, because of one man's trespass, death reigned through that one man, much more will those who receive the abundance of grace and the free gift of righteousness reign in life through the one man Jesus Christ. —Romans 5:15–17

IN THE PREVIOUS VERSES (12–14), PAUL ESTABLISHED THE analogy of the two Adams by comparing their likenesses, but here Paul begins to contrast the two to demonstrate the superiority of the latter: The free gift is *not* like the trespass.

There is the free gift that Paul has already established in the argument leading up to this passage. The free gift is the righteousness of God given to those who, like Abraham, have faith. The trespass is the disobedience of Adam in the garden that plunged humanity into its depraved state, as Paul demonstrated in chapters 1 and 2. The actions of these two Adams (sons of God or federal heads) are to be held in contrast.

The trespass of the first Adam brought death to *many* (euphemism for all mankind). The obedience of the Second Adam (that one man, Jesus Christ) brought grace in abundance to the *many.*

The judgment caused by the first Adam's *one trespass* brought an *abundance* of condemnation to the human race (the descendant of Adam) while the *singular obedience* of the second Adam brought justification to the many whose *sins are in abundance* after the manner of Adam.

Therefore, if *death reigned* as a result of the trespass of the first Adam, we can be sure that those who receive the abundance of grace and the free gift of righteousness given through the one man, Jesus Christ, will now *reign in life.* Instead of being tyrannized by death, they will tyrannize death because they have life more abundantly. Compare John 10:10: *The thief comes only to steal and kill and destroy. I came that they may have life and have it abundantly.*

In sum, the first Adam trespassed and brought sin into the world and by sin brought condemnation—eternal death—for all humanity. The second Adam brought grace and righteousness, and by that gift brought justification and life to all humanity (specifically to those who believe).

78. Reign in Life

For if, because of one man's trespass, death reigned through that one man, much more will those who receive the abundance of grace and the free gift of righteousness reign in life through the one man Jesus Christ. —Romans 5:17

BEFORE MOVING TO THE NEXT POINT OF PAUL'S ARGUMENT, it is worth considering more deeply the idea of "reign" in Paul's present contrast. He asserts that if death reigned as a result of the trespass of the first Adam, we can be sure that those who receive the abundance of grace and the free gift of righteousness given through the one man Jesus Christ will reign in life.

But when?

In one sense, we can understand Paul to be comparing the present suffering under the reign of death with the future joy under the reign of eternal life which Christ has secured for us as the second Adam. But he is clear that believers *will reign in life*. This seems to correspond with Daniel's prophecy and John's Revelation.

> And the kingdom and the dominion and the greatness of the kingdoms under the whole heaven shall be given to the people of the saints of the Most High; his kingdom shall be an everlasting kingdom, and all dominions shall serve and obey him. (Daniel 7:27)

> . . .and you have made them a kingdom and priests to our God, and they shall reign on the earth. (Revelation 5:10)

> Then I saw thrones, and seated on them were those to whom the authority to judge was committed. Also I saw the souls of those who had been beheaded for the testimony of Jesus and for the word of God, and those who had not worshiped the beast or its image and had not received its mark on their foreheads or their hands. They came to life and reigned with Christ for a thousand years. (Revelation 20:4)

> Blessed and holy is the one who shares in the first resurrection! Over such the second death has no power, but they will be priests of God

> and of Christ, and they will reign with him for a thousand years. (Revelation 20:6)

> And night will be no more. They will need no light of lamp or sun, for the Lord God will be their light, and they will reign forever and ever. (Revelation 22:5)

It seems that there is a sense in which those who believe have transcended the present reign of death. Although we must live out our seventy or eighty years in suffering and troubles and eventually pass through the Valley of the Shadow of Death where we will be delivered from the presence of sin, in Christ, we *presently* reign victorious over the power and penalty of sin (death).

There is another sense in which our reign will continue into everlasting glory after our bodies have been resurrected. Then we shall reign with Christ in the renewed world forever and ever.

79. Two Headships

Therefore, as one trespass led to condemnation for all men, so one act of righteousness leads to justification and life for all men. For as by the one man's disobedience the many were made sinners, so by the one man's obedience the many will be made righteous. —Romans 5:18–19

PAUL, CONTINUING HIS COMPARISON, SUMMARIZES THE FEDeral work of the two Adams. The contrast between the one and the many in verse 19 is a concept rooted in ancient political theory. This is an important concept to understand in order to comprehend Paul's argument. Some have by this passage misunderstood Paul to be teaching universalism. But to do so would be to impose modern democratic thinking on the ancient text.

The *one* is the monarch, the federal or seminal head of a people. The *many* are the people, those under the headship. The broader political treatment includes the few, the aristocrats or oligarchs.

To this end, the phrase *Cuius regio, eius religio* (literally, "whose realm, their religion" – the religion of the ruler was to dictate the religion of those ruled) held important meaning in the Middle Ages.

The first Adam trespassed (i.e., he transgressed God's law), an act that brought condemnation to all men under his federal headship; which is also seminal for all who are born have been born of the first Adam.

The second Adam obeyed the Father, even unto death (John 8:29), an act that brought justification and life to all men under his headship (i.e., all those who believe).

We can now begin to think of all humanity being under one of the two federal headships—the headship of the first Adam (to which all men are born) and the headship of the second Adam (to which only those who believe can be born).

Thus, Jesus told Nicodemus in John 3 that *he must be born again.*

80. Where Sin Increased, Grace Abounded All the More

Now the law came in to increase the trespass, but where sin increased, grace abounded all the more, so that, as sin reigned in death, grace also might reign through righteousness leading to eternal life through Jesus Christ our Lord.
—Romans 5:20–21

PAUL NOW EXPLAINS WHY THE LAW WAS BROUGHT INTO THE picture. In verses 13–14, Paul explains that men died before the law because sinned reigned even then. Without much explanation, he states that "sin is not counted where there is no law." Here is where he picks up the idea again and finishes that thought.

One of the reasons the law came into the picture was to increase the trespass—make it more noticeable, more apparent.

Of course, that is not the only use of the law, but it is the law's purpose in the context of Paul's present argument. The law was given to be a mirror so men could see the true nature of his sinful condition and recognize his condemned standing before God. Calvin has a helpful analogy for this. He writes,

> He indeed teaches us, that it was needful that men's ruin should be more fully discovered to them, in order that a passage might be opened for the favour of God. They were indeed shipwrecked before the law was given; as however they seemed to themselves to swim, while in their destruction, they were thrust down into the deep, that their deliverance might appear more evident, when they thence emerge beyond all human expectation. Nor was it unreasonable, that the law should be partly introduced for this end—that it might again condemn men already condemned; for nothing is more reasonable than that men should, through all means be brought, nay, forced, by being proved guilty, to know their own evils.[38]

38. John Calvin and John Owen, *Commentary on the Epistle of Paul the Apostle to the Romans* (Bellingham, WA: Logos Bible Software, 2010), 214.

The law forces men to see how guilty, how evil they really are.

But where the law has increased sin (revealed it more clearly), grace abounded all the more. No matter how deep, how ugly the sin is, it can not exceed the depth and beauty of grace that leads men to eternal life through Jesus Christ our Lord.

Yes, sin brings death. But grace also brings something: not just life, but eternal life. And this grace triumphs over death because it brings life, not through the law, but through the righteousness that can only be received apart from the law (Romans 3:21), through Jesus Christ.

81. By No Means!

What shall we say then? Are we to continue in sin that grace may abound? By no means! How can we who died to sin still live in it? —Romans 6:1–2

NOW WE SEE WHAT PROFOUND DEPTHS OF GOD'S WISDOM AND saving grace Paul must plunder in order to make the gospel, so clearly laid out already, understandable to those who willingly slander him. We must keep in view two things Paul has already stated if we are to grasp the depth of what seems to be such crude utterance: *by no means!*

First, he said in Romans 3:21–25:

> But now the righteousness of God has been manifested apart from the law, although the Law and the Prophets bear witness to it— the righteousness of God through faith in Jesus Christ for all who believe. For there is no distinction: for all have sinned and fall short of the glory of God, and are justified by his grace as a gift, through the redemption that is in Christ Jesus, whom God put forward as a propitiation by his blood, to be received by faith. This was to show God's righteousness, because in his divine forbearance he had passed over former sins.

It is clear as daylight that salvation—justification before God—can only be attained through faith in Jesus Christ because all are sinners and cannot please God by keeping the law. They must receive the gift of grace (unmerited favor) from God that was accomplished by Jesus for us. And the greater the sin, the greater the grace (cf. Romans 5:18–21).

Second, in Romans 3:7–8, he mentions in passing that he is often slandered as condoning sin so grace can abound. He says, "But if through my lie God's truth abounds to his glory, why am I still being condemned as a sinner? And why not do evil that good may come?—as some people slanderously charge us with saying. Their condemnation is just."

The answer to the claim that since where sin abounds, grace much more abounds, we should, therefore, continue in sin so grace will continue to abound (that which Paul had been accused of preaching) is: *by no means!* That's not the way it works.

Why? Because we cannot separate or compartmentalize the work of Christ who imputed his righteousness to us. The work of Christ is not merely justification. It is redemption too. It is sanctification and glorification as well.

If we have Christ's righteousness imputed to us as our just standing before God, the only way we could have attained it is by our union with Christ in his death and resurrection. If we died with Christ, we also died to sin.

Therefore, we cannot continue in sin that grace may abound because we died to sin and were raised to walk in newness of life in Christ (as we shall soon learn, cf. Romans 6:4).

82. Baptized into Christ's Death

Do you not know that all of us who have been baptized into Christ Jesus were baptized into his death? We were buried therefore with him by baptism into death, in order that, just as Christ was raised from the dead by the glory of the Father, we too might walk in newness of life. —Romans 6:3–4

HERE IS A PASSAGE THAT EXPLAINS IN FULL WHAT PAUL merely alluded to in the previous verses (1–2).

Baptism is not merely memorial as some would imply by calling it an ordinance. Baptism is sacramental in that it is the appointed sign which signifies the death of our old man, the one born under the headship of the first Adam. While baptismal water does not wash away sins per se, it is that unique and genuine symbol of our union with Christ in his death and resurrection by the Holy Spirit.[39] "For in one Spirit we were all baptized into one body—Jews or Greeks, slaves or free—and all were made to drink of one Spirit" (1 Corinthians 12:13).

This union of ours with Christ into his death further brings forth fruit by way of his resurrection. Like Christ, we are raised from the dead by the glory of the Father, that we might walk in newness of life.

This spiritual condition of this new life in Christ is real even now while we wait for the death of our bodies, that we might be resurrected in our new bodies at the appointed day.

Consider Paul's words from his two letters to the Corinthians:

> For this perishable body must put on the imperishable, and this mortal body must put on immortality. When the perishable puts on the imperishable, and the mortal puts on immortality, then shall come to pass the saying that is written: "Death is swallowed up in victory."

39. Sacraments, like baptism, truly offer what they signify, but they benefit only those who receive them in faith. Thus, a sacrament may be valid without being beneficial. The Latin terms are ex opere operato (referring to the objective validity of the sacrament) and ex opere operantis (referring to the subjective benefit of the sacrament, whether the recipient is submitting to the sacrament in faith or not).

"O death, where is your victory? O death, where is your sting?" The sting of death is sin, and the power of sin is the law. But thanks be to God, who gives us the victory through our Lord Jesus Christ. Therefore, my beloved brothers, be steadfast, immovable, always abounding in the work of the Lord, knowing that in the Lord your labor is not in vain. (1 Corinthians 15:53–58)

For in this tent we groan, longing to put on our heavenly dwelling, if indeed by putting it on we may not be found naked. For while we are still in this tent, we groan, being burdened—not that we would be unclothed, but that we would be further clothed, so that what is mortal may be swallowed up by life. (2 Corinthians 5:2–4)

83. United with Christ

For if we have been united with him in a death like his, we shall certainly be united with him in a resurrection like his. —Romans 6:5

THE WORD TRANSLATED *UNITED* IN THIS VERSE IS THE GREEK word συμφυτος (*symphytos*), meaning *organically united*. The KJV translates it *planted*. It could also be translated *engrafted*. The idea is that since we are engrafted into the death of Christ, we most certainly shall also be engrafted into his resurrection.

Our relationship to Christ is more than simply a conformity to his example. It is a spiritually organic union. So explains Paul again in his letter to the Corinthians:

> But in fact Christ has been raised from the dead, the firstfruits of those who have fallen asleep. For as by a man came death, by a man has come also the resurrection of the dead. For as in Adam all die, so also in Christ shall all be made alive. But each in his own order: Christ the firstfruits, then at his coming those who belong to Christ. (1 Corinthians 15:20–23)

Calvin summarizes the union as follows: "Hence as the graft has the same life or death in common with the tree into which it is ingrafted, so it is reasonable that we should be partakers of the life no less than of the death of Christ; for if we are ingrafted according to the likeness of Christ's death, which was not without a resurrection, then our death shall not be without a resurrection."[40]

40. John Calvin and John Owen, *Commentary on the Epistle of Paul the Apostle to the Romans* (Bellingham, WA: Logos Bible Software, 2010), 222–223.

84. No Longer Enslaved to Sin

We know that our old self was crucified with him in order that the body of sin might be brought to nothing, so that we would no longer be enslaved to sin.
—Romans 6:6

USING AN OLD MAN/NEW MAN NARRATIVE, PAUL NOW BEGINS to expound on the theological mechanics of what he asserted in response to his hypothetical interlocutor's question: *What shall we say then? Are we to continue in sin that grace may abound?*—along with his more concise statement made in verse 5 about sharing in resurrection also because we shared in the death of Christ.

In other words, he will attempt to explain to his Roman audience how it works.

The expression *our old self* and *body of sin* don't refer to the physical body but to our *sinful humanity*, our fallen condition brought about due to our sonship to the first Adam and subsequent sinful choices.

Those who have faith in God's promise are grafted into Christ by the Spirit so that we might be crucified with him. It is through our crucifixion with Christ that our old self, our body of sin is destroyed.

That being the case, we are liberated from the power of sin over us. We are no longer *enslaved* to it; we are dead to sin. Sin is still present but it is no longer a master over us.

In our union with Christ, we are not only delivered from the penalty of our sins, we are also delivered from the enslaving power of sin.

85. Set Free from Sin

For one who has died has been set free from sin. —Romans 6:7

DEATH, IT HAS BEEN SAID, IS THE GREAT EQUALIZER OF MEN. Death puts everyone it touches out of commission. It takes from him all his accomplishments and all of his future. For the man in prison, death frees him from his cell. For the one enslaved, death delivers him from his bondage.

Death puts an end to all the actions of life. Therefore, argues Paul, the one who has died in Christ has been set free from sin.

In other words, we who have died to sin should no longer participate with sin (i.e., exercise ourselves in it). Being dead to it, we must cease from all the actions in which sin operated during its existence in our lives.

Yet, a reasonable man may object, we have yet to see such a person who has wholly crucified sin in the flesh, even amongst those who identify as Christians.

Paul will answer this objection more fully as he fleshes out his argument; but we must, on one hand, acknowledge this circumstance to be real in our union with Christ, while also recognizing that while we still live in our old bodies, we must daily mortify the sin which raises itself in us.

In this sense, we realize our ransomed condition in degrees, gradually, and day by day, more and more, as we yield ourselves to the Holy Spirit who is accomplishing this great work in us.

86. We Will Also Live with Him

Now if we have died with Christ, we believe that we will also live with him.
—Romans 6:8

PAUL REPEATS WHAT HE SAID EARLIER (V. 4) THAT HE MIGHT set the stage for what follows, namely that Christians must pursue the newness of life while they remain in their earthly tabernacle the same way they mortify sin in the body as long as they live in this body.

As Christ died and rose again once and for all—never to die again—so *will* we and so *do* we. We too will be resurrected but it is also true that our pursuit of mortifying sin and living out the newness of our lives must never die.

One modern metaphor in which the proverbial rubber meets the road concerning Paul's point is to think about a car without brakes traveling uphill. There is no place on the hill of our sanctification where we can let off the accelerator without it resulting in a tragic reversal and crash.

Not to say, one could *lose* a salvation that was given to him by God and received by faith. That is not the case. Jesus is not so weak or incompetent.

It is to say that if one returns to his old life, he was none of Christ's and Christ was none of his. There are *possessors* and there are *professors.* To live according to the old nature is to deny Christ. To live according to the newness of life is to believe that we will also live with him.

87. Death Has No Dominion

We know that Christ, being raised from the dead, will never die again; death no longer has dominion over him. —Romans 6:9

ALL HUMANITY LIVES UNDER THE DOMINION OF DEATH. IN the modern era, humanity seeks to elude Death at all costs. Modern man is obsessed with his god, *Progress,* and with Progress's priest, *Scientism,* whom he believes will ultimately deliver him from Death's dominion.

But such idolatrous pursuits are a fool's errand. The wages of sin is death, and death will continue to rule over Adam's race as it has since the Fall.

But Christ, in taking on a human body—and taking up humanity into Divinity—submitted himself to Death's power and then crushed it permanently at his resurrection.

Having freed himself from the dominion of Death, by virtue of the power of his righteousness, he now, by that same power, frees all *his* people from Death's clutches.

All those who, by faith in Progress, pursue eternal life will be dismally disappointed.

But all those who, by faith in Christ, pursue eternal life, will be justified, sanctified, and glorified.

Christ's new humanity will not be disappointed, but pleasantly surprised by the glory that shall be revealed in them on that day (Romans 8:18).

88. You Also Must Consider

For the death he died he died to sin, once for all, but the life he lives he lives to God. So you also must consider yourselves dead to sin and alive to God in Christ Jesus. —Romans 6:10–11

PAUL NOW APPLIES TO THE PRESENT PURPOSE OF HIS LETTER his argument that we are in union with Christ in both death and resurrection through faith—as signified by our baptism.

Christ destroyed death for us by his own death—or as the theologian John Owen described it, he accomplished the death of Death—but now lives unto God (in the heavenlies, reigning at the Father's right hand) because he was resurrected.

So you also, says Paul, must live your lives in this way—dead to sin and alive to God in (union with) Christ Jesus.

We who are in Christ must *consider* ourselves dead to sin. The Greek word translated *consider* is *λογίζομαι* (*logizomai*) and means *reckon or take into account by reasoning.*[41]

While this is true in the spiritual sense of our being, true in our standing before God presently, it is a conscientious decision that must be made each day that we still live in the flesh.

Simultaneously, we must consider that we have also been resurrected in Christ (though it is yet to be accomplished in our flesh) and therefore alive to God.

As Christ *lives to God* reigning at his right hand in the celestial realm (Heaven), we too must *live to God* reigning in our terrestrial realm (Earth) as God's viceroys (cf. Matthew 28:18–20).

41. William Arndt et al., *A Greek-English Lexicon of the New Testament and Other Early Christian Literature* (Chicago: University of Chicago Press, 2000), 597.

89. Not Under Law but Under Grace

Let not sin therefore reign in your mortal body, to make you obey its passions. Do not present your members to sin as instruments for unrighteousness, but present yourselves to God as those who have been brought from death to life, and your members to God as instruments for righteousness. For sin will have no dominion over you, since you are not under law but under grace.
—Romans 6:12–14

HERE WE HAVE ONE OF THE MOST PROFOUND TRUTHS IN Christianity as well as one of the most profoundly misunderstood and abused verses in the Bible.

Paul has argued eloquently and cogently that the one who believes the promise of God regarding Christ has imputed to him the righteousness of Christ and is simultaneously ingrafted into a union with Christ in which he or she shares in both the death and resurrection of Christ.

This union transfers the believer's sonship from son of Adam to son of the second Adam via a new birth. And, although we still live in the flesh and are still yet to experience the physical death and resurrection of our bodies, we are, in God's mind's eye, already dead to sin and alive unto him.

Therefore, sin is no longer our master and we are not to allow it to reign in our mortal bodies. Instead of obeying its passions, we are to obey God's passions as one whom he has rescued and redeemed, as one whom he has brought from death to life.

We are not to present our bodies to sin to be used as instruments of unrighteousness, anymore; instead, we are to present ourselves to God so our bodies can be used as instruments for righteousness.

But here is the rub—the place where so many misinterpret and misuse the Scripture. These justify certain sins claiming they are "not under the law but under grace," as though grace frees them from righteousness or from being accountable to the Law's standard. They assume that because they have been freed from the penalty of the law, they are free to serve their sinful passions without consequence. But exactly the opposite is true.

What Paul is actually saying is that we Christians are called to righteousness now that we have been made righteous, because now sin no longer has dominion over us. Certainly, we will stumble and return to our old habits and will sin. For that, we have an advocate with the Father, Jesus (1 John 1:9; 2:1).

But we are no longer imprisoned under sin's dominion. We have been rescued and are now under God's regime. Sin is no longer our king. God is our king. The statement, *Since you are not under the law but under grace,* is a statement of promise and hope that what we could not do prior to our union with Christ (live righteously) is now possible because of grace. It is by no means a license to sin.

In short, Paul is saying, Don't let sin rule over you and make you think you are obligated to obey its passions. You've been set free by Christ and *sin will have no dominion over* you because you are *not under law* that provokes the flesh to obey the passions of sin; you are *under grace* (in union with Christ by the power of God's Spirit and by virtue of unmerited favor toward us) in which he grants us a new disposition toward righteousness and sin.

Live how God intended you to live and flourish as a human being!

90. Are We to Sin?

What then? Are we to sin because we are not under law but under grace? By no means! —Romans 6:15

AT THIS POINT PAUL IS COMPELLED TO PROVIDE A *REFUTATIO* for what he anticipates to be the next carnal argument against his teaching. In the previous verse (Romans 6:14), he had stated emphatically, "*For sin will have no dominion over you.*" The reason being is "*you are not under law but under grace.*"

But since the carnal appetites of mankind tend to clamor against the mysteries of God, Paul anticipates his last statement will be cherry picked as justification for licentious desires or as a means of proving him a heretic—as he has already stated some have tried to do (Romans 3:7–8).

Thus, he raises another rhetorical argument with his question: "What then? Are we to sin because we are not under law but under grace?"

And responds with another "By no means!"

But this is not some brush-off; it's not a simple denial that lacks an explanation or proof. It is the set up for an expanded explanation which will be treated in subsequent verses.

But what is important here is the fact that Paul readily anticipates the antinomian spirit of men, so he indirectly heads off their heretical treatment of the law.

The annulment of the Law's curse is by no means an annulment of its precepts. Those who are under grace are not free from the spirit of the Law's intent—to teach men how to live righteously.

They are now *empowered by grace* to do so, effectively.

91. We Are All Obedient Slaves

Do you not know that if you present yourselves to anyone as obedient slaves, you are slaves of the one whom you obey, either of sin, which leads to death, or of obedience, which leads to righteousness? —Romans 6:16

WHEN PAUL SAID *BY NO MEANS!* IN RESPONSE TO HIS RHETORICAL question as to whether or not Christians should continue in sin, he wasn't emphatically denouncing the proposition and moving on. He was denouncing the absurd proposition with a commonplace axiom, what we might think of as a Proverb: παριστάνετε ἑαυτοὺς δούλους (*Paristanete heautous doulos,* To whom you present yourself, you are their slave).

The word *slave* is a translation of the Greek word *δούλους* (*doulos*) and means *one who is solely committed to another, their subject.*

We might imagine the days of the monarchy when someone would say *Long live King Alfred!* Or *God save King Alfred!* (substitute any monarch's name here). Or even when a nobleman would respond to a king's request with, *As the King commands!* These were idioms of allegiance. People would make the statement as a public declaration of their subjection to the monarch.

So it is with all of us. If we obey sin, we are making ourselves sin's subject. That obedience will lead to death (The wages of sin is death, cf. v. 23). If we subject ourselves to obedience (to the Law; to the Lord), it leads to righteousness.

To be clear, this is not to be understood in terms of earning favor with the Lord; rather, it is to be understood as our *response* to having received imputed righteousness as part of God's unmerited favor toward us.

As Bob Dylan reminded us, "You're going to have to serve somebody. Well, it may be the devil or it may be the Lord, But you're going to have to serve somebody."[42] The question is: do we want to be slaves to sin which only always leads to death, or slaves to Jesus who liberates us from death and gives us righteousness and abundant life (John 10:10)?

42. Bob Dylan, "Gotta Serve Somebody," 1979.

92. Slaves of Righteousness: Free Indeed

But thanks be to God, that you who were once slaves of sin have become obedient from the heart to the standard of teaching to which you were committed, and, having been set free from sin, have become slaves of righteousness. —Romans 6:17–18

PAUL NOW GIVES THANKS TO GOD FOR THE CONVERSION THAT has taken place in the lives of these believers at Rome. Once slaves of sin, they have been set free by their heart-deep obedience to the gospel—faith in Christ alone—and are now slaves of righteousness.

By his giving thanks to God, we are reminded that Paul is writing a letter to real people, the Church that is at Rome. As we have been following his argument, Paul has shown that "no one can be a servant to righteousness except he is first liberated by the power and kindness of God from the tyranny of sin."[43]

And now he makes the application personal. Paul acts as a father who praises the good that his child does in order to both affirm him and to teach him specifically what he is being praised for so as to encourage the behavior.

Liberated from sin and death, the Roman Christians are free to live as they were intended to live, not as their fleshly passions led them to live. Once cleaned from the filth and stench of the miry pit, who in their right mind would return again to eat with the swine?

Living any other way than as slaves to righteousness would not make sense. Real freedom includes freedom from the necessity of returning to their sin (cf. Proverbs 26:11). As Jesus himself taught "If the Son shall free you, you shall be free indeed" (John 8:36).

43. John Calvin and John Owen, *Commentary on the Epistle of Paul the Apostle to the Romans* (Bellingham, WA: Logos Bible Software, 2010), 238.

93. So Now: The New Humanity

I am speaking in human terms, because of your natural limitations. For just as you once presented your members as slaves to impurity and to lawlessness leading to more lawlessness, so now present your members as slaves to righteousness leading to sanctification. —Romans 6:19

ALL OF GOD'S REVELATION IS A MATTER OF CONDESCENSION. Human reason cannot attain to God, so God must come down to us.

To do so requires that he make the mysteries of the Trinity understandable to simple and fallen human beings if we are to know anything of him. Furthermore, what he has revealed of the heavenly mysteries are, to use a cliché, just the very tip of the iceberg. What God has revealed to man is not all God knows, of course.

Here Paul tells the Christians at Rome that his *death-to-life* and *slavery* illustrations are simply everyday examples to make the doctrine more understandable. Jesus says similar to his disciples in John 3:12: *If I have told you earthly things and you do not believe, how can you believe if I tell you heavenly things?*

Salvation in Christ is a mystery but Paul has been speaking in human terms so they can understand how to live now that they are Christians. To yield one's members as slaves to impurity and lawlessness only leads to practicing more lawlessness and rendering one unfit for the presence of God (state of condemnation). But to yield one's members as slaves to righteousness not only leads to sanctification (the process of becoming more Christlike), but it also renders one fit for God's presence (state of grace).

The theologian, Robert Jewett, notes how Paul's exhortation here points to a 'new form of social life as the primary embodiment of holiness.'[44] In other words, Paul's "so now" is more than just an exhortation to personal holiness; he is laying down the principles for life in a new Christian Society—Christ's new humanity as it were.

44. Jewett puts it this way: "Although it [holiness] is ordinarily interpreted as an individual virtue, the second person plural imperatives throughout this pericope point to a new form of social life as the primary embodiment of holiness." (Jewett, *Romans*, 421) cited in Colin G. Kruse, *Paul's Letter to the Romans*, ed. D. A. Carson, The Pillar New Testament Commentary *(Grand Rapids, MI: Eerdmans, 2012)*, 284.

94. For When You Were Slaves of Sin

For when you were slaves of sin, you were free in regard to righteousness. But what fruit were you getting at that time from the things of which you are now ashamed? For the end of those things is death. —Romans 6:20–21 (ESV)

USING THE PRINCIPLE OF CONTRARIES (SLAVE VERSUS FREE, sin versus righteousness), Paul argues a slave can only have one master. When they were slaves to sin, they could not also be subjects of righteousness. This doesn't mean they never did any good—even a stopped watch is right twice a day—but they lived in the realm of sinfulness without much thought for righteousness.

And now reflecting on their former lifestyle, Paul uses an agricultural metaphor (reaping and sowing) to show how it was that they were indeed slaves to sin because they were reaping that which is, in their new spiritual frame of reference, shameful. And the end (telos) of those things they were reaping is death.

A slave can only have one master so being a slave to sin puts a man on a specific trajectory that is free of righteousness; it's a trajectory that yields shame and ends in death. Only by being purchased (ransomed or redeemed) by a new master, one who is righteous, can one be free from sin and its fruit of shame and death.

C. S. Lewis captures this idea about the trajectory of one's obedience rather remarkably in his acclaimed book, *The Great Divorce*. He says, "There are only two kinds of people in the end: those who say to God, 'Thy will be done,' and those to whom God says, in the end, 'Thy will be done.'"[45]

Lewis, like the apostle Paul, is asserting that our eternal destination is not imposed so much as it is chosen—the natural outworking of the will we cultivate. If we are slaves to God through Jesus Christ, we ascend toward righteousness and union with Him; if we insist on our own autonomy (i.e., which is actually being slaves of sin), we descend into shameful self-imprisonment—and ultimately, death.

45. C. S. Lewis, *The Great Divorce: A Dream* (New York: HarperOne, 2001), 75.

95. But Now: Eternal Life

But now that you have been set free from sin and have become slaves of God, the fruit you get leads to sanctification and its end, eternal life. —Romans 6:22

"FOR WHEN" IN THE PREVIOUS VERSES DESCRIBED THEIR CONdition before Christ.

"But now" describes their condition in Christ presently: they are no longer slaves to sin but have been set free from it and have now become slaves of God.

And as slaves of God, the fruit they are now harvesting is not shameful as the fruit was that they were harvesting before. And it doesn't lead to death as it did before.

Now, as slaves of God, the fruit they are harvesting is that of sanctification (i.e., being made holy) and its end result, abundant and eternal life!

96. Wages versus Free Gift

For the wages of sin is death, but the free gift of God is eternal life in Christ Jesus our Lord. —Romans 6:23

PAUL HAS BEEN ARGUING FOR A NEW AND BETTER LIFE IN Christ using death-versus-life and slave-versus-free analogies. Here he boils down his argument to this succinct and powerful summary of the two conditions of humanity.

The word *ὀψώνιον* (*opsōnion*), translated "wage," historically refers to the compensation Roman soldiers received for their service. This use of the word is striking as it refers to the compensation one receives for his service to sin—death! And not physical death merely.

As Paul has indicated throughout his argument and by contrasting it with eternal life here, it is clear he is speaking of *eternal* death—eternal separation from God. Serving sin leads to an unholy, shameful life and, ultimately, eternal death.

But the free gift of God (unmerited favor that can only be received by faith in Christ Jesus and not by the works of the Law) is *shamelessness* and *sanctification,* which increasingly leads to life more abundant and eternal.

It is notable that Paul uses the expression, *our Lord,* in reference to Christ Jesus. His whole argument has been based on who we serve, that is, who we acknowledge as our Lord (*kurios*) and who we obey, Sin or Jesus Christ.

97. The Limits of the Law

Or do you not know, brothers—for I am speaking to those who know the law—that the law is binding on a person only as long as he lives? —Romans 7:1

CHAPTER SEVEN SERVES AS A KIND OF PARALLELISM WITH chapter six. But where chapter 6 focused on the believer's relationship to sin, chapter 7 focuses on the believers relationship to the Law. Robert Utley summarizes it this way: "The analogy of death freeing a slave (6:12–23) is paralleled by death freeing the marriage bond (7:1–6)."[46]

Note the brief examples in the following table:[47]

CHAPTER 6	*CHAPTER 7*
6:1 "sin"	*7:1 "law"*
6:2 "died to sin"	*7:4 "died to law"*
6:4 "that we might walk in newness of life"	*7:6 "that we might serve in newness of spirit"*
6:7 "he who has died is freed from sin"	*7:6 "we have been freed from the law having died to that wherein we were held"*
6:18 "having been set free from sin"	*7:3 "free from the law"*

The institution of slavery in chapter 6 would be recognized by Jew and Gentile alike; and, by using this example, Paul is now better able to demonstrate why a person no longer under the law should not continue to be a slave to sin but a slave to righteousness.

Here in chapter 7, verses 1–6, Paul begins speaking specifically to those who know the law and makes a legal argument about marriage they will more easily apprehend. It is in at least one way more apropos to our real condition in Christ. Death nullifies the jurisdiction and subsequent curse of the law which is binding only on living men. Thus, Paul will show how a bride can only be

46. Robert James Utley, The Gospel according to Paul: Romans, vol. Volume 5, Study Guide Commentary Series (Marshall, Texas: Bible Lessons International, 1998), Ro 7:1–6.

47. (Borrowed from Anders Nygren's Commentary on Romans, translated by Carl C. Rassmussen, p. 268)

married to one man at a time. If the first husband dies (the first Adam), she can be married to another (Christ).

To be clear, the law is holy, and the commandment is holy and righteous and good, as Paul will affirm in a few verses later (Romans 7:12). But given its legal demands, the law was also a death sentence, a curse, since all human beings stand condemned under the law.

> Christ redeemed us from the curse of the law by becoming a curse for us—for it is written, "Cursed is everyone who is hanged on a tree . . . ." (Galatians 3:13)
>
> . . . by abolishing the law of commandments expressed in ordinances, that he might create in himself one new man in place of the two, so making peace . . ." (Ephesians 2:15)
>
> . . . by canceling the record of debt that stood against us with its legal demands. This he set aside, nailing it to the cross." (Colossians 2:14)

Having died and been raised with Christ, we are under the New Covenant, which means there is a real sense in which we are dead to the jurisdiction of the law of the Old Covenant.

98. Released from the Law

For a married woman is bound by law to her husband while he lives, but if her husband dies she is released from the law of marriage. Accordingly, she will be called an adulteress if she lives with another man while her husband is alive. But if her husband dies, she is free from that law, and if she marries another man she is not an adulteress. Likewise, my brothers, you also have died to the law through the body of Christ, so that you may belong to another, to him who has been raised from the dead, in order that we may bear fruit for God. —Romans 7:2–4

IN MUCH THE SAME WAY AS PAUL ARGUED FROM DEATH TO life and from one slave master to another—that we are no longer obligated to sin, to bear fruit unto unrighteousness and death but to bear fruit unto righteousness and eternal life—he argues now from covenantal ties. This means he has in mind for his audience those who know the law.

God's Law has declared marriage a sacred institution, a covenant between a single man and a single woman before the eyes of God that makes them as if they were one flesh. To break that sacred covenant is to commit adultery, literally to "mix seed" (Exodus 20:14; Deuteronomy 5:18). In much of the ancient Pagan world, adultery could only be committed by women. But God's Law as delivered to the Jews made it clear that both the man and the woman were culpable for the act (Leviticus 20:10–21). Jesus again clarifies further in Matthew 5:27–31 what constitutes adultery.

Thus, in the same way that a woman is free to remarry after her first husband dies, so we have died to the law (i.e., no longer under its decretive jurisdiction) via our union with Christ's death so that we can belong to him now through his resurrection. But how is this the case?

To fully understand Paul's analogy, we must understand the characters and their roles in this interplay. The married woman is the sinner bound by the law to her husband. Her husband to whom she is bound by the law until he dies is the first Adam. The law is what binds the woman to her husband. Christ's victory over sin and death (i.e., his resurrection v. 4) has, in effect, killed the first Adam, thus freeing the woman from the bondage of the law.

In this sense, she is free from the law, free to marry another and bear fruit for God.

The image Paul paints is the believer's relationship to the law. It no longer has jurisdiction over the former relationship since we have died to the law through the body of Christ.

99. The New Way of the Spirit

For while we were living in the flesh, our sinful passions, aroused by the law, were at work in our members to bear fruit for death. But now we are released from the law, having died to that which held us captive, so that we serve in the new way of the Spirit and not in the old way of the written code. —Romans 7:5–6

AS THE COVENANTAL POWER BINDING US TO OUR PROVERBIAL husband (i.e., our old man, Adam) while we were alive in the flesh, the Law only aroused our sinful passions which worked to bear unrighteous fruit in our members (physical bodies) and only led to death.

But now, being released from our former husband, because in Christ we died to that which held us captive (recall the slave analogy), we now serve God in the new way of the Spirit (Acts 2:33, cf. Ephesians 1:13) and not in the old way of the written code (Law).

To be clear, Paul's analogy of the Law must be kept in its proper context. The Law is still the revelation of God's holy character and is not nullified in that sense. It is nullified, however, in that we are no longer motivated by its precepts since in our fallen natures, it only did the opposite—provoked us to sin. Now we are motivated by the Spirit of God who opens our eyes of understanding and transforms our dispositions so that we are motivated to please God, not merely out of fear of trespassing the Law, but out of the sincerity of our new hearts:

> And I will give you a new heart, and a new spirit I will put within you. And I will remove the heart of stone from your flesh and give you a heart of flesh. And I will put my Spirit within you, and cause you to walk in my statutes and be careful to obey my rules. You shall dwell in the land that I gave to your fathers, and you shall be my people, and I will be your God. (Ezekiel 36:26–28)

Chrysotom sums up this whole scheme nicely for us when he writes, "Once again Paul spares the flesh and the law. He does not say that the law was discharged or that sin was discharged but that we were discharged. How did this happen? It happened because the old man, who had been held down by sin, died and was buried."[48]

48. Gerald Bray, ed., *Romans (Revised)*, Ancient Christian Commentary on Scripture (Downers Grove, IL: InterVarsity Press, 1998), 173.

100. If It Had Not Been for the Law

What then shall we say? That the law is sin? By no means! Yet if it had not been for the law, I would not have known sin. For I would not have known what it is to covet if the law had not said, "You shall not covet." —Romans 7:7

AGAIN PAUL ANTICIPATES THE POTENTIAL ERROR OF THOUGHT in his imagined interlocutor and responds with another *By no means!* If *now we are released from the law*, so that we can *serve in the new way of the Spirit and not in the old way of the written code* it would stand to reason that the Law must be bad in some way.

But it's not the law that has the flaw; it's our flesh (i.e., our old man, Adam) that has the flaw. "The law is holy, and the commandment is holy and righteous and good," says Paul a few verses later (Romans 7:12). Here he argues that it was the law that revealed sin in us. He illustrates this truth using the sin of coveting.

We have all, from time to time, desired something that was never intended for us to have. But how could we have known that it was displeasing to God and destructive to our souls if the Law had not commanded us to not covet? It is only in the mirror of the Law that we see how real, how ugly, and how exceedingly sinful our sin actually is.

101. The Opportunity Sin Seized

"But sin, seizing an opportunity through the commandment, produced in me all kinds of covetousness. For apart from the law, sin lies dead." —Romans 7:8

PAUL PERSONIFIES SIN AS IF IT WERE SOME SORT OF MILITARY operative waging war against every human being. The commandment, though good and just in itself, is weaponized to produce *in [him] all kinds of covetousness.*

It's important that the reader recognize the literary nature of Paul's language in giving sin personhood. He says that apart from the law, it lies dead. More technically speaking, it is the law/commandment which conveys to us the knowledge of sin. Without the law, the knowledge of sin is nonexistent. It has no vitality, so to speak, by which it is able to reveal our sin to us, unless it is animated by the knowledge of the law.

Nevertheless, we cannot understand Paul to mean that if there was no law, sin wouldn't exist in the world. He has already confirmed that it does when he explained that "*death reigned from Adam to Moses* . . ." (Romans 5:14); before the law was revealed in writing, the wages of sin were evidenced by human mortality. But without out the presence of the law, sin has no power to smite the conscience or arouse the rebelliousness inherent in our fallen nature.

102. When Sin Came Alive

I was once alive apart from the law, but when the commandment came, sin came alive and I died. —*Romans 7:9*

CONTINUING IN HIS ARGUMENT THAT THE LAW GIVES LIFE TO sin, Paul illustrates his argument that the law gives life to sin by using a reversal of conditions. He was alive before the law but when it came on the scene, sin was brought to life, and in turn, he died.

Paul's use of the "I" is synecdoche for "Israel." Alive until the Law was given at Sinai, Israel died as soon as the law revealed to them the knowledge of sin (brought it to life).

It is the same for us. We seem to be alive as long as the light of the law does not shine into our hearts. And like cockroaches or rats dwelling in the dark recesses of the basement, sin comes to life as soon as the light of the law shines into the dark recesses of our heart.

It is only then that we can realize just how full of corruption (death) we really are—and how much we need a Savior.

103. Death to Me

The very commandment that promised life proved to be death to me. For sin, seizing an opportunity through the commandment, deceived me and through it killed me. So the law is holy, and the commandment is holy and righteous and good. —Romans 7:10–12

IT IS A MOST UNFORTUNATE SURPRISE TO THOSE WHO DESIRE righteousness by obeying the Law. God, through the commandment, shows us the way of life as it reveals the pure righteousness of God. Further, it was given to Israel to this end: that they would see the righteousness of God in the Law and in keeping it they would keep covenant with God and obtain eternal life.

However, our own corruption stands in the way and betrays us to the Lord. Paul explains that sin, seizing an opportunity through the commandment, deceives us and by doing so kills us. To be clear, the law is holy, and the commandment is holy and righteous and good. But we are not: sin (our fallen sin nature) leverages that which is holy and righteous and good and not only reveals in us that which is not holy and righteous and good, but also provokes us to rebellion and disobedience.

This is Paul's point. The law is good but our sin nature is not and therefore the law cannot save us. Not because the law is faulty that it cannot save us but that we are faulty. We need a new disposition, one that is capable of keeping the law, one that is capable of loving God and hating sin—not the other way around, like the sin that lives in us.

104. Death in Me through What Is Good

Did that which is good, then, bring death to me? By no means! It was sin, producing death in me through what is good, in order that sin might be shown to be sin, and through the commandment might become sinful beyond measure. —*Romans 7:13*

SOMETHING DIFFICULT FOR ALL HUMANITY IS THE ABILITY to see the world in all of its complexities. We wish that all the good guys wore white hats and the bad guys wore black hats, like they do in the movies. This way we could see goodness for what it is and know clearly who possesses it. And in a similar fashion, we could see evil for what it is and clearly see who embraces it. Yet, as Alexander Solszinidtzen reminded the world,

> If only it were all so simple! If only there were evil people somewhere insidiously committing evil deeds, and it were necessary only to separate them from the rest of us and destroy them. But the line dividing good and evil cuts through the heart of every human being. And who is willing to destroy a piece of his own heart?[49]

This inability to grasp such complexities is why it's often difficult for us to understand how God can bring good out of sinful actions meant for death and destruction (Romans 8:28–30). It may also be the reason we find it difficult to see how that which is good and holy and just (the law) can be called a ministry of death (2 Corinthians 3:6–8).

Here Paul attempts to explain the case regarding the complexity that exists in understanding how the law (which is good) is used by sin (which is bad) to bring death to us.

Before sin is discovered by the law, there is a sense in which it exists disguised as good, even regarded as such in some cases. But when the law makes sin known for what it is by expressing the commandment clearly (i.e., thou

49. Aleksandr Solzhenitsyn, *The Gulag Archipelago*, trans. Thomas P. Whitney (New York: Harper & Row, 1973), 168.

shalt not covet), sin is discovered for what it really is and takes on its real name and identity (i.e., normal human desire is revealed as concupiscence). With the spotlight shined on it, we see it as it really is—sinful beyond measure—a transgression of the law that is worthy of death.

This is why Paul says it was sin producing death in me through what is good.

105. Sold under Sin

For we know that the law is spiritual, but I am of the flesh, sold under sin.
—Romans 7:14

THE POINT OF THIS VERSE IS TO HIGHLIGHT THE CONTRAST between spirit and flesh. The modern church has had two thousand years of experience with God's Spirit being poured out on and in his people, so the contrast may not be as stark as it would have been to Paul's original audience. To the ancients, however, spirit and flesh were on opposite ends of the spectrum.

The Greek word for spiritual *πνευματικός* (*pneumatikos*), in this context makes it clear that Paul is highlighting the law's divine nature. It is supernatural. As such, it is from God, and, therefore, it is just and good, and holy.

The Greek word for flesh, *σάρκινός* (*sarkinos*), in this context also makes it clear that Paul means that which is weak, sinful and transitory. Literally, it means that which is not spiritual or divine, but merely human. It is natural.

And not only is Paul a mere weak and mortal man, he is one who has been sold under sin. The language here is that of the slave market. The Greek phrase is literally, *πεπραμένος ὑπὸ τὴν ἁμαρτίαν* (*pepramenos hupo ton harmatia*) and the perfect participle means that this is not a one time occurrence but a continuing state of being. Leon Morris notes, "This is the only New Testament passage where this verb is followed by ὑπό."[50] *Hupo* is a marker of that which is in a controlling position in reference to power, rule, sovereignty, command, etc. Paul means to give the picture that as one who is of the flesh, he has been sold over to sin, and is under the control of sin's power or dominion.

It is important to recall the context of the larger argument here. Paul is not saying that he, in his current state as a Christian, has no choice but to sin. Rather, in the context of his human inability to keep the law, we see how sin, using the law against us, slays us. The law is of God. The sons of Adam are sold under sin. The result is death. This is the curse of Genesis 3.

50. Leon Morris, *The Epistle to the Romans*, The Pillar New Testament Commentary (Grand Rapids, MI; W.B. Eerdmans, 1988), 291, n. 86.

106. I Do Not Understand My Own Actions

For I do not understand my own actions. For I do not do what I want, but I do the very thing I hate. —Romans 7:15

WHAT PAUL MEANS EXACTLY IN THIS PASSAGE HAS BEEN, IN some theological circles, an ongoing debate; and, how one chooses to understand it carries notable implications. That said, the most straightforward translation seems to make the most sense and maintains consistency with the rest of Paul's present argument as well as his overall theology.

The word translated "for" means *because* and it connects this statement to the one in the previous verse as a statement of reason. In other words, he is explaining *why* he says as well as *what* it means, to be "sold under sin."

It means that we tend to do things without knowing why we do them. Sin is irrational. All we must do to understand Paul here is to recall trying to explain why we committed some sin that we are confessing.

Sometimes we know why (i.e., we were angry), but sometimes we don't really know why we sinned that way. When we give thought to such sinful actions, we know we don't want to do them because we hate such things. But we usually are only able to think through that after we have sinned, or when we are not in the midst of being tempted to sin.

St. Augustine's story in his Confessions of stealing pears just to sin is a prime example. He and his friends weren't hungry and they didn't want to eat them (they actually fed them to the pig.) They merely wanted to take them for the sake of doing what was wrong and he didn't know why. He later understood why. He was sold under sin until Christ delivered him.

Throughout his argument, Paul treats sin as unnatural, as an intruder which the good law of God arouses in us. But, it's important to note, Paul does not dismiss responsibility. He confesses responsibility for the sin he does, but without an understanding of why he does it, when he really doesn't want to do it. It is sin in us, sin which is not natural to our original design as human beings.

107. A Foreign Agent, A Good Law, and the Self

For I do not understand my own actions. For I do not do what I want, but I do the very thing I hate. Now if I do what I do not want, I agree with the law, that it is good. So now it is no longer I who do it, but sin that dwells within me. —Romans 7:15–17

THE POINT OF PAUL'S ARGUMENT IS THE MOST IMPORTANT take-away: the Law is good!

When Paul violates his best intentions and transgresses the Law, the sense of guilt that he experiences is proof that the Law is good. Therefore, by acknowledging that his best intentions are to follow the Law, but that he found himself acting against his own intentions to do good, it shows the Law itself is good, but sin that dwells in him, has betrayed him and prompted him to sin.

Again, this is not a blame shift. He is not abdicating responsibility for his actions. Paul is speaking in terms that would today be called psychological terms (the psyche = soul). The players in this scenario are the Law, his self, and the unwelcome resident, sin. And he speaks this way, not to discount human responsibility but to show that while Law is used to bring death to sinners, the Law itself is good.

It is the foreign agent, sin, that uses the good Law to bring death to the self.

108. Nothing Good Dwells in Me

For I know that nothing good dwells in me, that is, in my flesh. For I have the desire to do what is right, but not the ability to carry it out. For I do not do the good I want, but the evil I do not want is what I keep on doing. Now if I do what I do not want, it is no longer I who do it, but sin that dwells within me.
—Romans 7:18–20

CONTINUING WITH HIS USE OF THE RHETORICAL *I*, PAUL REINforces his refutation against those who claim that the gospel he is preaching includes the denigration of the Law. It is not the Law that has failed. It is the sin nature that dwells in him. That part of him which constitutes the "I" part of him desires to do good, but that which carries out his actions is the sin nature that dwells in him (his flesh), and nothing good dwells there. Therefore, there exists in one man a conflict of natures—the desire to do good but the inability to carry it out.

Again, recall Paul is not speaking necessarily of his present spiritual condition in Christ, but as one who represents Israel, and ultimately, humanity born of Adam, and living under the law of God.

It seems, however, we can all relate to Paul's scenario: The good we want to do, we don't; and the evil we don't want to do, we do. Why? Because each of us have inherited a nature foreign to our original design—a sinful nature that dwells in us—that is inconsistent with our desire to do good.

This is where the culpability lies, not in the Law.

109. Captive to the Law of Sin

So I find it to be a law that when I want to do right, evil lies close at hand. For I delight in the law of God, in my inner being, but I see in my members another law waging war against the law of my mind and making me captive to the law of sin that dwells in my members. —Romans 7:21–23

PAUL USES A BEAUTIFULLY CRAFTED RHETORICAL FRAMEwork using laws to make his point. The word law is the Greek word *νομος* (*nomos*) and means, in its most generic sense, an established procedure or principle or system. It is usually used in regard to a government or regime (i.e., The Mosaic Law) but it can also refer to a pattern, like the law of gravity—or, as in verse 21, "I find it to be a law that when I want to do right, evil lies close at hand."

The laws he mentions in this passage are, first, the law of sin which resides in his members (vv. 21, 23), the law of God (v. 22), and the law of his mind (v. 23).

The pattern is that the law of Paul's mind (note that he uses the rhetorical, unregenerate "I" that is representative of Israel, and ultimately, all humanity, so this is true of our own situation as well) delights to fulfill the law of God, but there is another law at work in his members which is the law of sin. This law wages war against the law of his mind and leverages his members to make him captive to the law of sin.

There is another contrast we need to be aware of as well. This is the contrast between his members and his "inner being." His members are literally his body parts but are used metaphorically to represent his fallen nature, his flesh, that is at war with his inner being, his self.

Paul is not a gnostic who believes the body is inherently evil and the soul is inherently good. He wrote an entire letter (i.e., Galatians) refuting the doctrine of gnosticism. But he uses this dualistic construction here to make the larger point that there are various laws at work in the unregenerate man.

Said another way: even when the law of one's mind is in harmony with the law of God, the law of sin, dwelling in one's members (i.e., one's flesh), stands in opposition to the law of God. This law of sin leverages every man's members in an effort to wage war against the law of his mind and make the man captive to sin instead of free to obey the Law of God.

110. Wretched Man That I Am!

Wretched man that I am! Who will deliver me from this body of death?
—Romans 7:24

PAUL CONCLUDES HIS ARGUMENT WITH THIS VEHEMENT exclamation: *ταλαίπωρος ἄνθρωπος ἐγώ! (Talaiporos anthropos ego!)*

Ταλαίπωρος (talaiporos) in this exclamation is a strong word and the only other time it is used in the New Testament is in Revelation 3:17:

"For you say, I am rich, I have prospered, and I need nothing, not realizing that you are wretched, pitiable, poor, blind, and naked."

It means to be miserable, wretched, or distressed and is the antonym of *μακάριος (makarios)*, the word Jesus used in the Sermon on the Mount in the Beatitudes (cf. Matthew 5:3), which means to be happy or fortunate. The state of mankind who, still in his flesh and having been confronted and judged by the law of God, is one of utter misery, wretchedness and distress.

Paul's question—Who will deliver me . . . ?—is rhetorical in nature as we shall see in the following verses; but, here he shows us the state of one who is repentant before God and teaches us to bemoan and deplore our own unhappy condition.

"To be delivered," *ῥύομαι (rhyomai)* is to be rescued, saved, or preserved from danger. And the danger here is the body of death. Again, we must be careful not to project on Paul's argument the same dualistic meaning held by the gnostics (spirit = good / body = evil).

Instead, we should recall that Paul is making a metaphorical contrast between his outer being (members, body) as representing flesh (sin nature) and his "inner being" his true self which delights in the law of God.

111. Thanks Be to God

Thanks be to God through Jesus Christ our Lord! So then, I myself serve the law of God with my mind, but with my flesh I serve the law of sin. —Romans 7:25

PAUL CONCLUDES HIS ARGUMENT THAT THE LAW IS NOT SINFUL, but sin is sinful, by assuring his readers that the answer to the sin dilemma is Jesus Christ. This whole dialogue has been a source of contention between those who believe Paul is describing the Christian experience (flesh and spirit wrestling match) and those who believe that Christians can reach or should reach a state of sinless perfection since they are filled with the Spirit of God.

For example, Colin Kruse asserts,

> Some see in 7:25 evidence for the view that Paul is depicting Christian experience in 7:14–25. On the one hand Christians are thankful to God for the hope of final deliverance, but on the other they acknowledge the actuality of their situation—desiring with the mind to be a slave to God's law, but still struggling with a propensity to yield themselves as slaves to sin, this being the eschatological tension in which believers live. However, it is unlikely that the apostle, who declares that "sin shall not be your master, because you are not under law, but under grace" (6:14) and adds in 7:5–6 that believers who were once controlled by the sinful nature are now released from the law to serve in the new way of the Spirit, would then speak of them as slaves "to the law of sin."[51]

On the other hand, John Calvin argues that Paul

> teaches us that the faithful never reach the goal of righteousness as long as they dwell in the flesh, but that they are running their course, until they put off the body. He again gives the name of mind, not to the rational part of the soul which philosophers extol, but to that which is illuminated by the Spirit of God, so that it understands and wills

51. G. Kruse, *Paul's Letter to the Romans*, ed. D. A. Carson, The Pillar New Testament Commentary (Grand Rapids, MI: Eerdmans, 2012), 312.

aright: for there is a mention made not of the understanding alone, but connected with it is the earnest desire of the heart. However, by the exception he makes, he confesses that he was devoted to God in such a manner, that while creeping on the earth he was defiled with many corruptions. This is a suitable passage to disprove the most pernicious dogma of the Purists, (Catharorum,) which some turbulent spirits attempt to revive at the present day.[52]

I want to suggest, first, that Kruse is correct in acknowledging the scope of Paul's argument. The point Paul is making here is not about the Christian experience, per se; it's about the source of sin (i.e., it's rooted in human flesh not the law of God). But Calvin is also correct—as are so many others who share his view—in recognizing the situation Paul describes as a regular state of being for most Christians. He says, "Though Paul then bewailed his lot, and sighed for his departure, he yet confesses that he acquiesced in the good pleasure of God; for it does not become the saints, while examining their own defects, to forget what they have already received from God."[53]

This latter must also have been in view for Paul, or at the very least, it was anticipated where Paul is headed in his argument because in chapter 8, Paul unpacks this very idea, as Kruse admits, "Yet once more in this chapter Paul firmly locates the root cause of the human dilemma with sin, not the law, and by so doing rejects all suggestions that his gospel involves a denigration of the law. At the same time he provides a negative foil for his presentation of Christian freedom that is to follow in chapter 8."[54]

Sin is rooted in the human condition, not the law of God. And Jesus is the answer to the sin problem. As Paul will show in chapter 8, although we do not reach our full potential as Christians while still in this body, we are free from the condemnation of our sin and have liberty to pursue the righteousness that is in Christ, the righteousness that pleases God.

52. John Calvin and John Owen, *Commentary on the Epistle of Paul the Apostle to the Romans* (Bellingham, WA: Logos Bible Software, 2010), 274.

53. John Calvin and John Owen, *Commentary on the Epistle of Paul the Apostle to the Romans* (Bellingham, WA: Logos Bible Software, 2010), 274.

54. Colin G. Kruse, *Paul's Letter to the Romans*, ed. D. A. Carson, The Pillar New Testament Commentary (Grand Rapids, MI: Eerdmans, 2012), 312.

112. Now No Condemnation

There is therefore now no condemnation for those who are in Christ Jesus.
—Romans 8:1

THERE IS A SIGNIFICANT SHIFT THAT TAKES PLACE HERE based on what Paul has previously argued. "Therefore" connects his words of consolation in 8:1 to what has already been established in 7:6 ("the new way of the Spirit").

Furthermore, it should be noted that Paul moves back to using first and second person plural (v. 2) instead of the rhetorical "I" he picked up in his argument made from 7:7–25.

The rhetorical "I" in that section denoted how the Law-follower, try as one might to follow the Law, was a transgressor of the Law because sin in the Law-follower was awakened by the Law and betrayed any attempt to obey the Law by making war against the mind of the Law-follower, and taking him captive. It is a wretched condition that can only be remedied by the gospel of Christ.

This switch in perspective means that Paul is now beginning a new argument—really an extension of the previous argument—based on this new condition in Christ he introduced back in 5:9, 6:22, and 7:6:

> Since, therefore, we have now been justified by his blood, much more shall we be saved by him from the wrath of God. (Romans 5:9)

> But now that you have been set free from sin and have become slaves of God, the fruit you get leads to sanctification and its end, eternal life. (Romans 6:22)

> But now we are released from the law, having died to that which held us captive, so that we serve in the new way of the Spirit and not in the old way of the written code. (Romans 7:6)

Now no condemnation means the Law can no longer touch the one who is in Christ Jesus. This is not a legal fiction; it's a real condition and one we can rejoice in.

To be clear, it does not give us a license to sin, as some suppose. Christians are not antinomians. God's Law forever remains good, just, and holy. But being in Christ Jesus—united to him in his death, burial, and resurrection—means we are safe from the Law's condemnation, beyond its jurisdiction (7:1–3). Moreover, it also means that our nature, our disposition toward God and sin, has changed—which is what verse 2 is about to explain.

113. The Spirit of Life Has Set You Free

For the law of the Spirit of life has set you free in Christ Jesus from the law of sin and death. —Romans 8:2

PICKING UP THE THEME OF LAW AGAIN, PAUL CONTRASTS THE two possible states of a human being to explain the reason for his bold statement that there is now no condemnation.

We see the law of the Spirit of life contrasted with the law of sin and death. In Christ Jesus, one has been set free by the Spirit of life—that is the Spirit of God—from the bondage of sin who has so long held mankind captive (7:14–24).

The law condemned us to death because sin had enslaved us but there is therefore now no condemnation for those who are in Christ Jesus because having been united with Christ Jesus by faith: the Spirit of life has set us free (5:1–2).

There is something in our flesh—even now as Christians—that tries to convince us that to be a follower of Christ we must give up our individuality and our identity. But nothing could be further from the truth. It is only in Christ that we are truly free to desire and to fulfill those things which bring us joy and make us flourish as human beings.

This recalls a line from Irenaeus in *Against Heresies* that speaks to God's redemptive intentions for us. He writes, "For the glory of God is a living man; and the life of man consists in beholding God. For if the manifestation of God which is made by means of the creation, affords life to all living in the earth, much more does that revelation of the Father which comes through the Word, give life to those who see God."[55]

He's speaking of the Incarnation and subsequent redemptive work of Christ (Word). Setting believers free from the law of sin and death is not a reluctant necessity on God's part. He's not acquiescing to give us our freedom; and we are not acquiescing to receive it at the expense of our personhood. It is the glory of God to set us free from the law of sin and death by imparting to us the Spirit of life in Christ Jesus.

55. Irenaeus of Lyons, "Irenæus against Heresies," in *The Apostolic Fathers with Justin Martyr and Irenaeus*, ed. Alexander Roberts, James Donaldson, and A. Cleveland Coxe, vol. 1, The Ante-Nicene Fathers (Buffalo, NY: Christian Literature Company, 1885), 490.

114. Weakened by the Flesh

For God has done what the law, weakened by the flesh, could not do. By sending his own Son in the likeness of sinful flesh and for sin, he condemned sin in the flesh, in order that the righteous requirement of the law might be fulfilled in us, who walk not according to the flesh but according to the Spirit. —Romans 8:3–4

SINCE THE LAW COULD NOT IMPUTE RIGHTEOUSNESS—NOT because it was anything other than good, holy, and just—because of the disease of sin in the flesh of man, the law was made impotent to this purpose.

As Paul has shown, this does not mean the law no longer serves any function or that it is impotent to reveal the holy standard of righteousness. It simply means that man, due to the impotency of his flesh, cannot attain righteousness by keeping the law.

So God has done for believers what the law could not do. He sent his Son (i.e., the second person of the Godhead, the Word, the Divine Logos) to take on the likeness of sinful flesh and become a sin offering, literally, to become a propitiation (i.e., and for sin, cf. Leviticus 16:5–22, Hebrews 13:11–12, and 1 John 2:2).

By sending Christ to be a sin offering, God condemned sin in the flesh; that is, he gave believers a righteous standing before God so that they could fulfill the righteous requirement of the law. But it is conditional. It must be received by faith cf. Romans 4:22–25.

What then is the evidence for this faith? It is seen in that the believer walks not according to the flesh (his old sinful habits) but according to the Spirit.

On this particular phrase, John Calvin notes, "But it was very proper for him, after having promised gratuitous remission to the faithful, to confine this doctrine to those who join penitence to faith, and turn not the mercy of God so as to promote the licentiousness of the flesh."[56]

In other words, true regeneration is seen in the person who not only confesses Christ, not in order to presume on God's grace (i.e., once saved,

56. John Calvin and John Owen, *Commentary on the Epistle of Paul the Apostle to the Romans* (Bellingham, WA: Logos Bible Software, 2010), 278.

always saved), but also walks in daily, humble repentance (i.e., perseverance of the saints).

115. Where Do You Set Your Mind?

For those who live according to the flesh set their minds on the things of the flesh, but those who live according to the Spirit set their minds on the things of the Spirit. —Romans 8:5

IT IS NECESSARY FOR PAUL TO CLARIFY THE DIFFERENCE between those who "walk according to the flesh" and those who "walk according to the Spirit" (v. 4). And he does so in a similar manner to unpacking a nesting doll. While his explanation remains fairly broad at this point, he will continue to narrow in as he unpacks the meaning and reveals the orientation of the opposing ways of life.

To live according to the flesh or according to the Spirit is to set one's mind on the things of that particular "way of life." The word for "set their minds" is φρονεω (*phroneo*) and refers to a kind of wisdom or discernment. In this context, it means to give careful consideration to something or someone so as to intend on taking up someone's side, or espousing someone's cause.

To set one's minds on the things of the Spirit is to take up the Spirit's side or cause—to approximate one's life accordingly—which is righteousness. Said another way, the one who puts their faith in Christ and receives Christ's righteousness imputed to them, is free from the condemnation of the law against all their sins: past, present, and future.

But it is only demonstrable that a person is in Christ by way of the cause he takes up. A person who is in Christ will not take up the cause of the flesh (sin nature). They will take up the cause of Christ—including repenting (i.e., confessing and forsaking their sins, Proverbs 28:13) when they stumble and sin.

116. Two Minds, Two Trajectories, Two Ends

For to set the mind on the flesh is death, but to set the mind on the Spirit is life and peace. —Romans 8:6

THE TWO WAYS OF LIVING HAVE TWO DIFFERENT ENDS. FOR the man who sets his mind on the flesh, his end is death. For the man who sets his mind on the Spirit is life and peace. The contrast of ends is stark: death or life and peace?

Regarding the expression to set the mind on the flesh, the Greek expression is *τὸ φρόνημα τῆς σαρκὸς* (*to phronema tēs sarkos*) and it is the abstract of "minding the things of the flesh," in the preceding verse and only used one other place in the NT (Romans 8:27). The trouble with the word *φρόνημα* (*phronema*) for English speakers is there is not an equivalent in our language, so it makes translating this Hebraistic expression that was originally written in Greek challenging.

On this expression, John Calvin asserts,

> Erasmus has rendered it "affection," (affectum;) the old translator (Jerome), "prudence," (prudentiam.) But as it is certain that the τὸ φρόνημα of Paul is the same with what Moses calls the imagination (figmentum—devising) of the heart, (Gen. 6:5;) and that under this word are included all the faculties of the soul—reason, understanding, and affections, it seems to me that minding (cogitatio—thinking, imagining, caring) is a more suitable word.[57]

Modern scholars suggest something similar to Calvin but more nuanced:

> The mindedness, rather than the minding of the flesh, would be most correct. But the phrase is no doubt Hebraistic, the adjective is put as a noun in the genitive case, so that its right version is, "The carnal mind;"

57. John Calvin and John Owen, *Commentary on the Epistle of Paul the Apostle to the Romans* (Bellingham, WA: Logos Bible Software, 2010), 285–286.

> and "mind" is to be taken in the wide sense of the verb, as including the whole soul, understanding, will, and affections. The phrase is thus given in the next verse in our version: and it is the most correct rendering. The mind of the flesh is its thoughts, desires, likings, and delight.[58]

For the one who sets his mind on the flesh there is only one solitary reward that encompasses everything about his existence—death. Death brings an end to everything except conflict since the mind of the flesh is at enmity with God. Death here is eternal; thus, the lack of peace.

For the one who sets his mind on the Spirit there is life—the opposite of death—and peace. Peace is the absence of turmoil, chaos, and suffering. Life here is that which flourishes in holiness and is therefore also eternal.

We understand Paul's use of life and death best when we keep in mind these two ways of "mindedness" in life are two different eternal trajectories that begin for us at birth. We are all born on an eternal trajectory toward death but Christ came into the world to put those who believe on a new trajectory toward life and peace.

58. Editor's footnote (fn1) in chapter 8 of John Calvin and John Owen, *Commentary on the Epistle of Paul the Apostle to the Romans* (Bellingham, WA: Logos Bible Software, 2010).

117. The Mind That Cannot Please God

For the mind that is set on the flesh is hostile to God, for it does not submit to God's law; indeed, it cannot. Those who are in the flesh cannot please God.
—Romans 8:7–8.

AS PAUL CONTINUES HIS EXPLANATION OF THE TWO POTENTIAL states of mindedness (*φρονημα/phronema*) of the individual and how it relates to two different trajectories—either life and peace or death—he brings the argument full circle to his original assertion in chapter one that mankind has rebelled against God.

> For his invisible attributes, namely, his eternal power and divine nature, have been clearly perceived, ever since the creation of the world, in the things that have been made. So they are without excuse. For although they knew God, they did not honor him as God or give thanks to him, but they became futile in their thinking, and their foolish hearts were darkened. (Romans 1:20–21)

This word *hostile* is remarkable in that it is the same word used in Luke 23:12 where it says, "And Herod and Pilate became friends with each other that very day, for before this they had been at enmity with each other." Again, in James 4:4, where he says, "You adulterous people! Do you not know that friendship with the world is enmity with God? Therefore whoever wishes to be a friend of the world makes himself an enemy of God."

The law of God reveals to us what pleases him and those who refuse to submit to God's law (to what pleases him) are at enmity with God. They are literally taking up arms against God, rebelling against his rightful authority. How could a man please God if he is rebelling against him? Indeed, he cannot! By setting one's mind on the flesh, one can never say, in good conscience, he is God's own. Such a one cannot trust that God is any longer for him or will hear his prayers, except he repent.

John Chrysostom, fourth-century bishop of Constantinople, notes, "Paul is not saying that it is impossible for a wicked person to become good but rather that it is impossible for one who continues in wickedness to be subject to God."[59]

And Calvin asserts, "they who wish really to find out how far they agree with God must test all their purposes and practices by this rule."[60]

59. Gerald Bray, ed., *Romans (Revised), Ancient Christian Commentary on Scripture* (Downers Grove, IL: InterVarsity Press, 1998), 201.

60. John Calvin and John Owen, *Commentary on the Epistle of Paul the Apostle to the Romans* (Bellingham, WA: Logos Bible Software, 2010), 287.

118. Not in the Flesh But in the Spirit

You, however, are not in the flesh but in the Spirit, if in fact the Spirit of God dwells in you. Anyone who does not have the Spirit of Christ does not belong to him. —Romans 8:9

A CONCISE SUMMARY OF WHAT PAUL WRITES HERE IS WE become Christians by God's Spirit. If the Spirit of God dwells in us, we are no longer in the flesh, but are Christ's. We are Christians. If the Spirit of God does not dwell within us, regardless of what we profess with our tongues, we are none of his because we remain in the flesh. Recall that the end for those in the flesh is death; but for those who are Christ's, the end is life and peace.

Using the second person perspective (you) to apply to their lives in practice the theology he is discussing in theory shows Paul's pastoral heart for the Roman Christians. No doubt the testimony Paul has heard of the Roman Christians warrants such certainty about their condition (Romans 1:8). Nevertheless, he asserts: if in fact the Spirit of God dwells in you. Paul is qualifying his assumption lest there be some within the body who profess Christ in vain.

He makes this qualifying statement to prompt them to examine themselves to make sure they are indeed in the Spirit and not in the flesh. Or to use Peter's wording, he wants them to "be all the more diligent to confirm your calling and election" (2 Peter 1:10). How do we know if we are in the Spirit? What does it look like practically? To continue using Peter's words, it looks like this:

> His divine power has granted to us all things that pertain to life and godliness, through the knowledge of him who called us to his own glory and excellence, by which he has granted to us his precious and very great promises, so that through them you may become partakers of the divine nature, having escaped from the corruption that is in the world because of sinful desire. For this very reason, make every effort to supplement your faith with virtue, and virtue with knowledge, and knowledge with self-control, and self-control with steadfastness, and

> steadfastness with godliness, and godliness with brotherly affection, and brotherly affection with love. For if these qualities are yours and are increasing, they keep you from being ineffective or unfruitful in the knowledge of our Lord Jesus Christ. For whoever lacks these qualities is so nearsighted that he is blind, having forgotten that he was cleansed from his former sins. Therefore, brothers, be all the more diligent to confirm your calling and election, for if you practice these qualities you will never fall. (2 Peter 1:3–10)

To return to Paul's choice of wording, he means everything Peter does in his more concise expression: "For those who live according to the flesh set their minds on the things of the flesh, but those who live according to the Spirit set their minds on the things of the Spirit" (Romans 8:5).

119. If Christ Is in You

But if Christ is in you, although the body is dead because of sin, the Spirit is life because of righteousness. —Romans 8:10

IT SHOULD GRAB OUR ATTENTION THAT PAUL SAYS, "IF CHRIST is in you." Up till now, he has said "If the Spirit of God dwells in you." And he will continue using Spirit in subsequent statements with no indication that he is changing the subject. It would be an overreach to say that Paul is equating the person of Christ with the person of the Spirit. In other words, he is not dissolving the distinct persons of the Trinity into one person with his statement. Yet, to say that the Spirit is in a believer is nothing less than saying Christ is in the believer.

Again, Paul makes a conditional statement by using if, but this is a continuation of his thought about the same subject in the former verse, verse 9 (this is one example of where chapters and verses can foster confusion in reading Scripture).

We could understand Paul to be saying (I'm paraphrasing vss. 9–10), "But we all know you Roman Christians are not in the flesh but in the Spirit, that is if it is in fact the case that the Spirit of God dwells in you, because as you know, anyone who does not have the Spirit of Christ does not belong to him. But, as I was saying, if Christ is in you . . ."

In the second clause, it would be wrong to understand Paul ascribing to the body the source of sin. As he has continued to do in this entire discussion, he uses "body" as synecdoche to represent that part of our old nature, our Adamic nature, that is not yet mortified by the Spirit of God. As a result, our physical bodies must still face death even though our spirit is alive in Christ. St. Augustine of Hippo (354–430) explains, "Paul shows that both life and death exist in a man living in his body—death in his body, life in his spirit."[61]

Paul is encouraging the believers at Rome with the knowledge that although there remains on us that judgment unto death as far as our old

61. The City of God (20.15.19) as quoted in Gerald Bray, ed., *Romans (Revised), Ancient Christian Commentary on Scripture* (Downers Grove, IL: InterVarsity Press, 1998), 205.

Adamic nature remains in us, because of the righteousness God has imputed to us, the Spirit that is life is also in us and is conquering that old nature and blessing us with new life.

Said another way: although there are vestiges of our old nature and the consequences of those vestiges still play a role in our lives, the seed of the new life we have in Christ has been planted in us by the Spirit of life and we are experiencing the first fruits of that new life.

120. His Spirit Who Dwells in You

If the Spirit of him who raised Jesus from the dead dwells in you, he who raised Christ Jesus from the dead will also give life to your mortal bodies through his Spirit who dwells in you. —Romans 8:11

PAUL CONCLUDES HIS POINT ABOUT THE POWER OF THE SPIRIT in the life of the believer by relating it to the work of the Father who will in due course raise the believer's body (that will die because of sin) just as he raised Christ from the dead.

This is the blessed hope of the believer—not that we will exist in eternity as bodiless spirits—but that God will give life to our mortal bodies through the Spirit that dwells in us. Jesus is the first fruits of the resurrected life of all believers.

"For since we believe that Jesus died and rose again, even so, through Jesus, God will bring with him those who have fallen asleep" (1 Thessalonians 4:14).

Colin Kruse offers a meaningful summary of Paul's thought extending from verses 9, that is worth citing here:

> In 8:9 Paul insisted that possession of the Spirit is the *sine qua non* of Christian existence, and he employs this fact in the protasis of the conditional sentence here in 8:11: And if the Spirit of him who raised Jesus from the dead is living in you, he who raised Christ from the dead will also give life to your mortal bodies because of his Spirit who lives in you. Paul speaks frequently of God as the one who raised Christ from the dead (4:24; 6:4; 8:11; 10:9; 1 Cor. 6:14; 15:15; 2 Cor. 4:14; Gal. 1:1; Eph 1:20; Col 2:12; 1 Thess. 1:10), but only here is the Spirit referred to as the one who raised him from the dead. Paul's assurance to his audience is that the Spirit who lives in them and who raised Christ himself from the dead will do the same for them—he will give life to their mortal bodies also (a reference to believers' resurrection on the last day).[62]

62. Colin G. Kruse, *Paul's Letter to the Romans*, ed. D. A. Carson, The Pillar New Testament Commentary *(Grand Rapids, MI: Eerdmans, 2012)*, 334.

121. We Are Debtors

So then, brothers, we are debtors, not to the flesh, to live according to the flesh. For if you live according to the flesh you will die, but if by the Spirit you put to death the deeds of the body, you will live. —Romans 8:12–13

BY USE OF AN ANTITHETICAL ENTHYMEME (ONE PART OF THE antithetical argument is left off because it is so obvious) Paul concludes with the practical implications of what he has been demonstrating. Since we are no longer under the debt of sin, since we owe our flesh nothing, we should not live our lives according to the dictates of the flesh.

And, since we are debtors to the Spirit (since by God's spirit we possess life and peace), then it is to the Spirit we owe our allegiance, and we should, by the Spirit's power, put the deeds of the body (our sins) to death so that we might live—and live more abundantly (John 10:10).

Let us always remember that death is the compensation for sin; and, life and flourishing are the blessed gifts of the Spirit.

122. Sons of God

For all who are led by the Spirit of God are sons of God. —Romans 8:14

PREVIOUSLY, PAUL STATED THAT BEING INDWELLED BY THE Spirit was the essential key to the Christian life. Here he establishes that those being led by the Spirit are, in fact, the children of God. This is likely an allusion to the many passages of Scripture that speak of Israel being led by God as a son out of slavery in Egypt and through the wilderness.

> Then you shall say to Pharaoh, "Thus says the LORD, Israel is my firstborn son, and I say to you, 'Let my son go that he may serve me.' If you refuse to let him go, behold, I will kill your firstborn son." (Exodus 4:22–23)

> . . . then your heart be lifted up, and you forget the LORD your God, who brought you out of the land of Egypt, out of the house of slavery, who led you through the great and terrifying wilderness, with its fiery serpents and scorpions and thirsty ground where there was no water, who brought you water out of the flinty rock, who fed you in the wilderness with manna that your fathers did not know, that he might humble you and test you, to do you good in the end. (Deuteronomy 8:14–16)

> When Israel was a child, I loved him, and out of Egypt I called my son. The more they were called, the more they went away; they kept sacrificing to the Baals and burning offerings to idols. Yet it was I who taught Ephraim to walk; I took them up by their arms, but they did not know that I healed them. I led them with cords of kindness, with the bands of love, and I became to them as one who eases the yoke on their jaws, and I bent down to them and fed them. (Hosea 11:1–4)

The connection Paul makes to Israel's deliverance and their wilderness journey is a powerful one, and worthy of contemplation. In any case, what seems to be certain from verses 12–13 is that the Spirit does not simply indwell believers, like air filling a balloon. He indwells the believer for the purpose of accomplishing a holy activity—mortifying the flesh or killing sin—so that the believer takes on the attributes of God (i.e., he emulates the manners of the son of God that he is).

To be possessed by the Spirit of God is to become more and more like God, our Father, as we grow up into Him. And to be led by the Spirit in this sense seems to be a moral condition, not merely a vocational one. Further, it is ultimately a work of the Spirit of God in the life of the believer rather than sheer human ability.

123. Adoption as Sons

For you did not receive the spirit of slavery to fall back into fear, but you have received the Spirit of adoption as sons, by whom we cry, "Abba! Father!"
—Romans 8:15

HAVING RECEIVED THE INDWELLING OF THE SPIRIT OF GOD, believers not only take on His communicable attributes—God likeness as sons (i.e., godliness)—believers are also called to intimacy with God, their Father.

Two stations of relationship and intimacy are contrasted here: slaves and sons.

Slaves relate to their master in terms of authority, obedience, fear, and chastisement; that is, slaves live under their master's authority, always fearing to displease him and receive chastisement if and when they do. Further, there is no inheritance, or even consideration for an inheritance, for a slave. We would do well to reflect on Israel's situation under Pharoah since Paul seems to be drawing from this narrative in Israel's history.

> Therefore they set taskmasters over them to afflict them with heavy burdens. They built for Pharaoh store cities, Pithom and Raamses. But the more they were oppressed, the more they multiplied and the more they spread abroad. And the Egyptians were in dread of the people of Israel. So they ruthlessly made the people of Israel work as slaves and made their lives bitter with hard service, in mortar and brick, and in all kinds of work in the field. In all their work they ruthlessly made them work as slaves. (Exodus 1:11–14)

> Then the king of Egypt said to the Hebrew midwives, one of whom was named Shiphrah and the other Puah, "When you serve as midwife to the Hebrew women and see them on the birthstool, if it is a son, you shall kill him, but if it is a daughter, she shall live." (Exodus 1:15–16)

> Then Pharaoh commanded all his people, "Every son that is born to the Hebrews you shall cast into the Nile, but you shall let every daughter live." (Exodus 1:22)

Sons, on the other hand, can cry Abba, Father! Yes, sons are also under authority and can be chastised (Hebrews 12:5), but the relationship is drastically different. The Father and son have mutual affection one for the other, and it is their glory to honor one another. Further, adopted sons acquire all the legal rights of a biological son; and under Roman law, since an adoption was a deliberate public decision, a son could not be easily disinherited; that is, the adoption could not be capriciously annulled.

124. The Spirit Bears Witness

The Spirit himself bears witness with our spirit that we are children of God, and if children, then heirs—heirs of God and fellow heirs with Christ, provided we suffer with him in order that we may also be glorified with him. —Romans 8:16–17

THAT THE SPIRIT HIMSELF BEARS WITNESS WITH OUR SPIRIT, means that internally, the Spirit of God confirms to our spirit, that we believers are in fact the children of God. This new life in Christ means a new relationship with the Father. We are adopted children which means we are also entitled to the inheritance of God. None of this is accomplished by our own merit but by the merit of Jesus Christ, our older brother, with whom we share in this inheritance. All that was promised to Jesus we will share in.

Recall, this inheritance was first promised to Abraham—and to his offspring—to all who believed.

> After these things the word of the Lord came to Abram in a vision: "Fear not, Abram, I am your shield; your reward shall be very great." But Abram said, "O Lord God, what will you give me, for I continue childless, and the heir of my house is Eliezer of Damascus?" And Abram said, "Behold, you have given me no offspring, and a member of my household will be my heir." And behold, the word of the Lord came to him: "This man shall not be your heir; your very own son shall be your heir." And he brought him outside and said, "Look toward heaven, and number the stars, if you are able to number them." Then he said to him, "So shall your offspring be." And he believed the Lord, and he counted it to him as righteousness. And he said to him, "I am the Lord who brought you out from Ur of the Chaldeans to give you this land to possess."" (Genesis 15:1–7)

Paul further explains in his letter to the Galatians that those who are in Christ are Abraham's seed: "And if you are Christ's, then you are Abraham's offspring, heirs according to promise" (Galatians 3:29).

This is because

> . . . the promises were made to Abraham and to his offspring. It does not say, "And to offsprings," referring to many, but referring to one, "And to your offspring," who is Christ. This is what I mean: the law, which came 430 years afterward, does not annul a covenant previously ratified by God, so as to make the promise void. For if the inheritance comes by the law, it no longer comes by promise; but God gave it to Abraham by a promise. (Galatians 3:16–18)

Paul capitalizes on the singularity of the word to prove that the true Israel was the only begotten of God, Jesus, who came through the Israelites, but not all Israel are Israel. Only Christ and believers in Christ are the Israel to whom the promises were made.

How then do we know we are fellow heirs with Christ? If we suffer with him so that we may be glorified with him. That is, if we have died with Christ and have been buried. And in a real sense, those who have truly died with Christ, will, should it be necessary, actually and really die for Christ. Just as Dietrich Bonhoeffer exhorted in *The Cost of Discipleship*, "When Christ calls a man, he bids him come and die."[63]

63. Dietrich Bonhoeffer, *The Cost of Discipleship* (New York, NY: Touchstone, 1995), 89.

125. An Eternal Weight of Glory

The Spirit himself bears witness with our spirit that we are children of God, and if children, then heirs—heirs of God and fellow heirs with Christ, provided we suffer with him in order that we may also be glorified with him.

For I consider that the sufferings of this present time are not worth comparing with the glory that is to be revealed to us. —Romans 8:16–18

THE EMPHASIS OF THIS ENTRY IS ON VERSE 18, BUT IT WOULD be difficult to accurately consider its meaning without the preceding verses which provide its context. Verses 16–17 reveal that we who trust Christ are more than forgiven; we are made sons, heirs of God and joint-heirs with Christ. This is our new status—provided we suffer with him. To suffer with him means to follow him, imitate his life, and go the way of Christ:

> And he said to all, "If anyone would come after me, let him deny himself and take up his cross daily and follow me. For whoever would save his life will lose it, but whoever loses his life for my sake will save it. For what does it profit a man if he gains the whole world and loses or forfeits himself? For whoever is ashamed of me and of my words, of him will the Son of Man be ashamed when he comes in his glory and the glory of the Father and of the holy angels." (Luke 9:23–26)

This way of living, Jesus taught us, always brings suffering, and often the ire of the ungodly. In his Sermon on the Mount, he taught, "Blessed are those who are persecuted for righteousness' sake, for theirs is the kingdom of heaven. Blessed are you when others revile you and persecute you and utter all kinds of evil against you falsely on my account" (Matthew 5:10–11).

Later, Paul echoes the words of Jesus when he tells Timothy, "Indeed, all who desire to live a godly life in Christ Jesus will be persecuted" (2 Timothy 3:12).

In verse 18 then, Paul offers his readers a consolation, a word of encouragement about suffering in their present situation. The expression "for I consider" is *γαρ λογίζομαι (gar logizomai)* in Greek, which means to make a judgment after careful consideration. Note its use by both Paul and Peter in other letters:

> Brothers, I do not consider that I have made it my own. But one thing I do: forgetting what lies behind and straining forward to what lies ahead . . . (Philippians 3:13)

> By Silvanus, a faithful brother as I regard him, I have written briefly to you, exhorting and declaring that this is the true grace of God. Stand firm in it. (1 Peter 5:12)

The expression sufferings of this present time may refer to this life on earth but the grammatical construction makes it appear that Paul is referring more specifically to the current era in which he was writing, than the general historical-salvation timeframe. At this time the church in Rome had recently faced severe persecution under Claudius and now Nero was the new Emperor.

In either case, whatever "sufferings" this sinful world, including works of wicked men, might bring about, they are nothing in comparison to the glory that shall be revealed to us and/or in us in the eternal kingdom of Christ. It is just as Paul told the Corinthians when writing to them, "For this light momentary affliction is preparing for us an eternal weight of glory beyond all comparison, as we look not to the things that are seen but to the things that are unseen. For the things that are seen are transient, but the things that are unseen are eternal" (2 Corinthians 4:17–18).

126. Creation Waits with Eager Longing

For the creation waits with eager longing for the revealing of the sons of God.
—Romans 8:19

IT IS NOT ONLY US WHO MUST WAIT WITH PATIENCE FOR THE day of resurrection, but creation waits with us eagerly. The Greek expression Paul uses here is ἀπεκδέχομαι ἀποκαραδοκία (*apekdechomai apokaradokia*) A literal translation would be "awaits eagerly with eager expectation." Although the expression seems redundant in English, the original seems to heighten the nature of the eagerness with which the creation awaits the full revelation of the sons of God.

The eager expectation for which the creation waits is the revealing of the sons of God! Nature and nature's creatures await the day of resurrection, when the glory of the children of God will be on display. John echoes Paul when he writes in his first epistle, "Beloved, we are God's children now, and what we will be has not yet appeared; but we know that when he appears we shall be like him, because we shall see him as he is" (1 John 3:2).

It is a matter of gentle dispute among Christians of all ages as to what is included in "the creation." Some have suggested it is referring only to the rational creatures (i.e, descendents of Adam and Eve), others include angels and spiritual beings in "the creation." Still others suggest the entire created order, the cosmos here personified by Paul, eagerly awaits the resurrection when everything is remade in its perfected state.

To whatever extent "the creation" is to be understood, we must at least acknowledge the fall of man has been catastrophic to all of creation (i.e., creatures as well as the material world, including the heavens). On the surface, we might think of the grave pollution the planet has incurred, not to mention the deep sufferings of sentient creatures. But as Paul continues to unpack his message of hope, pointing his reader to the eschaton, it seems there is something deeper going on. The full scope of the creation's eager longing is a mystery. We'll just have to wait together in hope as we anticipate the day when God makes all things new and fully glorious.

"And he who was seated on the throne said, 'Behold, I am making all things new . . .'" (Revelation 21:5).

127. Creation Itself Will Be Set Free

For the creation waits with eager longing for the revealing of the sons of God. For the creation was subjected to futility, not willingly, but because of him who subjected it, in hope that the creation itself will be set free from its bondage to corruption and obtain the freedom of the glory of the children of God.
—Romans 8:19–21

THE CREATION, PERSONIFIED HERE FOR LITERARY EMPHASIS, awaits alongside mankind with eager longing for the resurrection of the sons of God, because it too will be redeemed in the resurrection, the day the curse is finally and fully lifted. In the tradition of the Jewish rabbis and OT prophets, Paul reminds the Romans that creation was subjected to this curse of futility (bondage to corruption), not by its own choice, but as a result of God's judgment on mankind. He appears to have Genesis 3:17–19 in mind:

> And to Adam he said, "Because you have listened to the voice of your wife and have eaten of the tree of which I commanded you, 'You shall not eat of it,' cursed is the ground because of you; in pain you shall eat of it all the days of your life; thorns and thistles it shall bring forth for you; and you shall eat the plants of the field. By the sweat of your face you shall eat bread, till you return to the ground, for out of it you were taken; for you are dust, and to dust you shall return."

Paul does not say what this liberation of the creation will look like at the time when it shares in the 'freedom of the glory of the children of God', but it is certain that it will be vastly different than it is now, and likely opposite of Isaiah's description of its presently cursed condition:

Isaiah 24:4–6 (ESV):

> The earth mourns and withers; the world languishes and withers; the highest people of the earth languish. The earth lies defiled under its inhabitants; for they have transgressed the laws, violated the statutes,

> broken the everlasting covenant. Therefore a curse devours the earth, and its inhabitants suffer for their guilt . . .

In his *Homilies on Romans XIV*, Chrysostom explains, "Here Paul's discourse becomes more emphatic, and he personifies the creation in the way that the prophets do when they speak of the floods, clapping their hands and so on."[64]

> Let the sea roar, and all that fills it; the world and those who dwell in it! Let the rivers clap their hands; let the hills sing for joy together before the Lord, for he comes to judge the earth. He will judge the world with righteousness, and the peoples with equity. (Psalm 98:7–9)

Cyril of Alexandria in his *Explanation of the Letter to the Romans* is also helpful, asserting that

> The creation is waiting for the revelation of the sons of God at some point in the future which is still unknown. Who can know when this will be? But by the secret plan of God, which orders all things for the best, it will come to this end. For when the sons of God, who have lived a righteous life, have been transformed into glory from dishonor and from what is corruptible into what is incorruptible, then the creation too will be transformed into something better.[65]

64. Gerald Bray, ed., Romans (Revised), Ancient Christian Commentary on Scripture (Downers Grove, IL: InterVarsity Press, 1998), 215.

65. J.-P. Migne, ed. Patrologia Cursus Completus. 166 vols. Series Graeca. Paris: Migne, 1857–1886. Migne PG 74 col. 821. cited by Gerald Bray, ed., *Romans (Revised)*, Ancient Christian Commentary on Scripture (Downers Grove, IL: InterVarsity Press, 1998), 215. See also 1 Cor 15:54.

128. Groaning Together

For we know that the whole creation has been groaning together in the pains of childbirth until now. —Romans 8:22

PAUL'S LARGER ARGUMENT JOINS HUMAN AND NON-HUMAN creation as "groaning together." But given the next verse (v. 23) focuses on "not only the creation, but we ourselves," is an indication that Paul, in using the expression "the whole creation," has the subhuman creation in view in this particular verse.

There are two ditches Christians tend to fall into concerning the created order (i.e., environment) and passages like these serve to remind us of those ditches. The first ditch is to believe God is solely interested in the redemption of the human race and that the non-human creation serves simply as a background and exists peripherally to God's concerns.

The second ditch is the belief that God's need to do redemptive work in creation is proof that mankind should not use or take dominion of the earth. Both of these are false. Both humanity and the created order that God meant for us to steward stands together in need of redemption.

N. T. Wright's comment the liberation of both the subcreation and the believers is insightful:

> The basis of Paul's belief here must be a combination of two things: the biblical promise of new heavens and new earth (Isa 65:17; 66:22), and the creation story in which human beings, made in God's image, are appointed as God's stewards over creation. Putting the picture together, in the light of the observable way in which the created order is out of joint, and the clear biblical and experiential belief that the human race as a whole is in rebellion against God, Paul, in company with many other Jews, saw the two as intimately related. After the fall, the earth produced thorns and thistles, humans continued to abuse their environment, so that one of the reasons why God sent Israel into exile, according the Scriptures, was so that the land could at last enjoy

> its sabbaths (Lev 26:34–43 [cf. 25:2–5]; 2 Chr 36:21). But the answer to the problem was not (as in some New Age theories) that humans should keep their hands off creation . . . The answer, if the creator is to be true to the original purpose, is for humans to be redeemed, to take their place at last as God's imagebearers, the wise stewards they were always meant to be. Paul sees that this purpose has already been accomplished in principle in the resurrection of Jesus, and that it will be accomplished fully when all those in Christ are raised and together set in saving authority over the world (see 1 Cor. 15:20–28).[66]

All this reminds us of John's vision and potentially helps put our eschatology in better perspective.

> Then I saw a new heaven and a new earth, for the first heaven and the first earth had passed away, and the sea was no more. And I saw the holy city, new Jerusalem, coming down out of heaven from God, prepared as a bride adorned for her husband. And I heard a loud voice from the throne saying, "Behold, the dwelling place of God is with man. He will dwell with them, and they will be his people, and God himself will be with them as their God. He will wipe away every tear from their eyes, and death shall be no more, neither shall there be mourning, nor crying, nor pain anymore, for the former things have passed away." And he who was seated on the throne said, "Behold, I am making all things new." Also he said, "Write this down, for these words are trustworthy and true." (Revelation 21:1–5)

66. N. T. Wright, 'Romans', 596, quoted by Colin G. Kruse, *Paul's Letter to the Romans*, ed. D. A. Carson, The Pillar New Testament Commentary *(Grand Rapids, MI: Eerdmans, 2012)*, 345–346.

129. The Firstfruits of the Spirit

And not only the creation, but we ourselves, who have the firstfruits of the Spirit, groan inwardly as we wait eagerly for adoption as sons, the redemption of our bodies. —Romans 8:23

THE FIRST CLAUSE DISTINGUISHES OUR HUMAN REDEMPTION from the redemption of the non-human creation which also shares in our groaning. This does not mean there are two kinds of redemption or two parts of redemption. Paul is simply emphasizing one part of creation and then the other.

We who groan along with creation have the firstfruits of the Spirit. The firstfruits of the Spirit refers to the earnest payment God has made on our redemption by giving us the Holy Spirit while we wait for the full harvest of redemption (Ephesians 1:13–14). Paul uses the metaphor of the firstfruits to illustrate how, like at harvest time, the firstfruits are brought to the priests, then the full harvest is completed; so it is with our redemption. What God started by giving us the Spirit will be effected by God's Spirit and completed when he resurrects our bodies.

Though we walk in the Spirit with hopeful anticipation for the full adoption process to be completed, for now we groan inwardly because we are still in the process of mortifying sin in our flesh. That full adoption of sons is the finished redemption of our beings, which means our bodies must die so they can be resurrected in perfection. Then we will be whole.

130. In This Hope

For in this hope we were saved. Now hope that is seen is not hope. For who hopes for what he sees? But if we hope for what we do not see, we wait for it with patience. —Romans 8:24–25

THE EXPRESSION "WE WERE SAVED" IS IN THE AORIST TENSE which indicates it is a completed action. It happened when we entered into our union with Christ.

Then how is it that we still hope for it? What Paul refers to as "this hope" is the promised redemption that is still futuristic in its realization. In other words, though our salvation in Christ was completed as a transaction in the past (when the Father elected, when Christ died and rose again, and when we by the Spirit's power believed and were baptized), we have only received its fulfillment in part.

It is in hope that we await its future realization. This hope, to which Paul refers, is not a passive uncertainty, however; it's a positive perseverance. Leon Morris suggests, "It is the attitude of the soldier who in the thick of the battle is not dismayed but fights on stoutly whatever the difficulties."[67] With this hope before us, let us not be weary in well-doing, for in due season we shall reap if we faint not!

67. Leon Morris, *The Epistle to the Romans,* The Pillar New Testament Commentary (Grand Rapids, MI: W.B. Eerdmans, 1988), 325.

131. The Spirit Helps Us in Our Weakness

Likewise the Spirit helps us in our weakness. For we do not know what to pray for as we ought, but the Spirit himself intercedes for us with groanings too deep for words. —Romans 8:26

THOUGH WE BELIEVERS MUST RELY ON THE SPIRIT OF GOD for the fullness of adoption as sons—that is, the full realization of our redemption—by persevering in our present condition, we are not left without help. The same Spirit of God also helps us in our weakness. He helps us by interceding for us in prayer too.

Often we struggle not knowing exactly how to pray, or what to pray for. But the Spirit intercedes on our behalf when our groanings are too deep for words. The Greek word for groaning is *στεναγμός* (*stenagmos*) and means an involuntary expression of great concern, like a sigh. In a certain sense we might think of this groaning as that which is related to striving, or pushing toward some manifest end—like child birth.

Interestingly, Paul is clearly making a connection between ideas by using the word groanings for something that creation does, something humans do, and also something it appears the Spirit does.

The groaning that creation and humans make are similar to each other in that they are related to the burden of the curse upon us. However, the groaning associated with the Spirit is his intercession on our behalf through our inarticulate groanings. He helps us in our weakness, our inability to know what to pray for as we ought.

One clue here worth considering is the "Likewise" at the beginning of the verse. The "likewise" refers to the Spirit's helping us in our weakness, an antecedent to a previously-mentioned activity of the Spirit: bearing witness with our spirit about our adoption. "The Spirit himself bears witness with our spirit that we are children of God . . . "Likewise the Spirit helps us in our weakness" (Romans 8:16, 26).

The Spirit not only bears witness to our spirit, assuring us of our adoption, but also helps us in our weakness of not knowing what to pray for when our burdens are too heavy for words.

132. The Efficacy of the Spirit's Intercession

And he who searches hearts knows what is the mind of the Spirit, because the Spirit intercedes for the saints according to the will of God. —*Romans 8:27*

PAUL CONTINUES BY EXPLAINING HOW WE ARE HELPED IN our weakness; and he offers a powerful word of encouragement to this end.

The Spirit who makes intercession for us does so according to the will of God. This means he helps us by praying on our behalf in a way that is agreeable to the will of God; therefore, we can have confidence that God, who searches hearts, knows what is the mind of the Spirit who is interceding for us.

What may be of further encouragement to us is the fact that in 1 Corinthians 2:10–11, Paul tells the Corinthians that "the Spirit searches everything, even the depths of God. For who knows a person's thoughts except the spirit of that person, which is in him? So also no one comprehends the thoughts of God except the Spirit of God."

From these two passages, we get a partial glimpse into the Trinitarian nature of God. There is a mutually deep and abiding intimacy between God the Father and God the Spirit. Since God knows the mind of the Spirit and the Spirit knows the thoughts of God, and further, that the Spirit intercedes in accordance with the will of God, we can be assured that the Spirit's intercession for us will be effective.

And keep in mind to what end the Spirit's prayers will be effective: in the groanings of eschatological childbirth—the day of resurrection and renewal.

133. All Things Work Together for Good

And we know that for those who love God all things work together for good, for those who are called according to his purpose. —Romans 8:28

THIS VERSE HAS BEEN A PARTICULAR SOURCE OF COMFORT TO Christians for two millennia. Unfortunately, it has also frequently has been misapplied and taken out of context.

The context is the manner in which God is working out our redemption practically speaking, redemption in this life, while we are still in the flesh waiting with eager anticipation for the adoption of sons, which is the resurrection of our bodies, given that the transaction of our salvation (i.e., our justification) has already been completed and the future realization of our redemption is guaranteed.

In this already-not-yet period of the Christian's existence, the Spirit of God makes intercession for the saints according to the will of God, thus helping us in our infirmities. But this is not all that God is doing. Recall in the introduction of this letter, I laid out the chiastic structure of Paul's letter and suggested that the form of the letter was nearly as instructive as the content of the letter.

- 1:1–17 Introduction
  - 1:18–3:30 Chaos (Devolution of Humanity)
    - 4–5 Faith Saves
      - 6–7 Two Regimes
        - 8 The Glory of the Gospel
      - 9–11 Two Branches
    - 12–13 Faith Works
  - 14–15 Cosmos (Evolution of Humanity)
- 16 Farewell

Paul now begins to reveal what is often called "the golden chain" of redemption as he begins his ascent to the pinnacle of his letter. In the providential work of God, He is working all things—good and evil—together for good, specifically for those who love him, for those who are the called according to his purpose.

It is here so many misuse Paul's words to mean something other than what God is doing, as revealed through Paul. To understand the nature of God's covenant promise, one must understand what Paul means by "those who love God," and "those who are the called according to his purpose."

Further, one must understand how Paul is defining "good." In other words, to whom is such grace directed and what is the nature of this good that God is working all things together toward?

HINT: As will be revealed as we unpack this final part of the passage, the "promise" is for believers and the "good" is becoming conformed to the image of Christ.

134. Whom He Foreknew, He Also Predestined

For those whom he foreknew he also predestined to be conformed to the image of his Son, in order that he might be the firstborn among many brothers.
—Romans 8:29

HERE WE HAVE ARRIVED AT WHAT MANY THEOLOGIANS HAVE called the golden chain because here Paul lays out an order of events related to our redemption as having been predetermined by God so that we cannot possess one aspect of our adoption without possessing the other, as shall be demonstrated.

This is also a point of controversy for many Christians who have tried to wrest the Scriptures in an effort to make sense of what to our fallen human sensibilities appears to be unfathomable, namely that God has planned our redemption without our consent or participation. But we must also remember that the divine workings of our salvation do not belong to us, but what God has revealed does (Deuteronomy 29:29).

What we do know is that the Greek word translated foreknew, προγινώσκω (*progynosko*) means to ordain or determine beforehand. It is not a "bare prescience" as some try to argue. Because the English word, foreknew appears to have in it the idea of simply "knowing" as the Greek word γινώσκω (*gynosko*) carries with it, these have attempted to argue that God simply predestines those whom he knew beforehand would repent and believe. But this is not supported by the definition of the word, the grammatical structure of the sentence, or the larger argument Paul is making. What Paul is asserting quite plainly is that God has distinguished from the beginning, by the adoption of sons, his own children from the reprobates.

It is of interest to note that this word is only found in this place and in chapter 9:2; Acts 26:5; 1 Pet. 1:20; and 2 Pet. 3:17. And on this point, the editors of John Calvin and John Owen's Commentary on Romans reference those passages mentioned, stating that

> In the second, and in the last passage, it signifies merely a previous knowledge or acquaintance, and refers to men. In 1 Pet. 1:20, it is applied to Christ as having been "foreordained," according to our version, "before the foundation of the world." In this Epistle, chap. 11:2, it refers to God,—"God hath not cast away his people whom he foreknew:" and according to the context, it means the same as elected; for the apostle speaks of what God did "according to the election of grace," and not according to foreseen faith.[68]

From here, we can follow Paul's logical chain. Those who have been foreknown by God, have also been predestined (determined beforehand) to be conformed to the image of Christ to the end that his adopted sons will resemble their older, model brother.

Finally, we must not forget that all of this is meant to be an encouragement to those in Christ and in whom the Spirit of God is working to help their infirmities in this life. It's an assurance of sanctification.

As believers, we are set in hopefulness knowing that long before we were born, God chose us to be his sons, and has planned for our redemption via the death, burial, and resurrection of Christ and the imparting of his divine nature by the Holy Spirit who helps us by making intercession on our behalf according to the will of God that we might overcome our infirmities as we are conformed more and more into the image of our older brother, Jesus the Christ.

Nevertheless, God's plan as laid out here by the apostle is not in any way contrary to his proclamation that "everyone who calls on the name of the Lord will be saved" (Romans 10:13, cf. Joel 2:32 & Acts 2:21). Anyone who chooses by his own free agency to call on the name of the Lord *will be saved*!

68. John Calvin and John Owen, Commentary on the Epistle of Paul the Apostle to the Romans (Bellingham, WA: Logos Bible Software, 2010), 318, n1.

135. Our Glorious Destiny

And those whom he predestined he also called, and those whom he called he also justified, and those whom he justified he also glorified. —Romans 8:30

IT'S NOT UNCOMMON FOR THOSE WHO OBJECT TO GOD'S PREdestined plan of redemption, to point out that the previous verse (29) seems to limit God's predestinary work to that of *conforming believers to the image of his Son*. Yet, as Paul makes perfectly clear here, every part of our redemption in Christ is to be understood as inseparable. Just as those whom God foreknew to be his adopted sons, he also predetermined them to be conformed to Christ, and he further called them to this destiny.

It is helpful to remember also that this use of predestination refers to the predetermined purpose of God that his adopted sons proceed to their destiny in the same manner as Christ proceeded to his. In other words, we are to bear the cross in this life as Christ did. We are to be humbled that we might be lifted up.

This is the mind of Christ Paul exhorts the Philippians to adopt:

> Have this mind among yourselves, which is yours in Christ Jesus, who, though he was in the form of God, did not count equality with God a thing to be grasped, but emptied himself, by taking the form of a servant, being born in the likeness of men. And being found in human form, he humbled himself by becoming obedient to the point of death, even death on a cross. Therefore God has highly exalted him and bestowed on him the name that is above every name, so that at the name of Jesus every knee should bow, in heaven and on earth and under the earth, and every tongue confess that Jesus Christ is Lord, to the glory of God the Father. Therefore, my beloved, as you have always obeyed, so now, not only as in my presence but much more in my absence, work out your own salvation with fear and trembling, for it is God who works in you, both to will and to work for his good pleasure. (Philippians 2:5–13)

Those whom God has called to this destiny have also been justified, meaning they have received a gratuitous imputation of his righteousness, to the end that they too will be lifted up from bearing the cross of death and be glorified in resurrection to Christ's eternal kingdom.

All of this reminds us that while we are in this body on this earth suffering in our weakness and infirmities, all of it is part of God's plan toward our own glorious destiny of being conformed to the image of his son, Jesus Christ, to the end that we will occupy our place as adopted sons, where in God's mind's eye, we are already eternally accepted in the beloved.

In another letter, Paul unpacks the same truth this way:

> Blessed be the God and Father of our Lord Jesus Christ, who has blessed us in Christ with every spiritual blessing in the heavenly places, even as he chose us in him before the foundation of the world, that we should be holy and blameless before him. In love he predestined us for adoption to himself as sons through Jesus Christ, according to the purpose of his will, to the praise of his glorious grace, with which he has blessed us in the Beloved. (Ephesians 1:3–6)

136. If God is for Us . . .

What then shall we say to these things? If God is for us, who can be against us?
—Romans 8:31

IT IS A GOOD TIME TO RECALL THAT PAUL'S LINE OF REASONing is meant to encourage believers who are in the space of having been justified by God but still living in the infirmities of the flesh in hope of the bodily resurrection, the full realization of their redemption.

He has clearly articulated the work of Christ, the work of the Spirit, and finally, the work of the Father, in the loving redemption of the believer. And, although we may speak of the various works and aspects of our redemption in separate terms, they are inseparable. If one work has been accomplished (i.e., justification), all of them have been (or will be) accomplished (i.e., adoption, propitiation, intercession, calling, glorification, etc.).

Paul now raises the rhetorical question, "What then shall we say to these things?"

In other words, what are we to make of all this work accomplished on our behalf? The answer is the most encouraging and affirming truth we could possess: "If God is for us, who can be against us?" Let us make a list in our minds or on paper. If God, the Creator and Sovereign Monarch of the universe, be for us, then who can be against us? The answer is: there is no enemy, no scheme, and no weapon that could be raised against us that could possibly triumph over us.

We are safe; we are secure; we are accepted! And, even if the enemies of Christ kill us, we will not die!

137. He Who Did Not Spare His Own Son

He who did not spare his own Son but gave him up for us all, how will he not also with him graciously give us all things? —Romans 8:32

WHAT GREATER DEMONSTRATION OF PATERNAL LOVE COULD God have made for his adopted sons than to have offered up his own Son for us all. And if he wasn't unwilling to spare him for our sake, how will he not also, with Christ, graciously give us everything else that we need?

Those in Paul's audience familiar with the law and with Jewish history (Romans 7:1), will likely recognize his expression "*spare his own Son*" as an allusion to the story of Abraham tested by God and asked to sacrifice his son Isaac (Genesis 22:1–19). When Abraham demonstrated his willingness to sacrifice his only son, his son of promise, God ultimately spared Isaac. However, God did not spare his own Son, Jesus, but gave him up (i.e., delivered him to death) for the salvation of sinful human beings.

This is the most remarkable and most gracious evidence of God's good will toward us. Paul further asserts that if he was willing to give his son, how much more is he willing to give us our petitions. All we have to do is simply ask and we can be assured that we have what we need.

> And I tell you, ask, and it will be given to you; seek, and you will find; knock, and it will be opened to you. For everyone who asks receives, and the one who seeks finds, and to the one who knocks it will be opened. What father among you, if his son asks for a fish, will instead of a fish give him a serpent; or if he asks for an egg, will give him a scorpion? If you then, who are evil, know how to give good gifts to your children, how much more will the heavenly Father give the Holy Spirit to those who ask him!" (Luke 11:9–13)

> If you ask me anything in my name, I will do it. (John 14:14)

> . . . do not be anxious about anything, but in everything by prayer and supplication with thanksgiving let your requests be made known to God." (Philippians 4:6)

Another interesting implication of this verse is asserted by Origen, who reminds us that

> The Father gave up his Son not only for the holy and the great but also for the least and for all everywhere who are members of the church. Therefore anyone who offends the conscience of even the least and weakest of these is said to be sinning against Christ, because he is scandalizing a soul for whom Christ died.[69]

69. Gerald Bray, ed., *Romans (Revised)*, Ancient Christian Commentary on Scripture (Downers Grove, IL: InterVarsity Press, 1998), 229.

138. It Is God Who Justifies

Who shall bring any charge against God's elect? It is God who justifies.
—Romans 8:33

THERE IS, ABOVE ALL OTHERS, ONLY ONE COURT IN WHICH WE must all stand—the high tribunal of the creator, God. And what more consolation could we receive in this life than knowing that God is favorable toward us already. He has justified us by imputing to us the righteousness of Christ while accounting to him all charges brought against us, the elect of God.

When the accuser of the brethren (Revelation 12:10) or even our own consciences attempt to condemn us, it is God's absolution of our sins that will answer. There is no appellate or Supreme Court higher than this court to which our accusers can appeal. It is the foremost confidence of the believer to be persuaded of this glorious truth.

If we are in Christ, we can rest with great confidence in the certainty of this salvation. And if one is not in Christ, then by all means, he or she need only repent and believe the gospel so he or she might receive the righteousness of God which is apart from the law and that one will be justified in his sight.

139. Who Is to Condemn?

Who is to condemn? Christ Jesus is the one who died—more than that, who was raised—who is at the right hand of God, who indeed is interceding for us.
—Romans 8:34

COMMENTING ELOQUENTLY ON THIS PASSAGE, THE REFORMER, John Calvin, says, "As no one by accusing can prevail, when the judge absolves; so there remains no condemnation, when satisfaction is given to the laws, and the penalty is already paid."[70]

It is Jesus Christ who has paid the penalty for our sins in his death. Not only so, but the Father has approved of his payment (declared it satisfactory) by raising him from the dead in vindication of his righteousness. Now Christ sits at the right hand of God, the place of authority and highest honor.

Finally, Christ will come again to judge the living and the dead (Acts 10:42, 1 Peter 4:5), but this final clause gives us further confidence of our standing before God. By his very presence on the Father's throne, Christ indeed is interceding for us believers.

That is not to say he is continually offering his blood or perpetually pleading, as some have surmised. Rather, as Leon Morris notes in his citation of B.F. Westcott, "We should interpret the intercession passages in the light of frequent references to sitting at the right hand of God. His presence at God's right hand in his capacity as the one who died for sinners and rose again is itself an intercession. Wescott notes, 'His glorified humanity is the eternal pledge of the absolute efficacy of His accomplished work. He pleads, as older writers truly expressed the thought, by His Presence on the Father's Throne.'"[71]

70. John Calvin and John Owen, *Commentary on the Epistle of Paul the Apostle to the Romans* (Bellingham, WA: Logos Bible Software, 2010), 324.

71. Leon Morris, *The Epistle to the Romans,* The Pillar New Testament Commentary (Grand Rapids, MI: W.B. Eerdmans, 1988), 338.

140. Who Shall Separate Us?

Who shall separate us from the love of Christ? Shall tribulation, or distress, or persecution, or famine, or nakedness, or danger, or sword? —Romans 8:35

HERE PAUL ADDRESSES ANOTHER AREA OF CONCERN FOR THE believer, his well-being. The afflictions we face in this life are not only stressful, unsettling, and often painful, but like ominous, brooding storm clouds, they also tend to raise real doubts about God's love for us. Even John the Baptist, imprisoned by Herod for offending Herodias by preaching truth, felt the weight of doubt-producing distress and persecution.

> When Jesus had finished instructing his twelve disciples, he went on from there to teach and preach in their cities. Now when John heard in prison about the deeds of the Christ, he sent word by his disciples and said to him, "Are you the one who is to come, or shall we look for another?" (Matthew 11:1–3).

Paul bolsters the believers' confidence in God's love for them by raising the question: Who shall separate us from the love of Christ? His list of possibilities is rather exhaustive.

Tribulations are any kind of evil or trouble that afflicts us. Distress is the internal anxiety that weighs on us because of afflictions, tribulations, and persecutions. Persecution is the unjust oppression and violence done to God's own children.

Famine, nakedness, danger, and the sword are the various ways in which a believer may suffer and ultimately lose his or her life. Famine is the lack of proper nourishment or food, nakedness is the lack of proper clothing or shelter, danger are the many and varied perils one faces in an uncertain and fallen world; and of course, the sword is synecdoche for execution.

In all these afflictions, God's love for us stands assured. It is objective. It is not based on our merits or abilities. He loves us immutably because he is immutable. He knew us before the foundations of the world, his mercy was extended to us on the cross of Calvary, and his love is spread abroad in our hearts by his Holy Spirit, who leads, guides, and comforts us in all our afflictions.

Perhaps someone might raise the objection that sometimes, human afflictions are judgments from God. While this is true, for the believer no affliction is ever punitive in that sense. God does chasten his own sons (Hebrews 12:5), but even that is a reminder of His mercy toward us—not his wrath. In those scenarios, He is bringing us back into joyful fellowship with Himself by way of our repentance. So then, nothing shall separate us from the love of Christ!

141. Sheep to Be Slaughtered

Who shall separate us from the love of Christ? Shall tribulation, or distress, or persecution, or famine, or nakedness, or danger, or sword? As it is written,

> *"For your sake we are being killed all the day long;*
> *we are regarded as sheep to be slaughtered."*

—Romans 8:35–36

TO DEMONSTRATE HIS ASSURANCE TO BELIEVERS THAT though we suffer tribulation, distress, and persecution nothing shall separate us from the love of Christ, he quotes Psalm 44 to show that, historically, suffering is a condition of God's people. It is not a reason to believe one has been rejected or abandoned by God.

In the passage quoted, the Psalmist laments the fact that God's people had seemed to be abandoned by God, though they had apparently been faithful to him:

> All this has come upon us, though we have not forgotten you, and we have not been false to your covenant. Our heart has not turned back, nor have our steps departed from your way; yet you have broken us in the place of jackals and covered us with the shadow of death. If we had forgotten the name of our God or spread out our hands to a foreign god, would not God discover this? For he knows the secrets of the heart. Yet for your sake we are killed all the day long; we are regarded as sheep to be slaughtered. Awake! Why are you sleeping, O Lord? Rouse yourself! Do not reject us forever! Why do you hide your face? Why do you forget our affliction and oppression? For our soul is bowed down to the dust; our belly clings to the ground. Rise up; come to our help! Redeem us for the sake of your steadfast love! (Psalm 44:17–26)

Paul, when writing to the Corinthians, even asserts this is his own experience. He writes, "For we who live are always being given over to death for

Jesus' sake, so that the life of Jesus also may be manifested in our mortal flesh" (2 Corinthians 4:11).

God has a purpose in our suffering, and that purpose can be seen in our being conformed to the image of Christ. Suffering works for good for those who love God, for those who are called according to his purpose (v. 28). It works toward our being conformed to the image of Christ (v. 29, cf. 2 Corinthians 4:11).

142. More Than Conquerors

No, in all these things we are more than conquerors through him who loved us. —Romans 8:37

THE ANSWER TO THE QUESTION IN VERSE 35—SHALL TRIBULation, or distress, or persecution, or famine, or nakedness, or danger, or sword separate us from the love of Christ?—is an emphatic, No!

Those of us who are in Christ will still face tribulation and will still be possessed of the infirmities of the flesh even though we are now the justified, adopted sons of God, filled with his Holy Spirit. In God's providence, he will use all these things for our good—for our deification (i.e., being conformed to the image of Christ).

Suffering tribulations and persecutions do not mean we are abandoned or unloved by God. It may seem as though we are "being killed all the day long" and "regarded as sheep to be slaughtered," but this is not the final word. In all these things, because of the paternal love of the father toward us, we are more than conquerors. We are victors, we are occupiers of a better station. Remember Jesus's passion and crucifixion? That wasn't the end. The end was resurrection and a throne at the right hand of the Father.

For the believer, tribulations, distress, and persecution are sanctifying opportunities that demonstrate the power and lovingkindness of God toward us. In all these things we are being conformed more and more into the image of Christ. Through our suffering, he is making us worthy of our inheritance with him.

This is virtually the same message Paul gives to the Corinthian believers, but in more eloquent terms:

> But we have this treasure in jars of clay, to show that the surpassing power belongs to God and not to us. We are afflicted in every way, but not crushed; perplexed, but not driven to despair; persecuted, but not forsaken; struck down, but not destroyed; always carrying in the body the death of Jesus, so that the life of Jesus may also be manifested in our

bodies. For we who live are always being given over to death for Jesus' sake, so that the life of Jesus also may be manifested in our mortal flesh. So death is at work in us, but life in you. Since we have the same spirit of faith according to what has been written, "I believed, and so I spoke," we also believe, and so we also speak, knowing that he who raised the Lord Jesus will raise us also with Jesus and bring us with you into his presence. For it is all for your sake, so that as grace extends to more and more people it may increase thanksgiving, to the glory of God. So we do not lose heart. Though our outer self is wasting away, our inner self is being renewed day by day. For this light momentary affliction is preparing for us an eternal weight of glory beyond all comparison, as we look not to the things that are seen but to the things that are unseen. For the things that are seen are transient, but the things that are unseen are eternal. (2 Corinthians 4:7–18)

143. The Glory of the Gospel

For I am sure that neither death nor life, nor angels nor rulers, nor things present nor things to come, nor powers, nor height nor depth, nor anything else in all creation, will be able to separate us from the love of God in Christ Jesus our Lord.
—Romans 8:38–39

PAUL'S ARGUMENT ENDS IN A DOXOLOGY—A CONFESSION OF his faith. And now is a good time to recall what was set forth at the beginning of this journey through Romans. Paul's letter to the Romans follows a chiastic structure that reaches its pinnacle, its highest and most important point, at the center of the poetic structure: Chapter 8 The Glory of the Gospel.

1:1–17 Introduction
    1:18–3:30 Chaos (Devolution of Humanity)
        4–5 Faith Saves
            6–7 Two Regimes
                8 The Glory of the Gospel
            9–11 Two Branches
        12–13 Faith Works
    14–15 Cosmos (Evolution of Humanity)
16 Farewell

Another way of considering this letter is to see it as an ascent to the summit of a great mountain and then a descent down the other side. The mountain is the gospel and the summit is its glory. These two verses are like a flag posted at the summit.

Paul has led his readers up the front side of the mountain of the gospel (the theological side) and has posted his flag at the summit: Because of the gospel—this good news of which he is not at all ashamed (Romans 1:16–17)—nothing in all creation will be able to separate us from the love of God in Christ Jesus our Lord. Think of anything that arouses fear in us and present it to one of the categories Paul lists and see if it can separate us. Tyrants? Disease or Virus? Satanic forces? Nothing in all of creation can do it!

Hallelujah! We are sons of God! We are joint heirs with Christ! We are accepted in the Beloved! We are safe in the love of God. Though our redemption is not yet realized in time, it is complete in the omniscience of God. And in the meantime, God, through his Spirit in us, is conforming us more and more into the image of his Son, Jesus Christ. He is making us worthy of the station he has given us by his grace.

What do we then do with this knowledge and understanding of the gospel (this good news)? That is what we will discover as we make our way down the opposite side of the gospel mountain in chapters 9–16 (the practical side).

Theologians often refer to these two sides of the proverbial mountain as *orthodoxy* (correct belief) and *orthopraxy* (correct practice).

144. Truth in Christ

I am speaking the truth in Christ—I am not lying; my conscience bears me witness in the Holy Spirit . . . —Romans 9:1

WHAT SEEMS TO BE SO MUCH OF AN ABRUPT CHANGE IN SUBject matter as to raise doubts in the minds of some scholars about the place of chapters 9–11 is not so dubious if we keep in mind the broader purpose of the letter and the circumstances surrounding the person writing it.

First, Paul has just demonstrated that nothing in all of creation shall be able to separate the elect from the love of God. One question that comes to mind in light of Paul's declaration is "What about unbelieving Israel then?" Aren't they separated from God?

Next, it is well known both within the church and the Jewish community, that Paul has been a missionary to the Gentiles (Galatians 2:8, cf. Romans 11:13). Given the religious climate of the first century, this was no small indiscretion in the minds of the Sanhedrin as well as many Jewish believers. Paul has only added insult to injury. He has so far spent a large portion of his letter showing how the Jews are just as guilty of sin as the Gentiles. They are sinners just the same as Gentiles in the eyes of God; there is no difference (Romans 2:12–29, 3:9–20). Given Paul's ministry and now his articulation of the nature of the Jews' sins, there would certainly be a need for some clarification—some damage control (to speak in modern terms).

Paul will resume in chapter 12 his discussion of the implications of the gospel he has laid out in chapters 1–8. Before proceeding further, however, he must digress for the sake of laying out the big picture of God's historical-redemptive plan. And as shall be seen, redemption has all along been meant for Jews and Gentiles alike. As a matter of fact, the distinction is merely a temporary situation designed toward a particular end—the revelation of the Christ (Messiah)!

Here Paul begins with a strong oath, which in the Greek, begins with the word truth. He says, "*Ἀλήθειαν λέγω ἐν Χριστῷ, οὐ ψεύδομαι (alētheian lego en Christo ou pseudomai)*" "Truth I am telling in Christ; I'm not lying!" This is striking given the final celebratory tone with which he concludes chapter 8. He continues the oath with a promise that the Holy Spirit is witness to his conscience about the truthfulness of what he is about to assert.

145. Great Sorrow and Unceasing Anguish

I am speaking the truth in Christ—I am not lying; my conscience bears me witness in the Holy Spirit— that I have great sorrow and unceasing anguish in my heart. For I could wish that I myself were accursed and cut off from Christ for the sake of my brothers, my kinsmen according to the flesh. —*Romans 9:1–3*

PAUL WANTS IT TO BE CLEAR TO HIS READERS THAT IN NO uncertain terms is he merely a disinterested bystander regarding the plight of the Jews—their rejection of the Messiah.

He has great sorrow and unceasing anguish in his heart because of their condition. The language here appears to be superfluously pathetic in the rhetorical sense; but that does not diminish the reality of his anguish.

He is not like a child waiting for his breakfast who cries to his mother, I'm starving! It's much closer to someone who hasn't eaten for several days moaning, I'm literally starving! Paul is expressing in the strongest language possible just how distressed he is over their impending judgment and eternal condemnation. His emphatic expression of anguish is not sentimentalism; it's pastoral.

To demonstrate to what degree he is broken-hearted, he announces that he could wish he could change places with them if it would help them be saved. "Could wish" is the translation of *εὔχομαι* (*euchomai*), an imperfect, middle/passive verb, meaning he contemplates the idea as if it were possible to do so. In other words, Paul is not changing his theology or wishing something that could not actually be the case. Rather, he is continuing to express in the strongest possible terms just how deeply anxious he is over the plight of the unbelieving Jews.

Said another way, Paul wants the church at Rome to know he's not against the Jews. He's the kind of man who is so deeply burdened by their need for salvation, he is willing to risk everything for their conversion—even the damnation of his own soul if such a thing were possible.

146. That Which Belongs to the Israelites

They are Israelites, and to them belong the adoption, the glory, the covenants, the giving of the law, the worship, and the promises. —*Romans 9:4*

IN VERSES 4 AND 5, PAUL EXPOUNDS HIS REASONS FOR BEING willing to sacrifice himself for his kinsmen, if it were possible and if it meant they would be saved. The list is expansive and detailed.

First, to them belong the adoption, the adoption of sons that Paul has been discussing in previous verses. It is an adoption to which all believers were destined to be made part, but was first manifest and exercised with the people of Israel. Throughout the OT, Israel was called God's son (Exodus 4:22, Isaiah 63:8; Jeremiah 3:19, Hosea 11:1).

Second, theirs is the glory. The glory refers to that divine glory, the Shekinah glory revealed in the wilderness in a pillar of fire and a pillar of cloud, at Sinai, and when the temple was filled with the glory of God. No other people or nation received such a revelation of glory (Exodus 16:10; 24:15–17; 40:34–35; Leviticus 9:6, 23; Numbers 14:10; 16:19, 42; 20:6; Deuteronomy 5:24, 1 Kings 8:11; 2 Chronicles 5:13–14; 7:1–3). It is also the glory that will be manifest in the New Jerusalem, the consummated kingdom of Christ (Zechariah 2:5; Isaiah 60:19; Ezekiel 43:2, 4–5; 44:4).

Third, theirs is also the covenants. Using the plural, Paul seems to have in mind the covenant revealed and expanded through the ages (Noahic, Abrahamic, Mosaic, Davidic, and ultimately, the New Covenant with Christ).

Fourth, they were on the receiving end of the giving of the law. The Law of God was chief among the other privileges given to the Jews that made them distinct among the nations (Deuteronomy 4:5–8).

Fifth was the form of worship. The Jews were given the sacrificial system of Tabernacle/Temple worship which allowed their sins to be forgiven and gave them an open door to God's throne room. Not only this but also the Sabbath and Shema were part of their system of worship. All of this pointed to the Christ, his ultimate sacrifice for sins on the cross, and the rest of that which we receive in him for all eternity.

Sixth are the promises. All the promises given to God's people were first given to the Israelites, promises of blessing and fruitfulness in land and progeny (i.e., fruit of the ground and fruit of the womb). Further, the Israelites were given the promise of being the source of blessing for all the nations of the earth (Genesis 12:2–3; 18:18; 22:18; 26:14; Acts. 3:25).

But wait! There's more . . .

147. Christ, Who Is God

To them belong the patriarchs, and from their race, according to the flesh, is the Christ, who is God over all, blessed forever. Amen. —*Romans 9:5*

NOT ONLY TO THE ISRAELITES, BELONG THE ADOPTION, THE glory, the covenants, the giving of the law, the worship, and the promises," but also the lineage and revelation of Christ, the Messiah, who is God over all and blessed for ever.

The Patriarchs were not only the fathers of the nation of Israel, but they were also progenitors of Christ. It was through their lineage that Messiah was given. In his letter to the Galatians, he explains, "Now the promises were made to Abraham and to his offspring. It does not say, 'And to off-springs,' referring to many, but referring to one, 'And to your offspring,' who is Christ" (Galatians 3:16).

We are to understand from this that Christ is the true Israel, he alone is the promised seed. The promises given to Israel were made that they might be the physical or human seedbed of the Messiah. Later, again, in his letter to the Galatians, he further explains: "But when the fullness of time had come, God sent forth his Son, born of woman, born under the law, to redeem those who were under the law, so that we might receive adoption as sons" (Galatians 4:4–5).

Also, the fact that Paul names Christ as God who is over all and blessed forever is more than a doxology of sorts, it's a bold proclamation about the nature of Messiah. It is the boldest proclamation Paul makes to this end. In other letters, he remarks similarly but never this clearly.

Consider the following:

- In his second letter to the Corinthians he writes, "The God and Father of the Lord Jesus, he who is blessed forever, knows that I am not lying" (2 Corinthians 11:31).
- And in his letter to the Christians at Ephesus he writes, "Blessed be the God and Father of our Lord Jesus Christ, who has blessed

us in Christ with every spiritual blessing in the heavenly places . . ." (Ephesians 1:3).

Paul is emphatically proclaiming that Jesus (whom the Jews crucified) is the Christ, and Christ is God. It's no small declaration to unbelieving Israel.

148. Not All Israel Are Israel

But it is not as though the word of God has failed. For not all who are descended from Israel belong to Israel . . . —Romans 9:6

MOVING FROM HIS GLORIOUS PRAISE FOR THE BLESSINGS Israel has received and for the special distinction they possess among nations as the sons of God, the children of promise, Paul moves to a new and related argument.

Given the Jews, having received the promise, had outright rejected it and crucified their anointed offspring—their Messiah—it appears the covenant God made with Abraham has failed. It's as if Paul is responding to this fair assumption by raising the question of exactly who are the children of Abraham, the children of the covenant, that received these blessings and this distinction among the people of the earth?

The first thing Paul clarifies is that not all who are the physical offspring of Israel (Jacob) truly belong to the covenant. Not all are spiritual Israel because the covenant has conditions.

Paul will lay out the qualifications in full in the following verses; but, in short, he will explain that to qualify one must be a physical descendant of Abraham and Isaac who has received the sign of circumcision, and one must believe the promise. Therefore, the Jews who have rejected Christ have also rejected the covenant. They are not the children of promise.

149. The Children of the Promise

But it is not as though the word of God has failed. For not all who are descended from Israel belong to Israel, and not all are children of Abraham because they are his offspring, but "Through Isaac shall your offspring be named." This means that it is not the children of the flesh who are the children of God, but the children of the promise are counted as offspring. For this is what the promise said: "About this time next year I will return, and Sarah shall have a son." —*Romans 9:6–9*

HAVING ESTABLISHED THAT THE COVENANT HAD NOT FAILED but was being misinterpreted by the Jews, he explains that the plan of God is not according to their biological ancestry but according to the sovereign will of God by way of a promise.

As an example, he points to Abraham who had two sons. One was accepted, the son of promise, and one was rejected, the son of the flesh. The witness to Paul's argument is the Scripture itself (Genesis 18:10, 14).

This is only the beginning of Paul's proofs. He will not only demonstrate the case for God's sovereign election by highlighting Abraham, but will go on to include examples from Isaac's son's, Jacob and Esau.

For reasons that can only be attributed to the pride of our flesh, the thought that it is God, and not we ourselves, who superintends the plan for human redemption, causes many to bristle at the idea, even professed believers. But were it not for grace, none would be saved.

Let us recall what Paul so eloquently established previously:

> For by works of the law no human being will be justified in his sight, since through the law comes knowledge of sin. But now the righteousness of God has been manifested apart from the law, although the Law and the Prophets bear witness to it— the righteousness of God through faith in Jesus Christ for all who believe. For there is no distinction: for all have sinned and fall short of the glory of God, and are justified by his grace as a gift, through the redemption that is in Christ Jesus, whom God put forward as a propitiation by his blood, to

be received by faith. This was to show God's righteousness, because in his divine forbearance he had passed over former sins. It was to show his righteousness at the present time, so that he might be just and the justifier of the one who has faith in Jesus. Then what becomes of our boasting? It is excluded. By what kind of law? By a law of works? No, but by the law of faith. (Romans 3:20–27)

150. God's Purpose of Election

And not only so, but also when Rebekah had conceived children by one man, our forefather Isaac, though they were not yet born and had done nothing either good or bad—in order that God's purpose of election might continue, not because of works but because of him who calls— she was told, "The older will serve the younger." As it is written, "Jacob I loved, but Esau I hated." —Romans 9:10–13

PAUL CONTINUES TO ILLUSTRATE GOD'S SOVEREIGNTY IN election. Not only in Abraham's son, Isaac, but also in Isaac's sons, Jacob and Esau. The former is evidence of God working out his will through the son of promise rather than the son of the flesh. Each having different mothers, it might be easy enough to anachronistically assign the choice to sovereignty when it was already clear that Hagar was not part of the original promise.

But the latter illustrates God working out his purposes according to his sovereign will between two sons with the same mother. There is nothing to distinguish the sons in this case, except for God's will, seeing they are twins not yet born and having done neither good nor bad. As a matter of fact, before they were born, God established that the older would serve the younger (Genesis 25:21–23), an arrangement reverse of the natural expectation.

So it was not the natural order of an Ancient Near East custom that determined the lineage of Christ. Nor was it the works of the sons that determined the choice. It was done this way in order that God's purpose of election might be revealed and established.

Finally, Paul seals the argument with an affirmation from Scripture, Malachi 1:2–3, saying, As it is written, "Jacob I loved, but Esau I hated." The context of the reference is God's pleading with Israel to repent of their sinful worship by appealing to his enduring love for them.

"I have loved you," says the Lord. But you say, "How have you loved us?" "Is not Esau Jacob's brother?" declares the Lord. "Yet I have loved Jacob but Esau I have hated. I have laid waste his hill country and left his heritage to jackals of the desert."

The act of loving one and hating the other is not capricious or malicious on God's part. And, although the language seems shocking to our modern ear, the love/hate paradigm is one of comparison rather than one of emotion. Consider how Jesus told his disciples, ""If anyone comes to me and does not hate his own father and mother and wife and children and brothers and sisters, yes, and even his own life, he cannot be my disciple" (Luke 14:26)

From everything else we know about what Jesus taught (e.g., Mark 7:9–13), certainly it would be a grave error to believe he meant for his disciples to have any kind of malice for their families. Rather, by using this term of comparison, Jesus was illustrating just how much a disciple would need to be committed to him in order to be his disciple. One has to be more committed to Jesus than to his own family, whom we are commanded to honor in the decalogue (i.e., fifth commandment).

Returning to the passage in Romans, Paul reveals that the historical plan of redemption is not laid out by happenstance or caprice, but achieved by the purposes of our only-wise God, who sovereignly superintends his redemptive plan according to his good will.

151. Is There Injustice on God's Part?

What shall we say then? Is there injustice on God's part? By no means!
—Romans 9:14

THE CHARGING OF GOD WITH INJUSTICE IS EVIDENCE OF OUR fallen nature. How could it be that the Creator and Judge of the entire universe could be unjust.

Hypothetically speaking, what could motivate injustice on God's part? There is no one rich enough or powerful enough who could bribe him. There is no one or no thing that he himself did not create. There is no one to whom he answers since he is the source of all life, all knowledge, all light—everything! So the suggestion itself is absurd and without merit.

Paul raises the foolish question, rhetorically, then responds with an emphatic, "by no means!" Ridiculous as it is, the question of God's injustice is motivated by the rebellious human heart whose mind has fallen into futility (Romans 1:21ff). It is appalling to such a mind that God, the Sovereign of the universe, would act sovereignly and choose the destiny of his creation.

Paul will go on to reason through the principles of predestination; but to begin with, the most important thing for his audience to know is that because God alone is sovereign, by definition we are not. And because God is sovereign, whatever he wills, in his transcendent goodness, is therefore good—and never unjust!

152. God, Who Has Mercy

For he says to Moses, "I will have mercy on whom I have mercy, and I will have compassion on whom I have compassion." So then it depends not on human will or exertion, but on God, who has mercy. —Romans 9:15–16

PERHAPS PAUL'S INITIAL ARGUMENT AGAINST THE CHARGES of injustice from God seem cold and shallow—i.e., is there injustice on God's part? By no means!—but in defense of his assertion, he recalls Moses's intercession to God on behalf of Israel after they sinned in the wilderness by making golden calves in Moses's absence (Exodus 33:12–19).

God's reply to Moses is "I will have mercy on whom I have mercy, and I will have compassion on whom I have compassion." Paul elaborates on God's response to Moses, explaining that the perception of injustice directed at God in the matter of election is an error in the accuser's understanding regarding the nature of mercy.

It is God who owns the corner market, so to speak, on mercy. All mercy belongs to him. We, who are condemned in our trespasses and sins have no say in matters of mercy. We are justly condemned because we have sinned. And if God, in praise to the glory of justice, determines to allow one to receive what justly belongs to him, he is not unjust for doing so. And, if God chooses of his own good pleasure to distribute mercy to one who is condemned, it is his to do with as he pleases.

See Jesus's parable of the laborers in Matthew 20:1–16.

Ultimately, Paul is arguing for his readers to manage their expectations according to reality and not according to an inept sense of justice, perverted by a fallen nature. As Kruse notes in his commentary on Romans, "Paul establishes God's justice in the light, not of human standards, but of God's own revelation of himself. There is no higher standard to which the apostle could appeal."[72]

Further, the codifier of the Protestant Reformation, John Calvin, notes,

72. Colin G. Kruse, *Paul's Letter to the Romans*, ed. D. A. Carson, The Pillar New Testament Commentary *(Grand Rapids, MI: Eerdmans, 2012)*, 382.

> Monstrous surely is the madness of the human mind, that it is more disposed to charge God with unrighteousness than to blame itself for blindness. Paul indeed had no wish to go out of his way to find out things by which he might confound his readers; but he took up as it were from what was common the wicked suggestion, which immediately enters the minds of many, when they hear that God determines respecting every individual according to his own will. It is indeed, as the flesh imagines, a kind of injustice, that God should pass by one and show regard to another.[73]

Once we have, in humility, adjusted our expectations regarding who is the "owner of mercy," we can happily recall Paul's earlier proclamation, that ". . . the same Lord is Lord of all, bestowing his riches on all who call on him. For 'everyone who calls on the name of the Lord will be saved'" (Romans 10:12–13).

73. John Calvin and John Owen, *Commentary on the Epistle of Paul the Apostle to the Romans* (Bellingham, WA: Logos Bible Software, 2010), 354.

153. Whomever He Wills

For the Scripture says to Pharaoh, "For this very purpose I have raised you up, that I might show my power in you, and that my name might be proclaimed in all the earth." So then he has mercy on whomever he wills, and he hardens whomever he wills. —Romans 9:17–18

JUST AS GOD TOLD MOSES THAT HE WOULD HAVE MERCY AND compassion on whomever he wills, God also told Pharaoh that he raised the Egyptian king up for his own purposes: that I might show my power in you, and that my name might be proclaimed in all the earth (cf. Exodus 9:13–16).

Paul concludes by saying that God then shows mercy to whomever he wants and hardens whomever he wants in order to accomplish his good will. It is also important to keep in mind Paul's illustration of showing mercy or hardening whomever he wills in view the Jews' failure to accept Jesus Christ as their Messiah.

As he proceeds, he will unpack this further by explaining the Jews' rejection of Christ was not a surprise to God whose plan is to use their hardness to bring the Gentiles into the kingdom. God's will, it should be remembered, is always good. And his goodness, his justice, and his mercy far exceeds all that we could ever imagine in our finite minds. "For as the heavens are higher than the earth, so are my ways higher than your ways and my thoughts than your thoughts" (Isaiah 55:9).

154. Who Are You, O Man?

You will say to me then, "Why does he still find fault? For who can resist his will?" But who are you, O man, to answer back to God? Will what is molded say to its molder, "Why have you made me like this?" Has the potter no right over the clay, to make out of the same lump one vessel for honorable use and another for dishonorable use? —Romans 9:19–21

PAUL ONCE AGAIN USES THE HYPOTHETICAL INTERLOCUTOR to make his point. It is an effective rhetorician who anticipates potential objections from one's audience and then addresses them in such a tactful manner. By speaking to a hypothetical objector, the rhetorician can address his objector strongly, and in effect, "school him," while allowing his audience to listen in and learn the lesson from the hypothetical person's mistake without feeling belittled themselves.

The lesson Paul is teaching is that God is God and we are not! We are created beings and God is not unjust to do with his creation as he pleases. Paul retorts, "who are you, O man, to answer back to God? Will what is molded say to its molder, "Why have you made me like this?" Has the potter no right over the clay, to make out of the same lump one vessel for honorable use and another for dishonorable use?"

In his response, Paul is drawing upon a longstanding Jewish understanding of the relationship between creator and the created. It is an example every Jew who had even the slightest knowledge of the Holy Scriptures would have immediately recognized, that of the potter and the clay.

> You turn things upside down! Shall the potter be regarded as the clay, that the thing made should say of its maker, "He did not make me"; or the thing formed say of him who formed it, "He has no understanding"? (Isaiah 29:16)

> Woe to him who strives with him who formed him, a pot among earthen pots! Does the clay say to him who forms it, "What are you making?" or "Your work has no handles"? (Isaiah 45:9)

> So I went down to the potter's house, and there he was working at his wheel. And the vessel he was making of clay was spoiled in the potter's hand, and he reworked it into another vessel, as it seemed good to the potter to do. Then the word of the Lord came to me: "O house of Israel, can I not do with you as this potter has done?" declares the Lord. Behold, like the clay in the potter's hand, so are you in my hand, O house of Israel. (Jeremiah 18:3–6)

The example is even used in the the Wisdom of Solomon and the Sirach:

> A potter kneads the soft earth and laboriously molds each vessel for our service, fashioning out of the same clay both the vessels that serve clean uses and those for contrary uses, making all alike; but which shall be the use of each of them the worker in clay decides. (Wisdom of Solomon 15:7)

> All human beings come from the ground, and humankind was created out of the dust. In the fullness of his knowledge the Lord distinguished them and appointed their different ways. Some he blessed and exalted, and some he made holy and brought near to himself; but some he cursed and brought low, and turned them out of their place. Like clay in the hand of the potter, to be molded as he pleases, so all are in the hand of their Maker, to be given whatever he decides. (Sirach 33:10–13)

In his commentary, Brendan Byrne puts it this way: "The force of the image as Paul employs it . . . stems from the fact that the potter has to make vessels for a wide variety of uses, some noble (the banquet cup), some homely (the chamber pot); he will turn the same lump of clay in either direction as he sees fit. Like the potter, the Creator has a perfect right to turn the creature in whatsoever direction he chooses."[74]

All this being said, I cannot emphasize strongly enough that in none of what Paul is arguing does he suggest that God's will is capricious or even

74. Brendan Byrne, *Romans*, 297–98. Colin G. Kruse, *Paul's Letter to the Romans*, ed. D. A. Carson, The Pillar New Testament Commentary *(Grand Rapids, MI: Eerdmans, 2012)*, 385.

absolute. He doesn't treat his creation as a plaything; neither is he malicious or uncaring. Paul is only arguing that God, in his transcendent goodness and wisdom, is free to create and subsequently deal with his creation as he sees fit.

155. What If God?

What if God, desiring to show his wrath and to make known his power, has endured with much patience vessels of wrath prepared for destruction . . .
—Romans 9:22

IN AN ATTEMPT TO SHED FURTHER LIGHT ON HIS ARGUMENT that *the potter [has the] right over the clay, to make out of the same lump one vessel for honorable use and another for dishonorable use,* Paul follows up with a moving question: *What if?*

In other words, since the potter has the authority over his clay as can be seen in the cases of Moses (he will show mercy on whomsoever he will) and Pharaoh (God chose to harden him), then *What if God, desiring to show his wrath and to make known his power, has endured with much patience vessels of wrath prepared for destruction?*

In rhetorical language, Paul's argument is a kind of conditional *enthymeme,* a logical syllogism that uses *ellipsis* to make the point stronger. That is, he provides the *prostasis* (the clause containing the condition) but implies the *apodosis* (the clause in a conditional statement containing the conclusion).

The prostasis is "What if God . . . ?"

The apodosis is implied by proxy of his former conclusion back in verse 14 regarding God's justice in choosing one brother over the other: "What shall we say then? Is there injustice on God's part? By no means!"

In whole, it would go like this: "What if God, desiring to show his wrath and to make known his power, has endured with much patience vessels of wrath prepared for destruction? Can anyone charge him with unrighteousness? Is there injustice on God's part? By no means!"

The matter of who the *vessels of wrath* are is left unstated. But the inference seems to be pretty clear that Paul has in mind those who, like Pharaoh, God raised up for the purpose of showing his power. For he says to Pharaoh "But for this purpose I have raised you up, to show you my power, so that my name may be proclaimed in all the earth" (Exodus 9:16).

In conclusion, let us keep in mind, the example of the one God raised up to demonstrate his power is also the one who said: "Who is the Lord, that I should obey his voice and let Israel go? I do not know the Lord, and moreover, I will not let Israel go" (Exodus 5:2).

156. Prepared Beforehand

What if God, desiring to show his wrath and to make known his power, has endured with much patience vessels of wrath prepared for destruction, in order to make known the riches of his glory for vessels of mercy, which he has prepared beforehand for glory . . . —Romans 9:22–23

IN CONTRAST TO GOD'S HAVING "ENDURED WITH MUCH patience" vessels of wrath prepared for destruction, Paul raises the readers' attention to the flip side of this coin: the vessels of mercy, which he has prepared beforehand for glory.

Both are prepared beforehand, one for destruction and one for glory, all in order to make known the riches of such glory for those who are vessels of mercy. In other words, the Triune God has, from before the beginning of time, designed a plan according to the good counsel of his will to reveal both his wrath against sin and his mercy toward sinners who are in fact worthy of damnation.

"It was to show his righteousness at the present time, so that he might be just and the justifier of the one who has faith in Jesus" (Romans 3:26).

157. Even Us Whom He Has Called

What if God, desiring to show his wrath and to make known his power, has endured with much patience vessels of wrath prepared for destruction, in order to make known the riches of his glory for vessels of mercy, which he has prepared beforehand for glory—even us whom he has called, not from the Jews only but also from the Gentiles? —Romans 9:22–24

NOW THAT WE'VE EXAMINED THE PARTS OF PAUL'S SUB-ARGUMENT, we can see the whole as it is meant to be applied to the larger argument started in 9:6: "But it is not as though the word of God has failed. For not all who are descended from Israel belong to Israel . . ."

Ironically, the fact that the nation of Israel did not receive their Messiah was not because the covenant failed but because it was part of God's wise plan to save Israel—that is, the true Israel that includes both Jews and Gentiles. God was hardening the *vessels of wrath prepared for destruction* (rebellious national Israel) in order to show mercy to those of *us whom he called* (his *vessels of mercy prepared beforehand for glory*).

As Paul will further explain, he will use the salvation of the Gentiles to provoke the unbelieving Jews into receiving their true Messiah, Jesus; and the true Israel will be revealed as all those who believe on the One True Israel who kept the covenant, Jesus Christ.

For Paul explains it to the believers at Galatia like this: "Now the promises were made to Abraham and to his offspring. It does not say, "And to offsprings," referring to many, but referring to one, "And to your offspring," who is Christ . . . Why then the law? It was added because of transgressions, until the offspring should come to whom the promise had been made, and it was put in place through angels by an intermediary" (Galatians 3:16–19).

158. God's People Who Were Not His People

As indeed he says in Hosea,

> *"Those who were not my people I will call 'my people,'*
> *and her who was not beloved I will call 'beloved.'*
> *"And in the very place where it was said to them, 'You are not my people,'*
> *there they will be called 'sons of the living God."*

And Isaiah cries out concerning Israel: "Though the number of the sons of Israel be as the sand of the sea, only a remnant of them will be saved, for the Lord will carry out his sentence upon the earth fully and without delay." And as Isaiah predicted,

> *"If the Lord of hosts had not left us offspring,*
> *we would have been like Sodom*
> *and become like Gomorrah."*

—Romans 9:25–29

What is most ironic about our human nature is our proclivity to major on the minors, to focus on the periphery and not the center, to be overly concerned about the "what ifs?" This is not to say there is no place for such considerations and contemplations, but to be overly concerned over that which we have no influence, over that which is above our pay grade so to speak, is to miss the abundance of riches supplied by what concerns us. I'm speaking of the doctrine of election.

The tendency amongst modern, and particularly, democratically-minded, Christians is to focus on what appears to be unfair about God's elective purposes. Was it Pharaoh's fault that he was judged when it was, after all, God who hardened his heart? What about the Jews who rejected Christ as their Messiah—or Judas even of whom Christ said it would have been better for him to have never been born—is it fair that God would harden them in order to redeem the vessels of mercy prepared beforehand for glory?

Let us consider three things.

First, God is God and we are not. He is omniscient (he knows everything, the end from the beginning) and since wisdom is by definition based on knowledge, the foolishness of God (as if there could be such a thing) is higher than the wisdom of the wisest man (1 Corinthians 1:25–27). The goodness of God is "gooder" than the goodness of the "goodest" man. The mercy of God is more merciful than the most merciful man. You get the idea. God does not act capriciously, but wisely; and only because of his elective purposes has salvation been made possible for any human being.

Second, that God would reveal to us through his word that he has made such elective purposes is to know that God meant for us to know such things without telling us why. This is a curious thing God has done. Yet, since the earliest known writings of man, literary tragedy has been used to invoke fear and pity in the reader/listener for cathartic purposes (i.e., Homer, Sophocles, etc.). In other words, to learn of the tragic plight of another who is in some way like ourselves, or even better than ourselves, is to fear for ourselves and take pity on others. The catharsis is cleansing relief that causes us to say, "but for the grace of God there go I." While this is only conjecture on my part, there seems to be some likeness to it in such statements as Peter makes in his letter where he says to the believers: "*Therefore, brothers, be all the more diligent to confirm your calling and election, for if you practice these qualities you will never fall*" (2 Peter 1:10).

Third, the very point Paul is making in pointing to God's elective purposes—something which the Jews had no quarrel with—is to show that our salvation is a result of nothing less than God's gratuitous nature, grace! In our understanding of redemption, we must begin in the proper place. We are condemned already. We are by nature, children of wrath. On our own, there is no hope of salvation. Technically, if God would have allowed each of us to die in our sins, he would have done so justly. But he didn't. Because of grace alone, he has made those who are not his people into his people. If God would not have saved us, we would all end up like Sodom and become like Gomorrah!

159. The Gentiles Have Attained It

What shall we say, then? That Gentiles who did not pursue righteousness have attained it, that is, a righteousness that is by faith . . . —Romans 9:30

PAUL USES A JEWISH IDIOM, *PURSUE RIGHTEOUSNESS,* TO CONtrast the standing of the Gentiles with the standing of the Jews. This means we should not understand Paul to be saying that Gentiles didn't ever pursue righteousness. Many of them did. What they did not pursue is the righteousness of God. They weren't pursuing a right standing before God the way the Jews were.

To say they have attained it without pursuing it, Paul means that it was imputed to them by faith in Christ. They attained the righteousness which is apart from the law. "But now the righteousness of God has been manifested apart from the law, although the Law and the Prophets bear witness to it—the righteousness of God through faith in Jesus Christ for all who believe. For there is no distinction . . ." (Romans 3:21–22).

160. They Did Not Pursue It by Faith

What shall we say, then? That Gentiles who did not pursue righteousness have attained it, that is, a righteousness that is by faith; but that Israel who pursued a law that would lead to righteousness did not succeed in reaching that law. Why? Because they did not pursue it by faith, but as if it were based on works. They have stumbled over the stumbling stone . . . —*Romans 9:30–32*

IN CONTRAST TO THE GENTILES WHO DID NOT PURSUE RIGHTEOUSNESS but attained it by faith, Israel pursued the law as means of attaining righteousness but did not succeed because they neglected faith. Instead, they pursued the righteousness of the law by their works.

As had been prophesied, when the time came to receive their Messiah, Israel did not believe. They stumbled over Christ, the rock of offense, the very Rock that gave them water in the desert when their father in the law, Moses, led them into the wilderness (cf. 1 Corinthians 10:4).

God has determined beforehand that all would be saved by faith in Christ, not by keeping the law. Otherwise, who could be saved?

161. A Stone of Stumbling

Why? Because they did not pursue it by faith, but as if it were based on works. They have stumbled over the stumbling stone, as it is written, "Behold, I am laying in Zion a stone of stumbling, and a rock of offense; and whoever believes in him will not be put to shame." —Romans 9:32–33

PAUL CONCLUDES HIS ARGUMENT BY APPEALING TO ISAIAH, amalgamating a few different passages of Isaiah's prophetic writing (cf. Isaiah 28:16, 8:14, and 49:23) to support his theology from Scripture.

The point is, Israel failed, not because the covenant was no good but because Israel did not have faith and stumbled on the Rock that was laid to save them. God in his wisdom had chosen beforehand to lay this stone. For believers it would be a shelter and a foundation; for unbelievers, it would be a stone of stumbling. But God was not taken off-guard. He had planned "in advance" to steward the tragic failure of Israel as a means of bringing the Gentiles into the fold.

Paul concludes this part of his argument with a word of hope. Whoever believes in Christ, will not be put to shame. In other words, Israel's destiny was their own fault. No one else has to experience their tragedy—if they simply believe on Christ.

162. That They May Be Saved

Brothers, my heart's desire and prayer to God for them is that they may be saved.
—Romans 10:1

PAUL CONCLUDES THIS PART OF HIS ARGUMENT—THAT THE Jews failed to obtain the righteousness of God at no fault of the covenant but at the fault of their unbelief—with an *inclusio*. An *inclusio* is a literary device whereby the author restates his initial assertion, bringing his argument full circle. Back in Chapter 9:1–4, Paul started this line of reasoning by saying, "I am speaking the truth in Christ—I am not lying; my conscience bears me witness in the Holy Spirit—that I have great sorrow and unceasing anguish in my heart. For I could wish that I myself were accursed and cut off from Christ for the sake of my brothers, my kinsmen according to the flesh. They are Israelites, and to them belong the adoption, the glory, the covenants, the giving of the law, the worship, and the promises."

Now he repeats that his heart's desire and his prayers consist of wanting to see Israel saved. In other words, as the minister to the Gentiles, he has not turned his back on Israel. He longs to see them reconciled to God by faith in Christ Jesus. Might this be the longing and prayer of every one of us, that unbelievers will be reconciled to God by faith in Christ.

163. They Have a Zeal for God

Brothers, my heart's desire and prayer to God for them is that they may be saved. For I bear them witness that they have a zeal for God, but not according to knowledge. —Romans 10:1–2

PAUL FURTHER TESTIFIES THAT WHILE THE JEWS FAILED TO believe on Christ and did not attain the righteousness of God, it was not for a lack of zeal. The Jews indeed have a zeal for God, he argues, but it was not a zeal that was approximated to knowledge of God's plan of redemption.

To the Jews, a zeal for God was not unimportant. It had a long tradition in Israel. In their zeal, Simeon and Levi killed Shechem and his tribe for raping their sister Dinah (Genesis 34). Phinehas, in his zeal, killed the Israelite and the Midianite woman in a brazen sexual liaison that undermined the purity of Israel (Numbers 25). There was also the zeal of the prophets of God (1 King 19 & 2 Kings 9–10), and the zeal of the Maccabean revolt against Antiochus Epiphanes. There were even zealots in the midst of Israel during Christ's ministry (Matthew 10:4).

And Paul himself had been zealous of the Lord "circumcised on the eighth day, of the people of Israel, of the tribe of Benjamin, a Hebrew of Hebrews; as to the law, a Pharisee; as to zeal, a persecutor of the church; as to righteousness under the law, blameless" (Philippians 3:5–6, cf. Acts 8–9, 22:3).

But zeal without knowledge doesn't render salvation. As St. Augustine noted, "It is better to limp in the right way than to run with all our might out of the way."[75]

75. St. Augustine quoted in Leon Morris, *The Epistle to the Romans*, The Pillar New Testament Commentary (Grand Rapids, MI: W.B. Eerdmans, 1988), 379.

164. Ignorant of the Righteousness of God

For, being ignorant of the righteousness of God, and seeking to establish their own, they did not submit to God's righteousness. —Romans 10:3

AS HAS BEEN SHOWN, ZEAL WITHOUT KNOWLEDGE HAD LED the Jews to miss the mark of God's righteousness. Instead of submitting to God's revelation of himself, the Jews tried harder to do better on their own merits and ushered themselves toward damnation all the more quickly.

What it would have looked like to have had a zeal with knowledge, zeal that submitted to the righteousness of God, seems to be worked out in Paul's letter to the Philippians in his own testimony.

> For we are the circumcision, who worship by the Spirit of God and glory in Christ Jesus and put no confidence in the flesh— though I myself have reason for confidence in the flesh also. If anyone else thinks he has reason for confidence in the flesh, I have more: circumcised on the eighth day, of the people of Israel, of the tribe of Benjamin, a Hebrew of Hebrews; as to the law, a Pharisee; as to zeal, a persecutor of the church; as to righteousness under the law, blameless. But whatever gain I had, I counted as loss for the sake of Christ. Indeed, I count everything as loss because of the surpassing worth of knowing Christ Jesus my Lord. For his sake I have suffered the loss of all things and count them as rubbish, in order that I may gain Christ and be found in him, not having a righteousness of my own that comes from the law, but that which comes through faith in Christ, the righteousness from God that depends on faith . . . (Philippians 3:3–9).

165. The End of the Law

For Christ is the end of the law for righteousness to everyone who believes.
—Romans 10:4

WHAT PAUL MEANS BY "CHRIST IS THE END OF THE LAW" *Χριστὸς τέλος νόμος* (*Christos telos nomos*) is strikingly profound but simple. He is the telos, the goal, the target at which the law points all men. This is so that righteousness could be made available for everyone who believes.

In contrast to the righteousness the Jews sought to establish by their own works according to the law, Paul explains that God had given the law to show man his dire need for God's perfect, complete, whole righteousness, which can only be attained by faith in the person of Jesus Christ.

This is the ignorance that undermined the zeal of the Jews. This is also the simplicity that so often undermines the pride of the Gentiles. And, it's why Paul wrote to the church at Corinth, saying, "For Jews demand signs and Greeks seek wisdom, but we preach Christ crucified, a stumbling block to Jews and folly to Gentiles, but to those who are called, both Jews and Greeks, Christ the power of God and the wisdom of God" (1 Corinthians 1:22–24).

166. Righteousness Based on the Law

For Moses writes about the righteousness that is based on the law, that the person who does the commandments shall live by them. —Romans 10:5

HERE PAUL BEGINS TO EXPLAIN HIS ASSERTION IN VERSE 4, that *Christ is the end of the law for righteousness to everyone who believes* by contrasting two approaches to attaining righteousness—the first is based on law observance (v. 5) and the latter based on faith in Christ (v. 6).

Paul quotes Moses in Leviticus where he is teaching the people what the Lord would require of them to enter the promised land and remain part of the covenant community. Most scholars agree that for Israel, this promise of life for those who "do" the commandments extends naturally to eternal life as well. For Israel, there is not the kind of distinction between life in our natural state and life in our eternal state as some evangelicals have attempted to create. This means the focus for Israel is almost always on the natural state of things.

Moses had written in Leviticus 18:5, "You shall therefore keep my statutes and my rules; if a person does them, he shall live by them: I am the Lord." What Moses is telling Israel is that the Lord has commanded that every person who obeys the commandments (in their entirety) will live by them. And Paul, by quoting Moses, is saying that in order to attain the righteousness of the law, one must fulfill every part of it. Since all men at all times have always come short of this obedience—Israel is Paul's example—it would be foolish to pursue the law as a means of salvation.

The other kind, as we shall see in verse 6, is a righteousness based on faith that assures a person will live into the eternal state.

167. The Word Is Near You

But the righteousness based on faith says, "Do not say in your heart, 'Who will ascend into heaven?'" (that is, to bring Christ down) "or 'Who will descend into the abyss?'" (that is, to bring Christ up from the dead). But what does it say? "The word is near you, in your mouth and in your heart" (that is, the word of faith that we proclaim) . . . —Romans 10:6–8

TO SHOW WHAT RIGHTEOUSNESS BASED ON FAITH LOOKS like, he once again quotes Moses, but this time doing so by personifying "righteousness based on faith." This handling of the Scripture is consistent with the Jewish exegetical practices of his day as is the insertion of his own gospel application of this passage originally about the law of Moses. It's helpful to keep in mind that all of Moses' writings are considered "The Law" in one respect (cf. James 2:10).

Paul quotes another amalgamation of Deuteronomy. The first part is taken from Deuteronomy 9:4 whereas the second part is taken from Deuteronomy 30:11–14.

> Do not say in your heart, after the Lord your God has thrust them out before you, "It is because of my righteousness that the Lord has brought me in to possess this land," whereas it is because of the wickedness of these nations that the Lord is driving them out before you. (Deuteronomy 9:4)

> For this commandment that I command you today is not too hard for you, neither is it far off. It is not in heaven, that you should say, "Who will ascend to heaven for us and bring it to us, that we may hear it and do it?" Neither is it beyond the sea, that you should say, "Who will go over the sea for us and bring it to us, that we may hear it and do it?" But the word is very near you. It is in your mouth and in your heart, so that you can do it. (Deuteronomy 30:11–14)

Again, what Deuteronomy says about the law of Moses, Paul then applies to the gospel of Christ Jesus. Christ (the righteousness of God) does not have to be brought down to us or brought up for us. The righteousness of God is a person, Jesus Christ, and he has already descended and he has already resurrected. This was God's work (marvelous in our sight), a work of revelation to be received by faith.

The righteousness of God based on faith, Jesus Christ, is speaking now. It is the word of faith that Paul is preaching. God has revealed Christ to us; we don't need to go searching for him. We need only believe! As John notes, the Word (the Divine Logos) became flesh and dwelt among the apostles, and they had seen his glory, glory as of the only Son from the Father, full of grace and truth (cf. John 1:14).

168. Confess and Believe Jesus Is Lord

... because, if you confess with your mouth that Jesus is Lord and believe in your heart that God raised him from the dead, you will be saved. For with the heart one believes and is justified, and with the mouth one confesses and is saved.
—Romans 10:9–10

CONTINUING TO DRAW FROM MOSES AS RECORDED IN THE book of Deuteronomy, Paul expounds *the word of faith* that he is preaching. Moses says, "But the word is very near you. It is in your mouth and in your heart, so that you can do it" (Deuteronomy 30:14).

There must be a confession with the mouth that is believed in the heart. These are not meant to be understood as two separate things or specifically happening in this order. Rather, Paul is simply following the structure of Moses to argue for a sincere confession that is both spoken and believed in the heart.

If one was to "believe" without being willing to confess what was believed, it would not be a true confession, namely because it is not real belief if one cannot stand by it publicly. Alternatively, one would be a hypocrite to profess publicly what one does not sincerely believe in the heart. The confession then is that 'Jesus is Lord.' For a Jew to say this would be blasphemous—unless Jesus was YHWH.

As Cranfield explains in his critical commentary, Paul used the LXX (Septuagint), which was the commonly used translation of the Hebrew Bible into Greek. And, in the LXX, the word *κύριος* (*kurios*), translated *Lord* in English, is used as a translation for YHWH more than six thousand times. And while the use of the word κύριος could also be applied in non-religious terms, Jesus was often referred to as teacher, or Rabbi, by his disciples before his crucifixion and not κύριος until after the resurrection, which subsequently signified his connection to YHWH.

Additionally, it is notable that Paul applies the word Lord (*κύριος*) to Christ in his letters (e.g. Romans 10:12–14; 1 Thessalonians 5:2; 2 Thessalonians 2:2, 1 Corinthians 1:2, 1 Corinthians 16:2).

Consider Cranfield's explanation: "What then did the confession 'Jesus is Lord' mean for Paul? The use of κύριος more than six thousand times in the LXX to represent the Tetragrammaton must surely be regarded as of decisive importance here . . . and Paul approves of calling upon the name of the Lord Christ . . . but, for a Jew, to pray to anyone other than the one true God was utterly repugnant."[76]

So to confess that Jesus is Lord is to believe the God has raised him from the dead. Paul makes it superbly clear that the word of faith he is preaching is that justification before God (i.e., possessing the righteousness of God) is attained by faith in the Lord Christ alone, who died for our sins and rose again for our justification.

By believing, one is justified; and by confessing, one is saved. And in Paul's use of the term, saved, he means "salvation is *from* the wrath of God and *for* a share in the glory that is to come."[77]

76. C. E. B. Cranfield, A Critical and Exegetical Commentary on the Epistle to the Romans, International Critical Commentary (London; New York: T&T Clark International, 2004), 529.

77. Colin G. Kruse, *Paul's Letter to the Romans*, ed. D. A. Carson, The Pillar New Testament Commentary *(Grand Rapids, MI: Eerdmans, 2012)*, 410.

169. Not Put to Shame

For the Scripture says, "Everyone who believes in him will not be put to shame." *—Romans 10:11*

LIKE THE SOUND THEOLOGIAN AND RHETORICIAN THAT HE IS, Paul now appeals to Scripture to support his claim that "if you confess with your mouth that Jesus is Lord and believe in your heart that God raised him from the dead, you will be saved."

Quoting for a second time in this letter (the first time was in 9:33) from a passage in Isaiah, Paul universalizes the Prophet's words to be sure his audience accounts for the knowledge that the Gentiles are also included in the invitation. Isaiah wrote, "therefore thus says the Lord God, "Behold, I am the one who has laid as a foundation in Zion, a stone, a tested stone, a precious cornerstone, of a sure foundation: 'Whoever believes will not be in haste" (Isaiah 28:16).

To "be in haste" is a Jewish idiom that implies those who are in haste make foolish decisions that bring shame upon themselves. Paul doesn't at all change Isaiah's meaning; he uses clarifying language to assure his audience of the universality of the gospel: *Everyone who believes on Christ will not be acting foolishly; rather, he is wise because he will be glorified!*

170. The Same Lord Is Lord of All

For there is no distinction between Jew and Greek; for the same Lord is Lord of all, bestowing his riches on all who call on him. For "everyone who calls on the name of the Lord will be saved." —Romans 10:12–13

PAUL ASSURES HIS AUDIENCE THAT WHEREVER FAITH IS found, regardless of race, ethnicity, or nationality, the believer will be saved because there is only one Lord who is Lord of all.

Bestowing his riches refers to the magnanimity of God's grace—which includes not only an abundance of kindnesses and mercies for the believer but also spiritual gifts by which the believer may bless others.

And once again, to document his doctrine is not new but rooted in Scripture, he calls on the prophet Joel as a testimony: "And it shall come to pass that everyone who calls on the name of the Lord shall be saved . . ." (Joel 2:32).

171. How Then Will They Call On Him?

How then will they call on him in whom they have not believed? And how are they to believe in him of whom they have never heard? And how are they to hear without someone preaching? —Romans 10:14

AT THIS POINT, LET US REMEMBER THAT AT ITS ROOT, PAUL'S entire line of argument beginning from verse one of Chapter nine, is his chief concern that Israel might be saved and in explaining why not all have believed. He is certain that the covenant with Israel has not failed but that for reasons already explained, not all Israel (the nation) are Israel (the people of God).

Here he will begin a line of rhetorical questions in which each answer will naturally prompt the next question. He will unpack his point in this manner until it becomes clear that the natural way of things is that faith comes by hearing and hearing comes through the word of Christ. In other words, rather than viewing this line of reasoning as prescriptive, it should be understood as descriptive.

What this shows is that real faith is demonstrated in the prayer life of those who claim to be God's own (one cannot call on Christ if he doesn't believe in him) and that prayer life is actually initiated by another. Or as John Calvin notes, "We are in a manner mute until God's promise opens our mouth to pray, and this is the order which he points out by the Prophet, when he says, 'I will say to them, my people are ye;' and they shall say to me, 'Thou art our God'" (Zech. 13:9).[78]

78. John Calvin and John Owen, *Commentary on the Epistle of Paul the Apostle to the Romans* (Bellingham, WA: Logos Bible Software, 2010), 398.

172. Preaching Good News

And how are they to preach unless they are sent? As it is written, "How beautiful are the feet of those who preach the good news!" —Romans 10:15

HERE PAUL ENDS HIS RHETORICAL ASCENT WITH WHAT appears to be a plug for his own commission as a minister of the gospel, backed by the testimony of Scripture. He asserts that, clearly, one could not call on someone he hadn't believed in; and they couldn't believe in someone they had never heard of; and they cannot hear unless someone preaches to them; and there will be no one to preach to them if they are not sent.

Here is a good place to recall that Paul's main purpose in writing to the Church at Rome is to garner support for his mission work in Spain. To do so, he is inclined to lay out for the church the gospel he is preaching. Paul was sent—commissioned by Christ (Romans 1:4–5)—to preach the gospel as were all of the true apostles and missionaries of his day. To reemphasize the importance of this office, he cites Isaiah once again. Isaiah had prophesied the end of the Babylonian captivity and the return of the Jews to Zion. So Paul quotes the part of the prophecy where Isaiah had praised the beauty of the heralds of good tidings: "How beautiful upon the mountains are the feet of him who brings good news, who publishes peace, who brings good news of happiness, who publishes salvation, who says to Zion, 'Your God reigns'" (Isaiah 52:7).

Paul is comparing the preaching of the Old Testament heralds with the preaching of the New Testament heralds. Both are proclaiming the best of news with respect to each party's circumstance. And both preachers experience Jews who defiantly, and at great cost to themselves, reject the preachers' good news that, *Your God reigns!*

173. They Have Not All Obeyed the Gospel

But they have not all obeyed the gospel. For Isaiah says, "Lord, who has believed what he has heard from us?" —Romans 10:16

HERE PAUL BRIEFLY INTERRUPTS HIS LINE OF REASONING (which will resume in verse 17) in order to address what he anticipates will be an argument about the faith always following the word. One may ask, if the word precedes faith that way seed precedes corn, then why don't the Jews have faith? Since ambassadors have been sent, the gospel has been preached, and the Jews have heard the word of Christ, why is it that so many still have not believed?

Continuing to rely on the testimony of Isaiah—The quotation is taken from Isaiah's account of the suffering servant (Isaiah 53:1)—Paul shows that the problem is not with the covenant or the word. The problem lies in the hard heart of the Jews. He shows the Jews rejected the word in Isaiah's day as well. In a sense, the words of the prophet are actually prophetic for his own day. The covenant is good, the gospel is effective, but the people are hard-hearted.

While the natural working of this, as has been laid out, is that faith comes by hearing and hearing by the preaching and the preaching by the sending, hearing must be mixed with obedience, belief in the message sent via the messenger. "For good news came to us just as to them, but the message they heard did not benefit them, because they were not united by faith with those who listened" (Hebrews 4:2).

174. Faith Comes from Hearing

So faith comes from hearing, and hearing through the word of Christ. —Romans 10:17

HERE PAUL RETURNS TO THE LINE OF LOGIC AND CONCLUDES with "So . . ." The word *so* is translated from the Greek conjunction *αρα* (*ara*), which has a wide spectrum of meaning and usually indicates "a marker of intent, often with the implication of expected result—'for the purpose of, in order to." It can also mean something like, "Consequently," or "In conclusion of what has been said, we thus determine."

So having laid out the natural process, Paul concludes with a declaration about the efficacy of preaching. In other words, he is saying we can determine that faith comes from hearing the preaching which is the effective means through which the word of Christ is communicated to us.

To be clear, Paul is not suggesting it is merely the voice of man that can penetrate the hardened soul of a fallen human being, but that a preacher proclaiming the truth of the gospel is God's instrument of power by which he creates faith in some and hardens "disobedient and contrary people" (Romans 10:21, cf. 1 Corinthians 1:17–19).

> But of Israel he says, "All day long I have held out my hands to a disobedient and contrary people." (Romans 10:21)

> For Christ did not send me to baptize but to preach the gospel, and not with words of eloquent wisdom, lest the cross of Christ be emptied of its power. For the word of the cross is folly to those who are perishing, but to us who are being saved it is the power of God. For it is written, "I will destroy the wisdom of the wise, and the discernment of the discerning I will thwart" (1 Corinthians 1:17–19).

175. Have They Not Heard?

But I ask, have they not heard? Indeed they have, for

> *"Their voice has gone out to all the earth,*
> *and their words to the ends of the world."*

—Romans 10:18

FROM VERSES 18–21, PAUL AGAIN ADDRESSES A RHETORICAL interlocutor to answer what he anticipates will be the salient questions as to why Israel does not believe since he previously argued that faith comes to those who hear the word of Christ preached.

RHETORICAL INTERLOCUTOR: But I ask, have they not heard?

PAUL: Indeed they have! Haven't you heard what the Psalmist stated about the word of Christ? "Their voice goes out through all the earth, and their words to the end of the world. In them he has set a tent for the sun" (19:4).

> The heavens declare the glory of God, and the sky above proclaims his handiwork. Day to day pours out speech, and night to night reveals knowledge. There is no speech, nor are there words, whose voice is not heard. Their voice goes out through all the earth, and their words to the end of the world. In them he has set a tent for the sun, which comes out like a bridegroom leaving his chamber, and, like a strong man, runs its course with joy. Its rising is from the end of the heavens, and its circuit to the end of them, and there is nothing hidden from its heat. The law of the Lord is perfect, reviving the soul; the testimony of the Lord is sure, making wise the simple; the precepts of the Lord are right, rejoicing the heart; the commandment of the Lord is pure, enlightening the eyes; the fear of the Lord is clean, enduring forever; the rules of the Lord are true, and righteous altogether. More to be desired are they than gold, even much fine gold; sweeter also than honey and drippings of the honeycomb. Moreover, by them is your servant warned; in keeping them there is great reward." (Psalm 19:1–11)

Though scholars have made various and differing interpretations of Paul's quotation of this passage, his use of such a passage declaring the revelatory work of God as undeniable to all is striking (cf. Romans 1:19–21). However one interprets the variables of his statement and whatever particulars are drawn from it, it is undeniable that Paul, under the inspiration of God's Holy Spirit is declaring that *ignorance* is not the problem with those who deny Christ!

While it may sound pious, compassionate, or even philosophical to wonder what happens to some remote, obscure tribe of human beings who have hypothetically never heard of Christ, Paul would say: stop worrying; stop wondering. Ignorance is not their problem.

God's word has been so clearly revealed to all humanity that "his [own] invisible attributes, namely, his eternal power and divine nature, have been clearly perceived, ever since the creation of the world, in the things that have been made. So they are without excuse.

176. Jealous and Angry

But I ask, did Israel not understand? First Moses says,

> *"I will make you jealous of those who are not a nation;*
> *with a foolish nation I will make you angry."*

Then Isaiah is so bold as to say,

> *"I have been found by those who did not seek me;*
> *I have shown myself to those who did not ask for me."*

But of Israel he says, "All day long I have held out my hands to a disobedient and contrary people." —Romans 10:19–21

PAUL NOW ADDRESSES THE NEXT LOGICAL QUESTION OF HIS rhetorical interlocutor: If it is not from ignorance that Israel has not been saved, then from what?

To answer, Paul, being the good theologian that he was, appeals to Scripture for his answer. He quotes the prophets, Moses and Isaiah, to demonstrate the longevity of Israel's character flaw, the one that plagues them even at the time of his letter. Israel's sin has been a faithless disposition toward her covenant husband, YHWH, that eventually resulted in his divorcing her (i.e., her Babylonian captivity).

> The Lord said to me in the days of King Josiah: "Have you seen what she did, that faithless one, Israel, how she went up on every high hill and under every green tree, and there played the whore? And I thought, 'After she has done all this she will return to me,' but she did not return, and her treacherous sister Judah saw it. She saw that for all the adulteries of that faithless one, Israel, I had sent her away with a decree of divorce. Yet her treacherous sister Judah did not fear, but she too went and played the whore. Because she took her whoredom lightly, she polluted the land, committing adultery with stone and tree. Yet for all this her treacherous sister Judah did not return to me with her whole heart, but in pretense, declares the Lord." (Jeremiah 3:6–10)

Though Paul does not quote Jeremiah in this passage, and the Babylonian captivity, per se, is not in view, *the rebellious and unfaithful disposition* that led to their being put away is in view. As he notes in verse 21, *"All day long I have held out my hands to a disobedient and contrary people."*

To make such disobedient and contrary people angry and jealous, God is going to reveal himself to a people who did not seek him (i.e., the Gentiles) and allow this foolish people to find him. By the use of the word *foolish* here, Paul apparently has in mind the Psalmist's declaration that *a fool is one who says in his heart there is no God* (cf. Psalm 14:1, 53:1).

Subsequently, unbelieving Israel will be temporarily displaced by the Gentiles who believe the word of Christ preached to them:

> The next Sabbath almost the whole city gathered to hear the word of the Lord. But when the Jews saw the crowds, they were filled with jealousy and began to contradict what was spoken by Paul, reviling him. And Paul and Barnabas spoke out boldly, saying, "It was necessary that the word of God be spoken first to you. Since you thrust it aside and judge yourselves unworthy of eternal life, behold, we are turning to the Gentiles. For so the Lord has commanded us, saying, "'I have made you a light for the Gentiles, that you may bring salvation to the ends of the earth.'" And when the Gentiles heard this, they began rejoicing and glorifying the word of the Lord, and as many as were appointed to eternal life believed." (Acts 13:44–48)

177. Has God Rejected His People?

I ask, then, has God rejected his people? By no means! For I myself am an Israelite, a descendant of Abraham, a member of the tribe of Benjamin. —Romans 11:1

SINCE GOD HAS CALLED THE GENTILES TO HIMSELF AFTER such prolonged patience with Israel's disobedience (*All day long I have held out my hands*) is it safe to say that God has rejected his people? *By no means!* says Paul.

He uses his own testimony as an example. God called Paul, who was a Jew of no small pedigree. Here he identifies himself as *an Israelite, a descendant of Abraham, a member of the tribe of Benjamin.*

In other letters he identifies himself similarly:

> Are they Hebrews? So am I. Are they Israelites? So am I. Are they offspring of Abraham? So am I. (2 Corinthians 11:22)
>
> . . . though I myself have reason for confidence in the flesh also. If anyone else thinks he has reason for confidence in the flesh, I have more: circumcised on the eighth day, of the people of Israel, of the tribe of Benjamin, a Hebrew of Hebrews; as to the law, a Pharisee . . . . (Philippians 3:4–5)

Since Paul is a Jew and has been called by God and saved by Christ, it can be concluded that God has not given up on the Jews. He is still working out their salvation according to his sovereign will.

178. Chosen by Grace

God has not rejected his people whom he foreknew. Do you not know what the Scripture says of Elijah, how he appeals to God against Israel? "Lord, they have killed your prophets, they have demolished your altars, and I alone am left, and they seek my life." But what is God's reply to him? "I have kept for myself seven thousand men who have not bowed the knee to Baal." So too at the present time there is a remnant, chosen by grace." —Romans 11:2–5

NOW PAUL CLARIFIES WHAT HE MEANS IN VERSE ONE WHEN he refers to "his people." The assumption of his audience seems to be that Israel the nation are his people, but it must be remembered that *not all who are descended from Israel belong to Israel* (Romans 9:6). The people God has not rejected are *his people whom he foreknew.*

The word *foreknew* is the Greek word *προγινώσκω* (*proginosko*). The prefix *προ* (*pro*) means "beforehand." The word *γινώσκω* (*ginōskō*) means "to know." It is also uses to mean "choose" or "have intimate knowledge of" as in Genesis 4:1 when Adam *knew* his wife. The Septuagint, the Greek translation of the Hebrew Bible uses the same word in the case of Adam knowing Eve as Paul uses for God knowing his people beforehand.

See also Ephesians 1:4–5: "even as he chose us in him before the foundation of the world, that we should be holy and blameless before him. In love he predestined us for adoption to himself as sons through Jesus Christ, according to the purpose of his will . . ."

Paul confirms this with his appeal to Scripture in Elijah's conversation with God at a time when he believed all Israel had abandoned God and rejected the truth, that God reveals to him that "I have kept for myself seven thousand men who have not bowed the knee to Baal." And then adds, "So too at the present time there is a remnant, chosen by grace."

It is the remnant, chosen by grace (unmerited favor) before the world began, that are *his people whom he foreknew.* This doctrine is often repugnant to our fallen nature because it is humbling to know it is all of grace. We like to think we deserve salvation and it is entirely up to us whether we choose to accept Christ or not. But salvation is not like that. If it were left up to any one of us, none would be saved! As the Larnelle Harris song articulates so well, we would all be "Forever running but losing this race / Were it not for grace . . ." [79]

79. Larnelle Harris, *Were It Not for Grace*, Brentwood Music, 1998.

179. No Longer

But if it is by grace, it is no longer on the basis of works; otherwise grace would no longer be grace. —*Romans 11:6*

PAUL HERE EMPHASIZES THE FACT THAT GRACE HAS NO PART of works. It leaves nothing for it. It is all of God. Since God's choice is determined by his divine wisdom and immense gratuitousness before the world began, it must be, by necessity, independent of any human works.

Considering what Paul had already established back in 9:30–10:4, it follows that the use of the term *works* here refers to attempts by the Jews to establish their own righteousness by the works of the law.

If we were to consider his letters to other churches, this was obviously a struggle for many first-century Churches. See Paul's letter to the Galatians (1:6–9 and 3:1–5).

> I am astonished that you are so quickly deserting him who called you in the grace of Christ and are turning to a different gospel— not that there is another one, but there are some who trouble you and want to distort the gospel of Christ. But even if we or an angel from heaven should preach to you a gospel contrary to the one we preached to you, let him be accursed. As we have said before, so now I say again: If anyone is preaching to you a gospel contrary to the one you received, let him be accursed.

> O foolish Galatians! Who has bewitched you? It was before your eyes that Jesus Christ was publicly portrayed as crucified. Let me ask you only this: Did you receive the Spirit by works of the law or by hearing with faith? Are you so foolish? Having begun by the Spirit, are you now being perfected by the flesh? Did you suffer so many things in vain—if indeed it was in vain? Does he who supplies the Spirit to you and works miracles among you do so by works of the law, or by hearing with faith . . .

180. The Hardening of the Rest

What then? Israel failed to obtain what it was seeking. The elect obtained it, but the rest were hardened, as it is written,

> *"God gave them a spirit of stupor,*
> *eyes that would not see*
> *and ears that would not hear,*
> *down to this very day."*

And David says,

> *"Let their table become a snare and a trap,*
> *a stumbling block and a retribution for them;*
> *let their eyes be darkened so that they cannot see,*
> *and bend their backs forever."*

—Romans 11:7–10

USING THE RHETORICAL QUESTION AS A MEANS OF SETTING up the opportunity to answer, Paul brings together everything he has been saying in a neatly wrapped bundle. In doing so, he identifies three groups of people: Israel the nation, the elect, and the rest. Israel the nation failed to obtain what it was seeking (righteousness according to the works of the law, cf. Romans 9:30–10:4). The elect (the remnant chosen by grace, cf. Romans 11:5) obtained the righteousness of God. And, the rest (of Israel) were hardened like Pharaoh was hardened (cf. 9:17–18).

He follows up his neat summary with Scripture from the Law (Deuteronomy 29:4), the Prophets (Isaiah 29:10), and the Writings (Psalm 69:22–23) to back his conclusion. In sum, Israel had resisted God so long, and crucified their Messiah that he sent, he ultimately allowed them to have their way. He hardened them by removing his graciousness from them and gave them up to their own futile and darkened minds.

Said another way, because Israel closed her eyes to the truth of God's revelation (the Incarnation), he blinded her. Because she stiffened her back against God (and crucified their Messiah), God fused her spine so she could not bend. God's judgment on Israel is such that even her table (the symbol of God's graciousness and goodness in terms of sustenance, satisfaction, and safety) has become an obstacle to her salvation.

181. Salvation Has Come to the Gentiles

So I ask, did they stumble in order that they might fall? By no means! Rather, through their trespass salvation has come to the Gentiles, so as to make Israel jealous. —Romans 11:11

OUT OF HIS ARGUMENT THAT GOD HAS SAVED HIS ELECT AND hardened Israel, Paul offers a hopeful revelation: God is not through with Israel. This hardening of Israel, this sewing their rebellious eyelids closed, is not a permanent condition. It is a stumble rather than a fall. It is a temporary condition. As is so often the case with God, he is turning their evil into something good.

Israel's rejection of God has provided for the inclusion of the Gentiles. And, in turn, the inclusion of the Gentiles will serve to provoke Israel to jealousy. He will accomplish two goods with their one evil. Using their rebellion, God will save the Gentiles and ultimately save Israel as a result.

What should be most remarkable to us is that while human beings often fret about the secret counsels of God and sometimes fall prey to the delusion of Eve, namely that God is not fair and is withholding blessings from us (in this case withholding blessings from Israel), God is always gracious, even in justice. Here Israel has been *a disobedient and contrary people* all day long, and God, while executing judgment on them, is using it to their favor. This is by definition, an unmerited favor, which is the same thing as grace.

182. How Much More

Now if their trespass means riches for the world, and if their failure means riches for the Gentiles, how much more will their full inclusion mean! —*Romans 11:12*

USING AN ARGUMENT FROM THE LESSER, PAUL CLARIFIES that he does not mean that the salvation of the Gentiles depended on the ruin of the Jews. Far be it from that. It is how God worked providentially, that is he worked good out of evil contrary to the natural order of things. But how much more will the world be blessed when its redemption is worked out according the natural order of things?

If the trespass and failure of the Jews meant riches for the world, particularly riches for the Gentiles in terms of gospel blessings, how much more will the world be enriched by the full inclusion of the Jews?

Further, and contrary to some evangelical theology (i.e., John Murray), it doesn't appear Paul is suggesting this will only happen at the close of human history. As William Hendriksen points out, "[Paul's] words "their fulness" pertain to the salvation not of a physical unit, "the people of Israel"; but of the sum of all Israel's remnants."

In other words, the fullness of Israel will grow out of the remnant. Paul is not suggesting there will be a singular event that happens all at once at the end of the age. See Romans 11:1–7, cf. Romans 11:26.

> I ask, then, has God rejected his people? By no means! For I myself am an Israelite, a descendant of Abraham, a member of the tribe of Benjamin. God has not rejected his people whom he foreknew. Do you not know what the Scripture says of Elijah, how he appeals to God against Israel? "Lord, they have killed your prophets, they have demolished your altars, and I alone am left, and they seek my life." But what is God's reply to him? "I have kept for myself seven thousand men who have not bowed the knee to Baal." So too at the present time there is a remnant, chosen by grace. But if it is by grace, it is no longer on the basis of works; otherwise grace would no longer be grace. What then?

Israel failed to obtain what it was seeking. The elect obtained it, but the rest were hardened . . . (Romans 11:1–7)

And in this way all Israel will be saved, as it is written, "The Deliverer will come from Zion, he will banish ungodliness from Jacob" . . . (Romans 11:26)

183. The Reconciliation of the World

Now I am speaking to you Gentiles. Inasmuch then as I am an apostle to the Gentiles, I magnify my ministry in order somehow to make my fellow Jews jealous, and thus save some of them. For if their rejection means the reconciliation of the world, what will their acceptance mean but life from the dead? —Romans 11:13–15

HERE PAUL FOCUSES HIS AUDIENCE'S ATTENTION ON HIS MINistry to the Gentiles and asserts that in a very particular way, his ministry is accomplishing what he just explained God is doing in the more universal sense (cf. Romans 11:11).

It may be of help to note at this point that Paul's overarching purpose for writing this letter to the church at Rome in the first place was to introduce himself and justify his coming to them to have some fruit among them. Recall what he wrote in his introduction:

> For I long to see you, that I may impart to you some spiritual gift to strengthen you— that is, that we may be mutually encouraged by each other's faith, both yours and mine. I do not want you to be unaware, brothers, that I have often intended to come to you (but thus far have been prevented), in order that I may reap some harvest among you as well as among the rest of the Gentiles. I am under obligation both to Greeks and to barbarians, both to the wise and to the foolish. So I am eager to preach the gospel to you also who are in Rome. (Romans 1:11–15)

The historical context is equally important. Paul wrote his letter to the Romans sometime between 54–58 AD. The Roman historian Suetonius, tells us that in approximately 49 AD, Claudius had expelled the Jews from Rome because of a tumult that arose amongst the Jews of the city over someone named *Chrestus*. See also Luke's account in Acts 18:1–3.

As scholars have found no documentation supporting the existence of someone named *Chrestus*, it is largely believed to be a misspelling or alternate spelling of *Christos,* the Greek word for Christ. After the Jews were expelled, the church at Rome became predominantly Gentile, with Gentile leadership. After Claudias died in 54 AD, many of the Jews returned to Rome and were now part of a largely Gentile church (cf. Romans 14–15).

Paul's preaching to the Gentiles is a worthy ministry because he knows he is participating in God's plan for the redemption of the world—both Jews and Gentiles. If his preaching saves some Gentiles and makes some Jews jealous, then he is in line with God's plan. And, as he said before, *if [the Jews] rejection means the reconciliation of the [Gentile] world, what will [the Jews] acceptance mean but life from the dead [for the whole world]?*

184. Firstfruits and Roots

For if their rejection means the reconciliation of the world, what will their acceptance mean but life from the dead? If the dough offered as firstfruits is holy, so is the whole lump, and if the root is holy, so are the branches. —Romans 11:15–16

PAUL IS ARGUING THAT GOD'S REJECTION OF THE JEWS PROvoked reconciliation of the world, the inclusion of Gentiles into the people of God as a kind of firstfruits. In turn, this inclusion is meant to provoke the Jews to repentance. And when the Jews do repent, their inclusion will then mean an even greater reconciliation of the world. Compare Romans 11:12: "Now if their trespass means riches for the world, and if their failure means riches for the Gentiles, how much more will their full inclusion mean!"

To illustrate his point, Paul draws on a couple of examples that would be quite obvious to Paul's audience. The first is the illustration of firstfruits and the second is of a tree and its roots.

In the first example, the firstfruits were a portion of the whole that was to be offered to the priests before the whole of the bread was to be eaten. The firstfruits sanctified the whole (cf. Leviticus 23:9–14).

In the second example, the health of the roots of a tree determine the health of the rest of the tree. If the roots are healthy the rest of the tree will be healthy (cf. Job 18:16, Isaiah 11:1, Mark 4:6, Luke 13:6–9).

John Calvin summarizes Paul's argument this way: "Since then God has wonderfully drawn forth life from death and light from darkness, how much more ought we to hope, he reasons, that the resurrection of a people (the Jews), as it were, wholly dead, will bring life to the Gentiles."[80]

80. John Calvin and John Owen, *Commentary on the Epistle of Paul the Apostle to the Romans* (Bellingham, WA: Logos Bible Software, 2010), 424–425.

185. Grafted In

But if some of the branches were broken off, and you, although a wild olive shoot, were grafted in among the others and now share in the nourishing root of the olive tree . . . —Romans 11:17

PICKING UP FROM HIS SECOND ILLUSTRATION, PAUL BEGINS A longer discourse directed primarily at the Gentiles, warning them not to be haughty in their position but to be humble. He calls them "a wild olive shoot" that has been grafted in among the natural branches (the Jewish believers). The Gentiles now share in the nourishing root of the olive tree, which is Christ himself.

In what follows, Paul will tell them not to be arrogant but to be fearful, remembering

- who is the root and who is the branch (vs 18),
- that their standing is by faith (vs 19–20),
- how God dealt with the natural branches (vs 21),
- both the kindness and the severity of the Lord (vs 22),
- that those Jews who believe will be grafted back in (vs 23), and
- that the Jews were part of the tree naturally and will be again assuredly (vs 24).

186. Do Not Be Arrogant

Do not be arrogant toward the branches. If you are, remember it is not you who support the root, but the root that supports you. —Romans 11:18

THE ROOT IS THE HERITAGE THE NATURAL BRANCHES HAVE IN Abraham, Isaac, and Jacob. The Gentiles were grafted in and they derive their support from the roots; it's not the other way around. Just because the Gentiles (the ingrafted branches) are being used by God to bring the Jews (the natural branches that have been cut off) to repentance, doesn't mean the Gentiles have anything to add to the roots. The gentiles possess nothing here to brag about except for the grace of God.

"So that, as it is written, 'Let the one who boasts, boast in the Lord'" (1 Corinthians 1:31).

187. Stand Fast through Faith

Then you will say, "Branches were broken off so that I might be grafted in." That is true. They were broken off because of their unbelief, but you stand fast through faith. So do not become proud, but fear. —Romans 11:19–20

PAUL NOW ISSUES A MORE DIRECT WARNING TO THE GENTILES against any kind of boasting. It is true that the natural branches were broken off so that the Gentile could be grafted in, but the natural branch, the Jew, was broken off because of unbelief. The very reason the Gentile has been grafted in is because of belief. So, it is paramount to remember that salvation is all of grace through faith.

Paul warns the Gentiles to not become proud but to fear (cf. Proverbs 3:7). Peter had given a similar warning to the Christians in his letter:

> For if these qualities are yours and are increasing, they keep you from being ineffective or unfruitful in the knowledge of our Lord Jesus Christ. For whoever lacks these qualities is so nearsighted that he is blind, having forgotten that he was cleansed from his former sins. Therefore, brothers, be all the more diligent to confirm your calling and election, for if you practice these qualities you will never fall. For in this way there will be richly provided for you an entrance into the eternal kingdom of our Lord and Savior Jesus Christ. (2 Peter 1:8–11)

As did Paul in his letter to the Philippians: "Therefore, my beloved, as you have always obeyed, so now, not only as in my presence but much more in my absence, work out your own salvation with fear and trembling, for it is God who works in you, both to will and to work for his good pleasure" (Philippians 2:12–13).

And as did the author of Hebrews (Paul?) to his audience: "Therefore, while the promise of entering his rest still stands, let us fear lest any of you should seem to have failed to reach it" (Hebrews 4:1).

188. Kindness and Severity

For if God did not spare the natural branches, neither will he spare you. Note then the kindness and the severity of God: severity toward those who have fallen, but God's kindness to you, provided you continue in his kindness. Otherwise you too will be cut off. —Romans 11:21–22

AS PAUL HAS ALREADY NOTED IN VERSE 20, FEAR—NOT pride—is the proper response to God's gracious act of engrafting (us) Gentiles into the tree. He warns that if God would not spare the natural branches once they became an instrument of unbelief, do not think for a second God would spare us Gentiles if we too became such an instrument.

Paul then follows up with a final warning by comparing God's kindness toward belief and his severity toward apostasy. God is immutable. He never changes. Paul is not saying God is in flux here. Rather, God is the constant and where we choose to line up with God will determine whether we experience his kindness or his wrath.

Though all analogies for God eventually break down and should not be held in higher esteem than their usefulness merits, one is particularly helpful here. If God were to be compared to a river whose powerful waters flow in a single direction, our small rowboat will experience the benevolence of the mighty river when rightly oriented to the direction of its flow but experience violence if we try to row against its turbulent current.

Therefore, let us remain fearful of God's severity and continue to rest in his kindness that we never know the terrors of being cut off from the source of all goodness, truth, and beauty.

189. God Has the Power

And even they, if they do not continue in their unbelief, will be grafted in, for God has the power to graft them in again. For if you were cut from what is by nature a wild olive tree, and grafted, contrary to nature, into a cultivated olive tree, how much more will these, the natural branches, be grafted back into their own olive tree. —*Romans 11:23–24*

AS PAUL HAS ALREADY DEMONSTRATED BY HIS OWN TESTIMONY, God is not finished with Israel. They are not hopeless. If they repent of their unbelief, they will be grafted in again. Such a miracle is not above God's power. As an example, the Gentiles were unnaturally grafted into a cultivated olive tree; that is, they belonged to a different tree, a wild tree, and God grafted them in without any trouble. How much more would the natural branches take to grafting if they were added back to the tree they belonged to by nature? There are a few points of implication worth noting in Paul's argument.

First, the Gentiles are seen as unnatural branches because they are from a wild olive tree, which is contrasted with Israel who is seen as naturally belonging to the cultivated olive tree. The contrasted use of natural and unnatural, wild and cultivated, are meant to show the Gentiles as belonging to the class of historical unbelievers, while Israel belongs to the class of historical believers who are recipients of the privileges of God's grace.

Second, Paul does not imply, let alone ever state, that unbelieving Israel will be grafted back into the tree. Those who repent of their unbelief will find a place back in their natural tree, nourished by the cultivated root alongside the unnatural branches (Gentiles) who were grafted in because of their belief.

Finally, it is noteworthy that Paul says olive *tree* and does not say *trees* (in the plural). There is one tree in which all the faithful branches—natural and unnatural—receive the nourishment of the root of grace. Regardless of one's origin, there is only one tree, one church, the assembly of the redeemed of God to which all believers—Jew and Gentile alike—belong.

Paul lays this out again, but more straightforward, in his letter to the Ephesians. And it's worth reading carefully.

Therefore remember that at one time you Gentiles in the flesh, called "the uncircumcision" by what is called the circumcision, which is made in the flesh by hands— remember that you were at that time separated from Christ, alienated from the commonwealth of Israel and strangers to the covenants of promise, having no hope and without God in the world. But now in Christ Jesus you who once were far off have been brought near by the blood of Christ. For he himself is our peace, who has made us both one and has broken down in his flesh the dividing wall of hostility by abolishing the law of commandments expressed in ordinances, that he might create in himself one new man in place of the two, so making peace, and might reconcile us both to God in one body through the cross, thereby killing the hostility. And he came and preached peace to you who were far off and peace to those who were near. For through him we both have access in one Spirit to the Father. So then you are no longer strangers and aliens, but you are fellow citizens with the saints and members of the household of God, built on the foundation of the apostles and prophets, Christ Jesus himself being the cornerstone, in whom the whole structure, being joined together, grows into a holy temple in the Lord. In him you also are being built together into a dwelling place for God by the Spirit. (Ephesians 2:11–22)

190. A Partial Hardening

Lest you be wise in your own sight, I do not want you to be unaware of this mystery, brothers: a partial hardening has come upon Israel, until the fullness of the Gentiles has come in. —Romans 11:25

THIS STATEMENT IS A SUMMARY, AN EXPANSION, AND A WARNING.

It is a summary explanation of what has already been explained and illustrated: That God has partially hardened Israel for their unbelief; thus, he is working this way so that the Gentiles can be brought in, and in so doing, unbelieving Israel will repent and be saved themselves.

It is an expansion on what has been already explained in that there is a mystery that has been revealed. Paul's use of *mystery* is not the Pagan, esoteric use of the word (i.e., like that of the Gnostics). Rather, he means this is knowledge that could not have otherwise been known except that God has revealed it. The mystery is that God has partially hardened (ethnic) Israel until the fullness of the Gentiles has come in.

What does Paul mean by this phrase *until the fullness of the Gentiles has come in*? We see this near expression used by Jesus in Luke 21:24: "They will fall by the edge of the sword and be led captive among all nations, and Jerusalem will be trampled underfoot by the Gentiles, until the times of the Gentiles are fulfilled."

Given the olive tree illustration, it appears there is a specific period of time in which God will allow the engrafted branch on the olive tree to flourish before he engrafts the natural branch back into this tree. But Paul does not elaborate on when that will be or how that will look—except that we know. Instead, in verses 26, he will explain the manner in which this takes place.

Finally, Paul's statement is a warning or exhortation to the Gentiles to remain humble and not become wise in their own sight. This seems a clear warning against any kind of anti-semitism, which has unfortunately not always been heeded by Christians throughout the centuries. Nevertheless, let us "... who thinks that he stands take heed lest he fall" (1 Corinthians 10:12).

191. In This Way All Israel Will Be Saved

And in this way all Israel will be saved, as it is written,

> *"The Deliverer will come from Zion,*
> *he will banish ungodliness from Jacob";*
> *"and this will be my covenant with them*
> *when I take away their sins."*

—Romans 11:26–27

GOD WILL SAVE ALL ISRAEL IN THE WAY HE JUST DESCRIBED—and is about to finish describing in vss. 28–32—by hardening Israel until the fullness of the Gentiles has been achieved. It is in this way that the mystery will unfold. To support his argument, he references God's promises to Israel in the Prophets, namely, Isaiah 59:20–21 and Jeremiah 31:33–34:

> "And a Redeemer will come to Zion, to those in Jacob who turn from transgression," declares the Lord. "And as for me, this is my covenant with them," says the Lord: "My Spirit that is upon you, and my words that I have put in your mouth, shall not depart out of your mouth, or out of the mouth of your offspring, or out of the mouth of your children's offspring," says the Lord, "from this time forth and forevermore." (Isaiah 59:20–21)

> For this is the covenant that I will make with the house of Israel after those days, declares the Lord: I will put my law within them, and I will write it on their hearts. And I will be their God, and they shall be my people. And no longer shall each one teach his neighbor and each his brother, saying, 'Know the Lord,' for they shall all know me, from the least of them to the greatest, declares the Lord. For I will forgive their iniquity, and I will remember their sin no more." (Jeremiah 31:33–34)

But what does Paul mean by "all Israel"? There is a prominent view among modern evangelicals that Paul is pointing to an end-time event, Christ's return, when the Jews still living after the fullness of the Gentiles has been achieved, will suddenly repent and be instantaneously grafted back into the olive tree. All Israel are those saved at that time.

But following Paul's train of thought since the beginning of chapter 9 would not support such a view that only the Jews living at a particular time in history (i.e., Christ's return) will be grafted in.

It is clear Paul means all Israel in the sense he has already articulated in 9:6: ". . . For not all who are descended from Israel belong to Israel,"

And, given the fact that he contrasts the Gentiles with Israel, referring to Israel no less than 10 times since the beginning of Chapter 9, it is additionally clear that Pauls is speaking of the believing remnant of Israel in every generation, the total number of elect Jews.

In his commentary on Romans, William Hendriksen points out that

> The term "All Israel" means the total number of elect Jews, the sum of all Israel's "remnants." "All Israel" parallels "the fullness of the Gentiles." Verses 25. 26 make it very clear that God is dealing with both groups, has been saving them, is saving them, and is going to save them. And if "All Israel" indicates, as it does, that not a single elect Israelite will be lacking "when the roll is called up yonder," then "the fulness of the Gentiles" similarly shows that when the attendance is checked every elect Gentile will answer "Present."[81]

This is Henry Bavinck's position as well. God is saving his elect from both groups and making them one people of God (Ephesians 2:14, cf. Revelation 21:5).

What is most striking, and what should never be forgotten as we journey through Paul's letter to the church at Rome, is that all of Paul's arguments are made in light of the gospel, the unmerited favor of God toward hard-hearted sinners. Though God rightly judges deserving sinners (i.e., gives them justice), he also gives mercy and grace to innumerable undeserving sinners (i.e., gives them non-justice). What he never gives is injustice. He is both just and the justifier of the one who has faith in Jesus" (Romans 3:26).

81. William Hendriksen and Simon J. Kistemaker, Exposition of Paul's Epistle to the Romans, vol. 12–13, New Testament Commentary (Grand Rapids: Baker Book House, 1953–2001), 381.

192. Beloved Enemies

As regards the gospel, they are enemies for your sake. But as regards election, they are beloved for the sake of their forefathers. —Romans 11:28

FOR CLARITY'S SAKE, PAUL'S CATEGORIES ARE AS FOLLOWS:

- the Church at Rome to whom he is writing whose constituency is both Jew and Gentile believers where the majority group is apparently Gentile;
- broader Israel which includes both the elect remnant and the unbelieving ethnic Jews;
- the elect remnant, those who are currently in a state of unbelief but will believe because of the covenant God made with their fathers; and
- unbelieving Israel which has rejected true belief for religious form and identity.

As regards the gospel limits the context of Paul's first statement to God's mysterious work of redemption which is currently in view. The elect Israel, the remnant, are currently enemies of God (along with the rest of the unbelieving Israel) for the Gentile's sake. Had the elect remnant not been temporarily hardened along with the unbelieving Israel, the Gentiles would not have been brought in. But it is through this temporary hardening (or partial hardening as it relates to broader Israel) that grace has come to them.

But as regards election, remnant Israel are beloved because of the covenant made with their believing forefathers: Abraham, Isaac, and Jacob. What joins unbelieving Israel and remnant Israel together to make broader Israel is their ethnicity, their physical lineage. But what distinguishes remnant Israel from ethnic Israel is *faith*.

Although remnant Israel (along with unbelieving Israel) is currently in a state of unbelief, and therefore enemies of both God and believers, they will eventually be provoked into belief via the Gentile inclusion.

This will happen because they are elect of God as he promised through the covenant he made with their forefathers.

193. Without Regret

For the gifts and the calling of God are irrevocable. —*Romans 11:29*

PAUL AFFIRMS THE VALIDITY OF THE COVENANT PROMISE TO (remnant or believing) Israel by use of a *merism,* a kind of trope called a *synecdoche.* A merism is a rhetorical device (or figure of speech) in which a combination of two (usually contrasting) parts of the whole refer to the whole. Another example is "heaven and earth," which meant to imply all of creation.

Another way of understanding what Paul is saying would be to say the gift (or grace) of God's callings are irrevocable. The Greek word translated "irrevocable" is *ἀμεταμέλητος* (*ametamelētos*), which means "without regret." This calling that is an irrevocable gift is what theologians have often referred to as the inner or *effectual* call, "one that pertains only to the elect," says Hendriksen.[82]

It is not referring to those special gifts or privileges God grants to the people of Israel, the Jews, as Paul explains earlier (cf. Romans 3:1–2, 9:4–5). Those gifts pertain to the nation, ethnic Israel.

In his *Systematic Theology,* Berkhof explains the effectual call:

> It is in its most limited sense a change that occurs in the *sub-conscious* life. It is a secret and inscrutable work of God that is never *directly* perceived by man. The change may take place without man's being conscious of it momentarily, though this is not the case when regeneration and conversion coincide; and even later on he can perceive it *only in its effects.* This explains the fact that a Christian may, on the one hand, struggle for a long time with doubts and uncertainties, and can yet, on the other hand, gradually overcome these and rise to the heights of assurance.[83]

82. William Hendriksen and Simon J. Kistemaker, *Exposition of Paul's Epistle to the Romans,* vol. 12–13, New Testament Commentary (Grand Rapids: Baker Book House, 1953–2001), 384.
83. L. Berkhof, *Systematic Theology* (Grand Rapids, MI: Wm. B. Eerdmans publishing co., 1938), 469.

194. That He May Have Mercy on All

For just as you were at one time disobedient to God but now have received mercy because of their disobedience, so they too have now been disobedient in order that by the mercy shown to you they also may now receive mercy. For God has consigned all to disobedience, that he may have mercy on all. —Romans 11:30–32

THE ENTIRE POINT OF PAUL'S ARGUMENT NOW COMES INTO view. God has consigned all to the prison of disobedience—both Jew and Gentile—that he may have mercy on all. His *all* here does not mean every last person. To stretch the meaning that far would be to embrace universalism. *All* is all nations, Jews and Gentiles alike.

The way God has accomplished this is by showing mercy to the Gentiles when the Jews rejected him. By the mercy shown to the Gentiles, the Jews will be drawn to belief and receive mercy. It is now being done just the same way it was done when the Gentiles rejected the truth and God called Abraham out from Ur of Chaldeas to make himself a covenant nation of believers so the Gentiles then would be drawn to belief and receive mercy.

The fact that Paul is the minister of the Gentiles is evidence of God's providential strategy.

195. Oh, The Depth . . .

Oh, the depth of the riches and wisdom and knowledge of God! How unsearchable are his judgments and how inscrutable his ways!

> *"For who has known the mind of the Lord,*
> *or who has been his counselor?"*
> *"Or who has given a gift to him*
> *that he might be repaid?"*

For from him and through him and to him are all things. To him be glory forever. Amen. —*Romans 11:33–36*

PAUL CONCLUDES HIS ASSERTION THAT THE COVENANT HAS not failed and the explanation of the mystery which is God's plan for salvation with an impromptu doxology. Filled with praise and adoration for the infinite abundance of God's rich grace combined with his omniscience and subsequent wisdom, Paul delights in praise and quotes Scripture that affirms and amplifies his awe!

All things are from God and through God and to God! There is no one to whom God is indebted for anything. All are debtors to him. There is no one who could plumb the depths or scale the heights of his wisdom and ways. He alone deserves all glory forever!

196. A Living Sacrifice

I appeal to you therefore, brothers, by the mercies of God, to present your bodies as a living sacrifice, holy and acceptable to God, which is your spiritual worship. —*Romans 12:1*

THIS IS A GOOD PLACE TO RECALL THAT PAUL'S LETTER TO the Romans follows a chiastic structure that reaches its highest and most important point in chapter 8 where he breaks out with a doxology, praising and glorifying God for his grace and wisdom because of the mystery of the gospel.

- 1:1–17 Introduction
  - 1:18–3:30 Chaos (Devolution of Humanity)
    - 4–5 Faith Saves
      - 6–7 Two Regimes
        - 8 The Glory of the Gospel
      - 9–11 Two Branches
    - 12–13 Faith Works
  - 14–15 Cosmos (Evolution of Humanity)
- 16 Farewell

Another way we considered this letter is to see it as an ascent to the summit of a great mountain and then a descent down the other side. The mountain is the gospel and the summit is its glory. Paul has led his readers up the front side of the mountain of the gospel (the theological side) and has posted his flag at the summit. He is now leading his readers down the other side (the practical or application side) and making important stops on the way.

His first stop on the descent is to visit the mystery of the olive tree (chapters 9–11). He considers two particular branches of the tree: one natural branch which has been temporarily cut off for unbelief and one wild branch that has been grafted in because of faith. His treatment of the two branches mirrors his treatment of the two regimes: the regime of Adam and the regime of Christ (chapters 6–7).

At this stop, mirroring his treatment of the way faith saves (chapters 4–5), he will show how faith works. As Martin Luther noted in his study of Romans, we are saved by faith and not by works, but the faith that saves is a faith that works. Thus, Paul, with the mercies of God recently explained and highlighted as their motivation, appeals to the church at Rome to present themselves to God.

In particular, Paul exhorts them to present their bodies to God as a living sacrifice that is both holy and acceptable to one such as a one who gave Christ, his only begotten, for our sins. This, Paul says, is our *λογικὴν λατρείαν* (*logikēn latreian*). The ESV renders this "spiritual worship," and the KJV renders it as "our reasonable service." The EOB renders it "rational offering of divine service."[84]

In sum, presenting our bodies to God as a response to the mercies of God is a believer's *logical worship*. The first rational response of one who has been redeemed by faith in Christ, delivered from unbelief and damnation, is to set himself apart unto the Lord (be holy) and offer up his body in Christ's service instead of his own.

This response is acceptable and pleasing to God.

84. Laurent Cleenewerck, ed., *The Eastern/Greek Orthodox Bible: New Testament* (Laurent A. Cleenewerck, 2011), Romans 12:1.

197. Do Not Be Conformed

Do not be conformed to this world, but be transformed by the renewal of your mind, that by testing you may discern what is the will of God, what is good and acceptable and perfect." —Romans 12:2

THE FIRST STEP IN OUR REASONABLE SERVICE, OUR SPIRITUAL worship, is to refrain from conforming ourselves to the world. This means we are not to take on its shape or be molded by its values. The word *world* here means the system of life—the applied worldview—separated from the presence of God.

To illustrate, after God exiled Cain for refusing to repent for killing Abel, "... Cain went away from the presence of the Lord and settled in the land of Nod, east of Eden. Cain knew his wife, and she conceived and bore Enoch. When he built a city, he called the name of the city after the name of his son, Enoch" (Genesis 4:16–17).

A careful reading of the rest of the passage demonstrates that Cain's city was technologically advanced, had commerce and the arts, but it was lacking the presence of God. Subsequently, it lacked justice or a moral system of living and governance that honored God and provided for human flourishing (Genesis 4:19–24).

Like Paul does here, John also exhorts believers: "Do not love the world or the things in the world. If anyone loves the world, the love of the Father is not in him. For all that is in the world—the desires of the flesh and the desires of the eyes and pride of life—is not from the Father but is from the world. And the world is passing away along with its desires, but whoever does the will of God abides forever" (1 John 2:15–17).

198. Be Transformed

Do not be conformed to this world, but be transformed by the renewal of your mind, that by testing you may discern what is the will of God, what is good and acceptable and perfect. —Romans 12:2

THE REASONABLE SERVICE OR SPIRITUAL WORSHIP BEGINS with avoiding the temptation to conform—to be molded—to this world, which is the current regime or cultural system of society organized apart from the presence and influence of Christ. Instead, we are to be transformed *μεταμορφοῦσθε* (*metamorphoosthe*). This Greek word is the basis for our English word *metamorphosis*—the same word we use to describe the way a caterpillar changes into a butterfly.

Believers (i.e., followers of Christ) are to be transformed from what they were before they were part of the family of God into what is holy and acceptable to God, what is good and acceptable and perfectly aligned to his will. And we are to accomplish this by the renewal of our minds. The word 'renewal' is the Greek word ἀνακαινώσει (*anakainosei*) and means to be reborn or to cause something to become new and different, with the implication of becoming superior.

Further, our minds are renewed by testing our thoughts against the standard of the will of God and conforming to his will instead of the world's will. His will is good and acceptable and perfect. The more we are able to apprehend the mind of Christ and approximate our own minds to it, the more we are transformed and the less we are conformed to this world.

What is implied but not specifically stated here is that we learn the mind of Christ and thus the will of God by submitting ourselves to the influence of Scripture (the revealed word of God) and the "tested" traditions of the church (the covenant community of God). "But test everything; hold fast what is good" (1 Thessalonians 5:21).

199. Think with Sober Judgment

For by the grace given to me I say to everyone among you not to think of himself more highly than he ought to think, but to think with sober judgment, each according to the measure of faith that God has assigned. —Romans 12:3

EVEN IN HIS MINISTRY OF INSTRUCTING BELIEVERS IN THE grace of God, Paul appeals to the grace given to him for the task. His instruction is the natural outflow of what he has already stated, that " . . . by the mercies of God, [they would] present [their] bodies as a living sacrifice, holy and acceptable to God, which is [their] spiritual worship [and] not be conformed to this world, but be transformed by the renewal of [their] mind[s], that by testing [they] may discern what is the will of God, what is good and acceptable and perfect" (Romans 12:1–2).

First of all, then, believers need to think of themselves appropriately. The most common temptation is to think of oneself more highly than one ought. We are only what we are because of the grace given to us by the mercies of God. A right view of ourselves begins with a right view of God. This is how we "think with sober judgment." We don't have too lofty of a view of ourselves because we know we are sinners saved by the grace of God.

And we are not to have too low of a view of ourselves because God has assigned to each of us a measure of faith. In other words, there is a ditch on either side of sober judgment. One ditch is to fail to recognize we don't deserve what we have and the other ditch is to fail to recognize that even though we may not deserve it, we indeed have it. And that means we not only have value but we have a purpose.

One way I have often thought about this truth is to think about the value of one's thumb. Detached from the lifeblood and associated appendages of the hand, it is a worthless piece of flesh and bone. It would not, for example, make a beautiful ornament one would want to hang from the car mirror like fuzzy dice; that would be disgusting. But attached to the lifeblood and associated appendages, it is an invaluable piece of the body. It would be difficult to put a price tag on the value of one's thumb in its proper context.

200. One Body in Christ

For as in one body we have many members, and the members do not all have the same function, so we, though many, are one body in Christ, and individually members one of another. —Romans 12:4–5

PAUL WILL EXPOUND ON THIS IDEA OF THE CHURCH BEING A body more thoroughly in his letter to the Corinthians (1 Corinthians 12). But he was not the first to introduce this idea of a people being likened to a body. This was a thoroughly Roman idea that was first introduced in the 6th Century BC by Menenius Agrippa who defeated the Sabines and sought to win the sympathies of the plebs by likening the body politic to that of a human body.

Because the human body is made up of many parts but flourishes when all of the parts function properly and in harmony with each other, by Paul's day, Romans considered themselves to be a body politic that functioned best in similar manner.

Paul picks up this idea that is deeply embedded in the minds of these Roman Christians and shows them that the Church, the body of Christ, functions the same way. The difference being Christ is their new head. Having offered their own bodies as a living sacrifice to Christ because of the multitude of his magnanimous mercies, the Roman Christians were members one of another, each with different gifts and functions within the body of Christ.

And, thus, so are we believers in the twenty-first century, members one of another, functioning as one body, Christ being our head.

201. Having Gifts . . . Let Us Use Them

Having gifts that differ according to the grace given to us, let us use them: if prophecy, in proportion to our faith; if service, in our serving; the one who teaches, in his teaching; the one who exhorts, in his exhortation; the one who contributes, in generosity; the one who leads, with zeal; the one who does acts of mercy, with cheerfulness. —*Romans 12:6–8*

PAUL MAKES IT CLEAR THAT BELIEVERS—AND NOT ONLY ordained ministers—have been endowed with spiritual gifts meant to benefit the body of Christ in particular and the world around us in general. Scholars are divided as to whether this list is meant to be a list of examples or a comprehensive list. They are further divided with respect to the actual meaning of some of the functions. Because Paul provides similar lists that differ in number and function elsewhere in his writings (1 Corinthians 12:8–10, cf Ephesians 4:11), I tend to believe Paul's lists are illustrative of the various functions that are available to meet the needs of the congregation and community where believers are living in covenant with one another.

William Hendriksen and Simon J. Kistemaker give a summary of the seven functions mentioned in this passage as[85]

- prophesying,
- rendering practical service,
- teaching,
- exhorting,
- contributing to the needs of people,
- exercising leadership, and
- showing mercy.

85. William Hendriksen and Simon J. Kistemaker, *Exposition of Paul's Epistle to the Romans*, vol. 12–13, New Testament Commentary (Grand Rapids: Baker Book House, 1953–2001), 409.

Prophecy is always listed in the place of preeminence but it is by no means limited to prognostication (declaring of future events). It also includes instruction, reproof, and rebuke. It is, in essence, the declaration of the will of God. But Paul makes clear this is to be done in proportion (in accordance with our faith). The prophecy must be in accordance with revealed truth, namely Scripture and apostolic preaching (which would be recorded as NT Scripture).

The word for service is *διακονία (diakonia)*, meaning practical service or ministry. It is from this word, we get the ministry of the deacon.

Teaching is from *διδασκαλία (didasko)*, which means to instruct. In the context, it means specifically to instruct believers how to apply the teachings of the Old Testament, of Jesus, and of the apostles.

Exhorting is from *παρακαλέω (parakeleo)* and means to urge or encourage into action.

Contribute means to give to the needs of others without any ulterior motives. Paul says the those who are disposed to meet the needs of others with material goods should do so with generosity.

One who leads refers to overseers and elders (1 Thessalonians 5:12; 1 Timothy 3:4; 5:17). This work of governing, organizing, and overseeing should be done with zeal (i.e., diligence).

One who does acts of mercy refers to those who minister to the bereaved, ill, or dying—the Mother Theresas of the church. These are to carry out this heavy burden with cheerfulness.

202. Genuine Love

Let love be genuine. Abhor what is evil; hold fast to what is good. —*Romans 12:9*

PAUL MOVES FROM ENCOURAGING BELIEVERS TO USE THEIR spiritual gifts for the benefit of others to a general statement about *the attitude that should motivate* the believers' use of gifts—genuine love.

In the next verse, he will home in on more specific applications of love but here he makes a general and inclusive statement about ἀγάπη (*agape*). The Greek word translated love in this case has a variety of applications but it is typically used when it applies in the most generous and unrestricted sense possible.

Love should be genuine, Paul says. The word genuine is from the Greek word, ἀνυπόκριτος, (*anhypokritos*) meaning without pretense or hypocrisy; literally, *αν* means *without* and ὑποκριτής means *pretending* or *acting*.

What naturally accompanies such love is that one is oriented rightly toward that which is good and evil, abhorring what is evil (the privation or corruption of good) while holding onto or standing by that which is good.

Genuine, sincere love can *only* be oriented this way.

203. Love One Another

Love one another with brotherly affection. Outdo one another in showing honor.
—Romans 12:10

PAUL CLEARLY CONCEIVES OF THE GOSPEL AS CREATING A new humanity, one which will grow up alongside the old humanity, the wheat with the tares. And this new humanity can be conceived of as a new spiritual family all from the same father (Romans 8:15, cf. Matthew 12:46–50), a kind of priestly family that will act as a model for the rest of the world. This does not mean the new family is perfect, but it is righteous and therefore expected to model redemption rather than perfection.

Believers are called to love all humanity genuinely, but here Paul is calling for more intimacy and affection among family members. Love toward members of our spiritual family must not only be genuine, abhorring evil and holding fast that which is good, but it must also, in particular, be done with *φιλαδελφία* (*philadelphia*), translated "brotherly affection." Elsewhere he says the same: "So then, as we have opportunity, let us do good to everyone, and especially to those who are of the household of faith" (Galatians 6:10).

The way this looks is to outdo one another in showing honor. The Greek verb translated "outdo" is *προηγέομαι* (*proegeomai*) and means to preside or show leadership in this calling. Another way to possibly render the verb is to say that each family member ought to be trying to lead the way in showing honor to what is honorable. In this case what is honorable is our brothers and sisters in Christ.

John Lennon wanted us to imagine a world where there was no religion, no heaven or hell. In contrast, Paul wants us to imagine a world where love for one another is genuine and all of us are striving to outdo the other in showing honor.

204. Earnest Worship

Do not be slothful in zeal, be fervent in spirit, serve the Lord. —*Romans 12:11*

THIS IS AN INTERESTING STATEMENT, PRIMARILY BECAUSE the language is fairly unfamiliar to us. The first thing one might notice is the trifecta of words that all have to do with one's enthusiasm: *not slothful, zeal, and fervent.*

Slothful is the opposite of zeal and fervency, so Paul says to not be slothful. And the exhortation to avoid slothfulness seems to be aimed at a person's zeal. The first question, then, is what is zeal? "In zeal" is from *τῇ σπουδῇ* (*spoude*) meaning the earnest commitment in discharge of an obligation. The obligation in this case is our spiritual worship, our service to the Lord as a reasonable response to his abundant mercies (Romans 12:1,2).

Following up, Paul says, in contrast to his exhortation to avoid sloth, be fervent in spirit. And serve the Lord. Paul is exhorting the Roman believers, the new humanity that has been born again by the Spirit of God, to not be lazy in their service to the Lord. Instead, they are to be fervent (enthusiastic) in spirit about serving God and discharging their worship.

While some passages of Scripture are descriptive (tell us what happened or what was said without necessarily condoning the behavior or statement), other passages are prescriptive, meaning they teach us what all Christians everywhere and in every era should believe and do. Even though Paul's letter to the Romans was not written *to* us, it is written *for* us. Thus, being diligent in the discharge of our worship to God is a command every Christian should heartily and gratefully obey.

205. Cheerfully and Prayerfully Hopeful

Rejoice in hope, be patient in tribulation, be constant in prayer. —Romans 12:12

PAUL'S LIST FOR THE FAMILY OF GOD CONTINUES WITH AN exhortation for living in the present circumstances. One day, the redeemed of God will be saved not only from the penalty and power of sin, but from the very presence of sin. Until then, we must run our race here on earth with patience (cf. Hebrews 12:1–2). When the fullness of the kingdom is revealed, there will be no more suffering or tribulation. But for now, we must endure cheerfully.

Therefore, Paul exhorts the believers at the church in Rome to rejoice in hope, that is to remain in a state of mental well-being and happiness because of our expectation. In other words, we have a future, a good future, regardless of the present circumstance. Secondly, believers are to be patient (steadfast in our rejoicing) in the face of tribulation—and there will be tribulation (John 16:33, cf. 2 Timothy 3:12). Finally, believers are to be content in prayer, which is the same thing as saying, "Pray without ceasing" (cf. 1 Thessalonians 5:17).

While there are three different emphases, it is all one thing Paul is exhorting the church to do: be cheerfully and prayerfully hopeful amidst tribulations in front of a despairing broken world.

206. Philoxenia

Contribute to the needs of the saints and seek to show hospitality. —Romans 12:13

PAUL CONTINUES HIS EXHORTATION WITH TWO SPECIFIC admonitions. First, Christians are to contribute to the needs of the saints (recall Romans 12:6–8). Contribute comes from the Greek word, *κοινωνοῦντες* (*koinonountes*), share, which is closely related to *κοινωνία* (*koinonia*), communion. To contribute to the needs of the saints is to *share in the interests of others*, or *participate in being responsible for others' needs*.

Second, Christians are to seek to show hospitality, which is another very interesting word in Greek, the compound noun, *φιλοξενίαν* (*philoxenia*) [*philo* + *xenia*]. *Philo* means "love," as in *philosophy* (love of wisdom) and *Philadelphia* (brotherly love). *Xenos* means "stranger" or "guest" or "host," and *xenia* refers to the exchange or carrying out of a guest-host relationship for a stranger. One may think of the word *xenophobia* (fear of strangers) for context. That said, *philoxenia* means "the love of being a host to a stranger."

In the ancient world, there were weighty rules regarding *xenia* and to violate those rules meant judgment. An example of this is the Trojan War, which was started because *xenia* was violated. Paul exhorts believers to be eager to host others in need, especially those of the household of faith. Christians are exhorted to be enthusiastic to welcome strangers and those in need. "For I was hungry and you gave me food, I was thirsty and you gave me drink, I was a stranger and you welcomed me" (Matthew 25:35).

207. Bless the Persecutors

Bless those who persecute you; bless and do not curse them. —*Romans 12:14*

AS PAUL CONTINUES TO LIST THESE PRECEPTS FOR THE NEW gospel-centered humanity, the church, it doesn't appear that he is taking any great pains to lay them out in any precise order. Rather, he exhorts the church with a barrage of simple principles that would be most relevant for the new humanity in the present circumstances.

This present directive calls on believers to go further than the mere stoic discipline of simply avoiding retaliation for wrongs suffered; Instead, Christians are called to bless those who persecute us. Though the precept is admittedly wholly contrary to human nature, it is consistent with the divine nature granted to us who believe. "His divine power has granted to us all things that pertain to life and godliness, through the knowledge of him who called us to his own glory and excellence, by which he has granted to us his precious and very great promises, so that through them you may become partakers of the divine nature, having escaped from the corruption that is in the world because of sinful desire" (2 Peter 1:3–4).

To bless (from the Greek word *εὐλογέω* (*eulogeo*) from which we also get *eulogize*) is to ask God to bestow special favor; to call down God's gracious power. In Hebrew and other Ancient Near East cultures, to be blessed is to flourish in field and fertility. We are to seek God's blessings on our persecutors, asking God to make them flourish in righteousness, which is also to ask God for their salvation.

208. Rejoicing and Weeping

Rejoice with those who rejoice, weep with those who weep. —*Romans 12:15*

ADDING TO HIS LIST OF CHARACTER TRAITS BECOMING OF Christ's new humanity (Christians), Paul next lays down an exhortation toward true love for one's neighbor, that of mutual affection.

Genuine gospel-generated love is compelled to share in the celebrations as well as the heartaches of one's neighbor. We are to rejoice with those who are celebrating good news and blessings in their lives, and we are to have real sympathy for those who are suffering and carrying heavy burdens.

An unfortunate tendency that seems more prevalent among professed believers than it should be is the begrudging of a brother or sister for blessings they receive (i.e., a promotion at work, a pregnancy, a book deal, etc.) and the avoidance of the same in their brother or sister's time suffering (i.e., injury, lost loved one, lost job, etc.).

Let it not be so named amongst those whom Christ has redeemed.

209. Mind Your Mind

Live in harmony with one another. Do not be haughty, but associate with the lowly. Never be wise in your own sight. —Romans 12:16

THIS NEXT EXHORTATION IS ONE OF HUMILITY. PREVIOUSLY, Paul told believers not to think of themselves more highly than they ought to think (v. 3), which is a general exhortation to humility. Here he adds that believers are to live in harmony with one another. This means every potential display of sinful pride must be put to death.

Next, he reminds believers, as James also did (James 2:1–9), to not show partiality among the brethren by being haughty, but associate with (the KJV says to *condescend to*) the lowly.

While in our modern democratic culture the idea of reminding people to condescend to another or associate with the lowly may seem off-putting or haughty, we must avoid anachronistic tendencies to dismiss the aristocratic mind-set of the age.

It took the gospel two millennia to cultivate our modern sensibility for equality. (Note: the Christian idea of *equality*, as manifest in Paul's writings or even the writings of eighteenth-century deists like Locke and Jefferson, is something quite different than the postmodern idea of *equity*. The two should not be confused.)

In any case, it is of further interest to note Paul's double use of the Greek word, *φρονοῦντες* (*phronountes*), which is not expressed as clearly in the ESV as it is in other translations:

> Be of the same *mind* one toward another. Do not set your *mind* on exalted things, but [associate] with the humble. Do not think that you are wiser than you really are. (EOB)[86]

> Be of the same *mind* one toward another. *Mind* not high things, but [condescend] to men of low estate. Be not wise in your own conceits. (KJV)

86. Laurent Cleenewerck, ed., *The Eastern/Greek Orthodox Bible: New Testament* (Laurent A. Cleenewerck, 2011), Romans 12:16.

Phronountes is first translated *harmony* and then translated *haughty* in the ESV, the latter modified by *ὑψηλὰ* (hypselos). In the other translations it's translated *mind. Phronountes* means to give careful consideration to something; to set one's mind on that thing. *hypselos phronountes* means to cherish proud thoughts or harbor exalted thoughts.

Thus, we are called to set our minds on the same thing (Christ) and not cherish proud thoughts that exalt ourselves above our neighbors. In other words, never be wise in our own sight.

210. Repay No One Evil

Repay no one evil for evil, but give thought to do what is honorable in the sight of all. —Romans 12:17

PAUL FURTHER EXHORTS BELIEVERS THAT THEY ARE NOT VINdictive for wrongs suffered but instead think about the best way to respond in such a way that unbelievers, those outside the church, and even the persecutors, will have no legitimate reason to disapprove. Paul tells Timothy something similar in his pastoral epistle to him, as does Peter in his general epistle to believers.

> So I would have younger widows marry, bear children, manage their households, and give the adversary no occasion for slander. (1 Timothy 5:14)

> But even if you should suffer for righteousness' sake, you will be blessed. Have no fear of them, nor be troubled, but in your hearts honor Christ the Lord as holy, always being prepared to make a defense to anyone who asks you for a reason for the hope that is in you; yet do it with gentleness and respect, having a good conscience, so that, when you are slandered, those who revile your good behavior in Christ may be put to shame. (1 Peter 3:14–16)

As Paul will declare shortly, vengeance belongs to God, not to us. We are called to love even our enemies, and persecutors.

211. Live Peaceably with All

"If possible, so far as it depends on you, live peaceably with all." —Romans 12:18

PAUL BEGAN HIS LIST OF EXHORTATIONS TO CHRISTIANS WITH the charge that we love genuinely, abhorring what is evil and holding fast to what is good. Each of the exhortations are, in one sense, independent of the others; but, in another sense, they are collectively aimed at healthy community life.

Here Paul provides a sort of bookend to the series, exhorting believers to live peaceably with everyone so far as it is in their power to do so. He is not the only apostle to exhort believers to this end.

The author of Hebrews (maybe Paul) charges Christians, "Strive for peace with everyone, and for the holiness without which no one will see the Lord" (Hebrews 12:14).

And James also reminds the church, "But the wisdom from above is first pure, then peaceable, gentle, open to reason, full of mercy and good fruits, impartial and sincere" (James 3:17).

There are more examples, but all of them are simply echoing the words of our Lord Jesus in his Sermon on the Mount when he said, "Blessed are the peacemakers, for they shall be called sons of God" (Matthew 5:9).

The truth is, however, it is not always possible to keep the peace. This is why he says, *if possible* and *so far as it depends on you*. As Christians, we ought to bear many things and forgive many sins for the sake of peace, but we must not ever excuse compliance with or affirmation of sin for the sake of peacekeeping.

Let it never be said of believers that we have not done all that we can to keep the peace; but let it also never be said that we have flattered the vices of men for the sake of preserving peace.

212. Never Avenge Yourselves

Beloved, never avenge yourselves, but leave it to the wrath of God, for it is written, "Vengeance is mine, I will repay, says the Lord." —Romans 12:19

PAUL APPEALS TENDERLY TO THE BELIEVERS, CALLING THEM *beloved*. Certainly, it is a sensitive charge. Human nature wants to retaliate, seek what we, in our limited view, believe will serve justice. But Paul warns the believers that it is not our place. Vengeance belongs to God, the omniscient, all-wise judge of the universe.

Paul is not suggesting there will be no retribution to those who sin against us. He assures there is a place for the wrath of God, and we can be certain God will judge the wicked.

One way to look at this is to leave vengeance to the professional, commending the injustice done to us to God's care. That way we are free to live out God's will for us, trusting he will do better than we could ever do at meeting out justice properly and satisfactorily against those who sin against us.

213. Heap Burning Coals

"To the contrary, "if your enemy is hungry, feed him; if he is thirsty, give him something to drink; for by so doing you will heap burning coals on his head." Do not be overcome by evil, but overcome evil with good." —Romans 12:20–21

INSTEAD OF WHAT SEEMS NATURAL TO THE FLESH—TO TAKE vengeance on one's enemies—the believer is called to act contrary. Paul exhorts believers to overcome evil by doing good. How? Feed the hungry enemy and give him something to drink when he thirsts. In other words, by the power of the Spirit of God, we are to love even our enemy as a human being by meeting his needs.

The idea of heaping burning coals on his head is likely a metaphor for the grace of shame. Recall what Paul said previously about the work of godly kindness: "Or do you presume on the riches of his kindness and forbearance and patience, not knowing that God's kindness is meant to lead you to repentance?" (Romans 2:4).

214. No Authority Except from God

"Let every person be subject to the governing authorities. For there is no authority except from God, and those that exist have been instituted by God." —*Romans 13:1*

THE WORD TRANSLATED *PERSON* IN THIS PLACE IS THE GREEK word, *psyche,* or soul. Paul says, Let every soul be subject to the governing authorities. This begins his next series of exhortations to the new humanity, the gospel-people, the church. He moves from the general exhortation to love one another genuinely to loving one another politically.

The question that most conflicts believers about this exhortation is *to what extent?* Does Paul mean believers are to obey the human magistrates without qualification, without exception? The first principle that must be established, Paul says, is that without God, there is no authority, and all authority that does exist has been instituted by God. In subsequent verses, he will unpack this further, but here let us be mindful of the fact that Paul was a Pharisee, formerly, and therefore an astute student of the Old Testament Scriptures.

He would be precisely familiar with the stories of both Pharaoh and Daniel. As a matter of fact, he quotes the following passage about Pharaoh earlier in this letter (Romans 9:17).

> But for this purpose I have raised you up, to show you my power, so that my name may be proclaimed in all the earth. (Exodus 9:16)

> When Daniel knew that the document had been signed, he went to his house where he had windows in his upper chamber open toward Jerusalem. He got down on his knees three times a day and prayed and gave thanks before his God, as he had done previously. (Daniel 6:10)

It is from Scriptural passages like the former that Paul would derive the principle of recognizing all authority is from God. He raises up one and puts down another (cf. 1 Chronicles 36:22–23; Psalm 75:7).

But we should not make the mistake of thinking he has forgotten or neglected the latter. He undoubtedly knew the story of the disciples who resisted the unlawful law against preaching in the name of Jesus (Acts 4 and 5:29).

215. What God Has Appointed

Therefore whoever resists the authorities resists what God has appointed, and those who resist will incur judgment. —Romans 13:2

FROM THE TIME ISRAEL FIRST BECAME A TRIBUTE NATION (subservient to Gentile nations) to the time of Paul's writing, there had always been zealots whose goal it was to raise enough support to overthrow the occupying armies. Further, in Jewish teaching, Gentile magistrates were seen as illegitimate leaders of God's chosen people. Consider the second Psalm of David:

> Why do the nations rage and the peoples plot in vain? The kings of the earth set themselves, and the rulers take counsel together, against the Lord and against his Anointed, saying, "Let us burst their bonds apart and cast away their cords from us." He who sits in the heavens laughs; the Lord holds them in derision. Then he will speak to them in his wrath, and terrify them in his fury, saying, "As for me, I have set my King on Zion, my holy hill." (Psalm 2:1–6)

Even during Jesus's earthly ministry, many thought of Messiah in terms of a military and political leader in the way of Judas Maccabeus who led the Maccabean Revolts in the second century BC. Simon was called a Zealot by Luke (Luke 6:15), and in AD 66, the Jewish Zealots would revolt against the Romans leading to the destruction of the Temple in AD 70.

Paul's exhortation that the followers of Christ be subject to the ruling authorities is given in this context. He establishes the authority of his exhortation by reminding them that by resisting the civil authorities they were resisting what God had appointed and they would certainly incur judgment for doing so. We must remember that God is the author of authority and in his sovereignty, he raises one up and puts another down.

Paul's exhortation is a universal principle based on Jesus's teaching that we are to render to Caesar what is Caesar's and to God what is God's (Mark

12:17). That makes it a precept to be applied at all times, by every generation of believers. It also means there are qualifications to the precept—that it is not without its restrictions.

We are to give to Caesar what is Caesar, but we are not to give to Caesar what is the Lord's. Nor are we to give to those merely claiming to be Caesar what is Caesar's.

216. Do What Is Good

Let every person be subject to the governing authorities. For there is no authority except from God, and those that exist have been instituted by God. Therefore whoever resists the authorities resists what God has appointed, and those who resist will incur judgment. For rulers are not a terror to good conduct, but to bad. Would you have no fear of the one who is in authority? Then do what is good, and you will receive his approval . . . —Romans 13:1–3

THE REASON PAUL EXHORTS THE BELIEVERS TO OBEY authority is because God has ordained it, and ordained it toward a particular end—justice. Authority is ordained by God for judging bad conduct. And, assuming, as Paul does here, the authority is fulfilling its purpose, it is in the best interest of the believer to obey. Obeying the authority will earn the approval of the magistrate.

To put this exhortation in a contemporary context, it is good and right for the believer to obey the traffic laws, pay their taxes, and support civil policies that are designed to serve the greater good, even if the believer is not fully in support of a particular program. As a matter of fact, Christians should be the best examples of this as far as they are able.

But here is the rub. Sometimes the magistrate legislates and/or attempts to execute unjust laws. Laws that promote evil instead of good. When the lower authority contradicts the higher authority, we have an obligation to obey, and thus receive the approval of, the higher authority (God)—even at the expense of the disapproval and punishment of the lower authority.

Examples of such cases abound throughout history: when the apostles were commanded to stop preaching in the name of Jesus, they did so anyway, and were beaten and jailed for it (Acts 5:29); when the early Christians were told to offer incense to Caesar (an act of total submission) or be thrown in the arena, many died untimely, cruel deaths in the jaws and claws of wild animals.

May we always be found seeking the approval of the highest authority.

217. The Servant of God for Your Good

. . . for he is God's servant for your good. But if you do wrong, be afraid, for he does not bear the sword in vain. For he is the servant of God, an avenger who carries out God's wrath on the wrongdoer. —Romans 13:4

THIS IS ONE OF THE CLEAREST DECLARATIONS IN SCRIPTURE that the civil magistrate is a servant of God to execute judgment on evildoers, whether the magistrate acknowledges God or not. In addition to the obvious straightforward implications of this declaration, there are some more subtle implications as well.

First, the magistrate is God's servant. This means that in those things which fall to the magistrate, the believer (as well as unbelievers) has a divine responsibility to obey God by obeying said magistrate. This also means the magistrate is accountable to God, whether he acknowledges God or not. It is true God can raise up and put down at his discretion, but it is also true that God can delay judgment and allow an evil magistrate to store up wrath against the day of wrath (Romans 2:5).

Second, the magistrate is ruling for the good of the believer. Of course, he is ruling for the good of all humanity, but the believer who possesses the Spirit of God should, of all people, desire goodness and recognize the work required to achieve goodness in civic matters. Therefore, the believer should pray for the magistrate to carry out his duties faithfully, and show support and appreciation for his office and duties (1 Timothy 2:1–4).

Third, the believer should genuinely fear the power the magistrate possesses to execute judgment on evildoers and be far from ever being considered an evildoer according to just laws (1 Peter 2:13–17). This also implies that the magistrate, who bears not the sword in vain, should be wise in legislating just laws and mindful to carry out God's wrath faithfully on wrongdoers. He is, after all, God's servant (mentioned 2x in this one passage).

NOTE: There are technically only three regimes with some possible hybrids (i.e., republic) and all are legitimate forms of government: monarchy, aristocracy, and polity. The monarch is a ruler of one for the good of the many.

The aristocracy is the rule of the few noble for the good of the many. Polity is the rule of the many over themselves according to virtue.

Where government goes bad is not in its form but in its "for"—it's motivation. When the monarch ceases to rule "for" the benefit of the people and rules instead for the benefit of himself, he is called a tyrant or despot. When the aristocracy ceases to rule *for* the benefit of the people and rules instead *for* the benefit of the powerful and wealthy elite, they are called an oligarchy. And when the many cease to rule over themselves according to virtue and rule instead *for* the benefit of their baser passions—the bed and the table—they are called a democracy.

A proper apprehension of both the fact and the gravity of the fact that both ruler and subject are under the authority of God goes a long way toward a peaceful civil society.

218. Be in Subjection

Therefore one must be in subjection, not only to avoid God's wrath but also for the sake of conscience. —Romans 13:5

PAUL GIVES TWO REASONS TO OBEY THE MAGISTRATE: TO avoid God's wrath and to avoid a guilty conscience. In this case, God's wrath can be understood primarily as the magistrate's *work of carrying out God's wrath on the wrongdoer.*

Our consciences will accuse us when we are not living in subjection to God. In other words, we should obey the magistrate out of a heart of pure worship toward God. Peter says similar: "in your hearts honor Christ the Lord as holy, always being prepared to make a defense to anyone who asks you for a reason for the hope that is in you; yet do it with gentleness and respect, having a good conscience, so that, when you are slandered, those who revile your good behavior in Christ may be put to shame" (1 Peter 3:15–16).

219. Authorities Are Ministers of God

For because of this you also pay taxes, for the authorities are ministers of God, attending to this very thing. —Romans 13:6

THE DEMONSTRATIVE PRONOUN *THIS* IS NEUTER AND LIKELY refers to the whole of what Paul is saying: namely, rulers are ministers of God executing judgment on evildoers so you should obey them as having been appointed by God. Although, it could be referring more specifically to the clause, *for the sake of conscience*. Either way, it amounts to the same thing generally speaking: the reason believers should not begrudge paying taxes is because they are raised to support the execution of the ruler's duties. Taxes are necessary in order to create and maintain the conditions that allow for ordinary, normal life.

And the authorities that collect the taxes are also ministers of God attending to this very work, so they should be respected as well.

There are at least a few important implications to take away from all this. First, taxes are affirmed by God, and therefore should be considered normal and appropriate. Second, the fact that Paul addresses taxes and tax collectors here shows the context for his exhortation concerning the normal and expected functions of government.

Finally, what Paul *does not suggest* is that every conceivable, despotic act imposed by rulers or authorities is approved by God and therefore should be automatically obeyed.

But in the normal function of things, rulers have authority to administer justice against evil doers. Christians should, therefore, be in subjection to lawful authorities and should pay their taxes in support of the work they are doing.

220. Pay What You Owe

Pay to all what is owed to them: taxes to whom taxes are owed, revenue to whom revenue is owed, respect to whom respect is owed, honor to whom honor is owed.
—Romans 13:7

HAVING WORKED THROUGH THE LOGIC OF THIS LAST EXHORtation to obey the rulers and pay the taxes, Paul concludes with a command. *Pay* is an imperative verb and shows that Paul is moving beyond the general appeal to the believers' conscience and stating emphatically that Christians need to discharge their debts to society—even the society which doesn't honor God.

He begins with a general command to pay everyone what is owed them, and then moves to particular examples. Taxes are those monies levied against person and property. Revenue seems to be those monies levied against traded goods (i.e., imports and exports). But the debt to be discharged is not merely monetary; it is also personal. Christians are to pay the appropriate respect or honor due to those who hold office or stations that afford them honors. (i.e., rulers, Luke 20:22–25; spiritual leaders, Philemon 2:12; masters, 1 Peter 2:18; spouses, Ephesians 5:33, etc.)

In our postmodern, democratic state there is a general disdain for the concepts of authority and hierarchy. Equity is the modern man's virtue. And because this is the case, those tasked with exercising authority often become tyrannical in their office either out of pride or out of necessity—often out of both.

What might be a worthy exercise is to read through the New Testament letters with an eye to see the way the apostles treat authority and how they emphasize the manner in which the gospel prioritizes love, not force or rebellion, as the means of transcending conventional authority.

221. Owe No One Anything

Owe no one anything, except to love each other, for the one who loves another has fulfilled the law. —Romans 13:8

PAUL MAKES A BRILLIANT TURN OF PHRASE HERE TO DEMONstrate how the law is fulfilled in our exciting love toward one another. Beginning in verse 7, he says to the believers, pay what you owe and owe no one anything but love. Discharge all debts to one another including the debt of love we owe one another—which cannot be completely discharged. We will always owe this debt so we should continually pay it.

Paul then reminds the believers at Rome that to love one another is literally the fulfillment of the law as says the law: "You shall not take vengeance or bear a grudge against the sons of your own people, but you shall love your neighbor as yourself: I am the Lord" (Leviticus 19:18).

And so says Jesus: "And he said to him, 'You shall love the Lord your God with all your heart and with all your soul and with all your mind. This is the great and first commandment. And a second is like it: You shall love your neighbor as yourself. On these two commandments depend all the Law and the Prophets'" (Matthew 22:37–40).

This exhortation of Paul's suggests at least two practical applications:

First, don't steal by not paying your debts. "The wicked borrows but does not pay back, but the righteous is generous and gives . . ." (Psalm 37:21).

Second, love is a debt that can never be discharged and it looks a certain way. Pauls taught us what it looks like in his letter to the Corinthians:

> If I speak in the tongues of men and of angels, but have not love, I am a noisy gong or a clanging cymbal. And if I have prophetic powers, and understand all mysteries and all knowledge, and if I have all faith, so as to remove mountains, but have not love, I am nothing. If I give away all I have, and if I deliver up my body to be burned, but have not love, I gain nothing. Love is patient and kind; love does not envy or boast; it is not arrogant or rude. It does not insist on its own way;

it is not irritable or resentful; it does not rejoice at wrongdoing, but rejoices with the truth. Love bears all things, believes all things, hopes all things, endures all things. Love never ends. As for prophecies, they will pass away; as for tongues, they will cease; as for knowledge, it will pass away. (1 Corinthians 13:1–8)

222. Love Your Neighbor as Yourself

For the commandments, "You shall not commit adultery, You shall not murder, You shall not steal, You shall not covet," and any other commandment, are summed up in this word: "You shall love your neighbor as yourself." —Romans 13:9

WHAT PAUL IS EMPHASIZING HERE IS NOT AN ORDERLY TREATment of the Mosaic Law, but the one overarching commandment that sums up all the commandments directed at one's fellow man, namely, "You shall love your neighbor as yourself."

This is, of course, a summary of Jesus's teaching that all the law can be summed up in two commandments, one directed toward God, and another similar commandment directed toward one's fellow man, one's neighbor: "And he said to him, 'You shall love the Lord your God with all your heart and with all your soul and with all your mind. This is the great and first commandment. And a second is like it: You shall love your neighbor as yourself. On these two commandments depend all the Law and the Prophets'" (Matthew 22:37–40).

Recall that everything Paul is exhorting the believers to observe and to practice is a result of the regenerated life in Christ. The new gospel-oriented humanity has been empowered by the Holy Spirit of God to now live as the sons of God here on earth amidst an unbelieving and, therefore, unregenerate and untoward humanity whose inheritance is death.

> If the Spirit of him who raised Jesus from the dead dwells in you, he who raised Christ Jesus from the dead will also give life to your mortal bodies through his Spirit who dwells in you. So then, brothers, we are debtors, not to the flesh, to live according to the flesh. For if you live according to the flesh you will die, but if by the Spirit you put to death the deeds of the body, you will live. For all who are led by the Spirit of God are sons of God. For you did not receive the spirit of slavery to fall back into fear, but you have received the Spirit of adoption as sons, by whom we cry, "Abba! Father!" The Spirit himself bears witness with

our spirit that we are children of God, and if children, then heirs—heirs of God and fellow heirs with Christ, provided we suffer with him in order that we may also be glorified with him. (Romans 8:11–17)

223. Love Does No Wrong

Love does no wrong to a neighbor; therefore love is the fulfilling of the law.
—Romans 13:10

THIS VERSE IS MERELY A SUMMARY OF PAUL'S EXHORTATION to not withhold from any that which is due them, be it money, honor, or obedience, but especially love. When we truly love our neighbors, we are doing the very opposite of wronging our neighbors. Because this is the case, love is actually the fulfilling the law.

One word of caution, however. Loving our neighbor this way is not a means to salvation; it is a result of our salvation. It is the fruit of our faith in Christ who *loved us* with an everlasting love.

Christ, who loved us, fulfilled the law on our behalf, when he became a man, died for us, and rose the third day to take his place at the right hand of the Father.

224. Discerning the Time

Besides this you know the time, that the hour has come for you to wake from sleep. For salvation is nearer to us now than when we first believed. —*Romans 13:11*

NOT ONLY DOES PAUL WANT THE BELIEVERS AT ROME TO BE motivated by love for one another, but he also appeals to their knowledge of "the time." When he says, "you know the time," he is asking them to acknowledge their understanding of the critical nature of their present circumstances. (Nero is the Emperor at the time of his writing.) He exhorts them to lay aside their slumber and make notable progress in sanctification since salvation is nearer than when they first believed.

Clearly, Paul is thinking eschatologically. In the spirit of Christ's teaching and that of the other apostles, and as he has in other letters, Paul is referring to the return of Christ. (See Philippians 4:4–7; 1 Thessalonians 5:1–11, 23; Hebrews 10:24ff; James 5:7–11; 1 Peter 4:7–11; and Matthew 25:31–46; Mark 13:33–37 etc.).[87]

Because of the American evangelical affinity to the novel and modern belief in a dispensational and premillennial eschatology it is possible to miss the urgent nature of Paul's exhortation.[88] Until the nineteenth century, much of the church understood Paul (along with Jesus and John; see Matthew 24 and Revelation 1:3,19, respectively) to be anticipating the end of the Old Covenant epoch.

Paul's urgency about the end of the epoch would take place with the fall of Jerusalem and the final destruction of the Temple in AD 70. Ever since, Temple Judaism has been extinct but the church has flourished with the preaching of the word, the witness of the saints, and the power of the Holy Spirit.

> But in fact Christ has been raised from the dead, the firstfruits of those who have fallen asleep. For as by a man came death, by a man

87. William Hendriksen and Simon J. Kistemaker, Exposition of Paul's Epistle to the Romans, vol. 12–13, New Testament Commentary (Grand Rapids: Baker Book House, 1953–2001), 441.
88. John Darby and his followers circa. 1820.

has come also the resurrection of the dead. For as in Adam all die, so also in Christ shall all be made alive. But each in his own order: Christ the firstfruits, then at his coming those who belong to Christ. Then comes the end, when he delivers the kingdom to God the Father after destroying every rule and every authority and power. For he must reign until he has put all his enemies under his feet. The last enemy to be destroyed is death. For "God has put all things in subjection under his feet." But when it says, "all things are put in subjection," it is plain that he is excepted who put all things in subjection under him. When all things are subjected to him, then the Son himself will also be subjected to him who put all things in subjection under him, that God may be all in all. (1 Corinthians 15:20–28)

225. Cast Off the Works of Darkness

Besides this you know the time, that the hour has come for you to wake from sleep. For salvation is nearer to us now than when we first believed. The night is far gone; the day is at hand. So then let us cast off the works of darkness and put on the armor of light. —Romans 13:11–12

THE METAPHOR OF NIGHT AND DAY IS A CLASSIC ARCHETYPE of good and evil, right and wrong, past and future (i.e., turning over a new leaf). In the present context, Paul has time in mind as much as good and evil in mind (cf. v. 11, *you know the time; the hour has come*, etc.).

When he says *the night is far gone,* he means the old epoch is coming to an end; thus, in like manner, the old way of sinful living has come to an end. And when he says, the day is at hand, he means the epoch of Christ's light shining upon us has come into view; it is upon us even now.

Eschatologically, Paul appears to have in mind the closing of the Old Testament period and the emerging age of Christ's kingdom—the mustard seed if you will (Matthew 13:31–32). In 70 A.D., Christ visited Jerusalem in her day of judgment and not a stone of the Temple was left standing (cf. Luke 21:5–24). It was the end of the Jewish epoch. From that point in history forward, the new humanity would take the gospel of the already-but-not-yet kingdom of Christ to the ends of the earth (Matthew 28:18–20).

Paul is exhorting the believers in the Church at Rome, who are even now part of the family of God, to live as Kingdom believers by casting off the works of the old way, the old man, the old epoch, and put on the armor of light, the vestiges of the church militant—to live as citizens of Christ's kingdom, as citizens of the new redeemed humanity.

226. Walk Properly

Let us walk properly as in the daytime, not in orgies and drunkenness, not in sexual immorality and sensuality, not in quarreling and jealousy. —Romans 13:13

GIVEN THEIR PLACE IN HISTORY AS THE NEW HUMANITY, THE new Israel, the new people of God, Paul urges them to join him in walking properly: "Let us walk properly as in the daytime . . ."

The daytime is indicative of the opposite of darkness. The imagery is rather intuitive given the tendency in human decadence to put on the image of decency in the daylight, during the normal course of human interaction, and slip into something more vicious after the sun goes down. John tells us "people loved the darkness rather than the light because their works were evil" (John 3:19).

The list of vices Paul addresses is not meant to be all-inclusive (cf. Gal. 5:19–21) but representative of the deeds men do under the cover of darkness. In other words, Paul is exhorting the believers at Rome to behave properly, and proper behavior is that which one does in the open, under the light of Christ, and wouldn't mind doing even if everyone knew about it.

227. Put On the Lord Jesus Christ

But put on the Lord Jesus Christ, and make no provision for the flesh, to gratify its desires. —*Romans 13:14*

PAUL FIRST EXHORTED FROM THE *VIA NEGATIVA* (I.E., V. 13—not in not in orgies and drunkenness, not in sexual immorality and sensuality, not in quarreling and jealousy); he now exhorts *via positivia.*

In other words, to walk properly as in the day has both a negative aspect to avoid and a positive aspect to pursue. The positive is to *put on the Lord Jesus Christ.* This means we are to robe our lives in Christ (Galatians 3:27), to emulate Christ (1 Peter 2:21), and to fashion our minds after Christ (Philippians 2:5). The metaphor of adornment is a common metaphor of the time for what a man wears either honors him or dishonors him. What he is robed in on the outside typically says something about this character on the inside.

If every part of our life is consumed by Christ, then there will be no room for the flesh, no way to make provision for it, to gratify its desires. It is also of note that Paul does not repudiate legitimate human desires here. He uses the word *σαρκὸς* (*sarkos*), which is translated "flesh." He is talking about fleshly desires, inordinate desires (e.g., lust, envy, covetousness, etc. from which come orgies and drunkenness, sexual immorality and sensuality, and quarreling and jealousy).

NOTA BENE: It is of interest that Romans 13:13–14 was the Scripture St. Augustine read when he was in the garden crying over his sin and heard a child nearby say repeatedly, "Tolle, lege; tolle, lege" ("Take up and read; take up and read"). He took it as the voice of the Lord, picked up a Bible which fell open to this passage.

228. Welcome One Who Is Weak in Faith

As for the one who is weak in faith, welcome him, but not to quarrel over opinions. —Romans 14:1

AT THIS POINT, PAUL NARROWS HIS FOCUS FROM GENERAL exhortations to community life, or church-oriented exhortations. Recall the chiastic structure that guides us through Paul's thoughts as he is writing to the Romans.

- 1:1–17 Introduction
  - 1:18–3:30 Chaos (Devolution of Humanity)
    - 4–5 Faith Saves
      - 6–7 Two Regimes
        - 8 The Glory of the Gospel
      - 9–11 Two Branches
    - 12–13 Faith Works
  - 14–15 Cosmos (Evolution of Humanity)
- 16 Farewell

Sin brought chaos into the good and ordered world (1:18–3:30); but now the gospel changes everything. From chapter 4–8, we are instructed in the gospel, the specific operation of faith in God's saving grace through Christ. In chapters 9–11, he explains how the gospel works amidst the two branches of God's people, Old Testament Israel and the New Testament Israel (grafted Gentiles and a remnant of believing Israel). And in chapters 12–13, Paul explains how faith works itself out in our day-to-day lives, making us a peculiar and godly people i.e., saints.

Now, beginning here in chapter 14, we are introduced to the gospel's work in community life. Immediately, we are made aware of the gradations of maturity that exist in the church. This is actually a model for a healthy church. A church that is continually receiving new believers and helping them grow up in the Lord will continually have a gradation of maturity existing in it.

The first exhortation is one of welcome. The church is to welcome those who are more immature in their faith (weak in the faith), but not with the goal of arguing with them about their opinions.

Plato notably explained that opinions are a strongly held belief that rests on a spectrum between ignorance and absolute certainty, which is an aphorism that is in itself worthy of contemplation. Opinions, even strongly held opinions, ought to be held humbly enough that when new evidence is revealed that might change our belief, we would be wise enough to recognize it. But it also ought not to be held so loosely that our minds are changed by every wind of doctrine.

Paul recognizes the human tendency to want to convince the other of his strongly held belief, his liberty in Christ; but such matters of conscience must be addressed gently and wisely, recognizing that the one who is weak in the faith also has been welcomed by God through Jesus Christ. This one is, therefore, most importantly, our brother or sister in Christ.

229. Liberty in Christ

One person believes he may eat anything, while the weak person eats only vegetables. —Romans 14:2

AS PAUL EXHORTS THE BODY OF CHRIST TO UNITY, HE HIGHlights one of the areas most prone to cause division among believers, laws concerning eating and drinking. In his letter to the Colossians, Paul encouraged them not to submit to "judgment . . . in questions of food and drink, or with regard to a festival or a new moon or a Sabbath," as these were merely "a shadow of the things to come, but the substance belongs to Christ" (Colossians 2:16–23).

But in our passage currently under consideration, Paul is encouraging believers to be loving and patient with one another as they work through the changes that are taking place during this time of transition. He is acknowledging that the "strong" or mature believers are settled in the knowledge that it is now lawful to eat all things, freely. But the "weak" or immature believer should not be compelled to walk by the same rule.

As long as the weak believer is not depending on his adherence to dietary laws for his salvation, he is equally free to eat—or not eat in this case—what he pleases.

As was previously mentioned, there will always be gradations of maturity that exist in the church body that is continually receiving new believers and helping them grow up in the Lord. And as will be clearly established later in Paul's letter, it is the responsibility of the strong—by virtue of their strength—to bear with the infirmities of the weak.

230. God Has Welcomed Him

Let not the one who eats despise the one who abstains, and let not the one who abstains pass judgment on the one who eats, for God has welcomed him.
—Romans 14:3

PAUL NOW LAYS OUT AN EXAMPLE OF THE POTENTIAL KINDS of conflict between believers in matters of personal persuasion regarding dietary laws (14:5). One party has a weak conscience regarding the consumption of meat (the one who abstains) and the other party has a strong conscience regarding the same (the one who eats). One note of interest is that Paul ceases to refer to the two conflicting parties as the weak (14:1) and the strong (15:1) in this verse and refers to them only as "the one who eats" and "the one who abstains." Perhaps it is because the point has been established in the greater context and to highlight it here again would distract from the more important point.

On the one hand, he commands the one who eats to not *despise* the one who abstains. The Greek word translated "despise" is *ἐξουθενείτω* (*exoutheneo*) and means "to show by one's attitude or manner of treatment that an entity has no merit or worth," to "disdain" the other.[89]

And on the other hand, he commands the one who abstains "to not pass judgment" on the one who eats. The Greek word translated as "pass judgment," is κρινέτω (*krineto*) and means pass an unfavorable judgment upon, criticize, find fault with, condemn.[90]

The implications of these commands are also remarkable. The temptation of the one who eats (the one with strong faith) is to demerit or look down on the one who abstains, to have disdain for him or her because of their standards of prohibition. The temptation for the one who abstains is to be judgmental of the one who eats for what the abstainer believes is a licentious behavior

89. William Arndt et al., A Greek-English Lexicon of the New Testament and Other Early Christian Literature (Chicago: University of Chicago Press, 2000), 352.
90. William Arndt et al., A Greek-English Lexicon of the New Testament and Other Early Christian Literature (Chicago: University of Chicago Press, 2000), 567.

(eating meat) on the part of the eater. In both cases, it is the sin of pride that creates the breach in fellowship.

The reason for both parties to avoid falling into their respective sinful traps is because God has welcomed both to the same ground at the foot of the cross, equally. If God has welcomed *the other* despite his differing personal persuasions, it is not for us to judge the same on what we perceive to be the strength of his faith. It is for us to welcome all who are of the faith—weak or strong—for all are deserving of the same condemnation and yet are all redeemed by the same Savior, Jesus Christ.

231. Who Are You to Pass Judgment?

Who are you to pass judgment on the servant of another? It is before his own master that he stands or falls. And he will be upheld, for the Lord is able to make him stand. —Romans 14:4

PAUL HAS ALREADY ESTABLISHED THAT IT IS THE WEAKER brother who abstains from eating (v. 1). So be it. None of us has yet grown up into mature manhood, to the measure of the stature of the fullness of Christ (Ephesians 4:13). Therefore, it's not for the stronger brother to despise his weaker brother for his weakness (v. 3). Such a disposition would only reveal that the brother who is strong in matters of eating and drinking is also weak in matters of love and hospitality. And the weak brother who judges his brother who is stronger in matters of eating and drinking is only demonstrating his immaturity in the faith all the way around.

What Paul is saying here is that each is responsible to his own master, the Lord Jesus Christ. We all stand or fall before him and not before one another. And Paul assures them that in a case where one may be in error regarding such matters, it is not a matter of salvation. Both are believers. Both have been redeemed. Both have been welcomed by God. Both answer to the same master and not to each other.

It is also essential to remember, that while we may be persuaded differently in our own minds on secondary issues like dietary laws, *the record of debt that stood against us with its legal demands has been canceled. It has been set aside, nailed to the cross* (Colossians 2:14). Further, we are reminded that Jesus said of those he has saved, "My sheep hear my voice, and I know them, and they follow me. I give them eternal life, and they will never perish, and no one will snatch them out of my hand" (John 10:27–28).

Those who have been welcomed by God are not in jeopardy of losing their standing with him because they each approach such matters differently. However, to be clear, this is not a matter of relativism in terms of truth. It is a matter of personal understanding regarding the sense of the Scriptures and how to apply them accurately. In this matter, even the strongest in their faith still have growing to do. At the end of the day, the faith once delivered to the saints is about unity in Christ, not uniformity in preferences.

232. Fully Convinced in Our Own Minds

One person esteems one day as better than another, while another esteems all days alike. Each one should be fully convinced in his own mind. —*Romans 14:5*

THE FACT THAT PAUL MOVES FROM USING DIETARY LAWS AS his example in matters of personal persuasion to now using holy days as his examples implies that he is concerned with general disputes about the ceremonial laws that are coming to an end with the close of this epoch (AD 70).

In other words, not every belief or matter of personal persuasion in the Christian life is a matter of subjective opinion as some attempt to claim. Scripture is clear, for example, that "there is salvation in no one else, for there is no other name under heaven given among men by which we must be saved" (Acts 4:12). And, in matters of morality, "do you not know that the unrighteous will not inherit the kingdom of God? Do not be deceived: neither the sexually immoral, nor idolaters, nor adulterers, nor men who practice homosexuality, nor thieves, nor the greedy, nor drunkards, nor revilers, nor swindlers will inherit the kingdom of God" (1 Corinthians 6:9–10).

So then, in what kinds of matters are believers to not take issue with one another, but be fully convinced in his own mind? In the case Paul is addressing, there was a period of transition between the resurrection of Christ and the destruction of the Jewish temple in 70 A. D. when the epoch of the Mosaic Law came to an end. The early Christians began meeting on the first day of the week, but others continued to observe the Jewish Sabbath on the seventh day of the week. Additionally, there were days of fasting to be observed under the Mosaic Law that believers who followed Christ no longer felt the need to observe since they were only shadows of the reality (Colossians 2:17, cf. Hebrews 10:1).

Paul is saying that, in matters that are not clear from Scripture or where there seems to be ambiguity in the application of the Scriptures, we should be gracious toward our brothers and sisters in Christ who observe diets and days (for example) differently than we do. Simultaneously, we are to faithfully live out those things of which we are fully convinced in our own minds (Romans 14:23).

233. In Everything Give Thanks to God

One person esteems one day as better than another, while another esteems all days alike. Each one should be fully convinced in his own mind. The one who observes the day, observes it in honor of the Lord. The one who eats, eats in honor of the Lord, since he gives thanks to God, while the one who abstains, abstains in honor of the Lord and gives thanks to God. —Romans 14:5–6

BY COMPARISON WITH THE EARLIER CONSTRUCTION OF PAUL'S argument, the one who esteems one day better than another is the *weaker* believer. By weaker, he does not mean one who has a shaky foundation in Christ; rather, he means one who has a more sensitive conscience about particular matters of custom. Therefore, we must remember that while the observance of diets and days by the weaker believers was ultimately a matter of indifference in light of their common salvation and exhortation to unity, Paul is not affirming any wrongheaded notions held by any believer. And the reason why some things can be a matter of indifference, especially at this point in the church's development, is because both parties do so out of honor for and thanksgiving to God.

> "There are six things that the Lord hates, seven that are an abomination to him: haughty eyes, a lying tongue, and hands that shed innocent blood, a heart that devises wicked plans, feet that make haste to run to evil, a false witness who breathes out lies, and one who sows discord among brothers." (Proverbs 6:16–19)
>
> "Behold, how good and pleasant it is when brothers dwell in unity!" (Psalm 133:1)

234. We Are the Lord's

For none of us lives to himself, and none of us dies to himself. For if we live, we live to the Lord, and if we die, we die to the Lord. So then, whether we live or whether we die, we are the Lord's. —Romans 14:7–8

THE BROADEST POSSIBLE MEANINGS OF THESE VERSES ARE brought into clear focus by the preceding verses (5–6). The reason we need to be patient and welcome each other without taking opportunities to argue about differences in understanding of things like diets and days is because both parties—the weak and the strong—are doing what they do to honor God.

None of us lives to himself, says Paul. We are not our own; we were bought with a price; we live unto the Lord and not unto man (1 Corinthians 6:20; 7:23). Furthermore, if we die, we also die to the Lord and not ourselves (Philippians 1:20–24). We belong to the Lord in life and in death, and everything we do, we do for his praise and his glory (Colossians 3:23–24).

Otherwise, if it were a matter of difference regarding a practice not commended by the Lord, it would not fall into this category of gracious tolerance. If it was not for the honor and glory of the Lord, then it is obviously not to be tolerated.

For example, in his letter to the Ephesians, Paul says, "But sexual immorality and all impurity or covetousness must not even be named among you, as is proper among saints" (Ephesians 5:3).

235. Lord of the Dead and of the Living

For to this end Christ died and lived again, that he might be Lord both of the dead and of the living. —Romans 14:9

IT IS TO "THIS END," THE END THAT WE ALL BELONG TO THE Lord and seek to honor the Lord, that Christ "died and lived again." Why then should we wrongfully despise or judge our brothers and sisters in Christ about matters not clearly commanded in Scripture? Instead, we are to welcome one another with love and be patient and deferential in matters of personal conviction.

Note the construction of language Paul uses here, *died and lived again*; he does not say, *lived and died*. His point being, that by dying on the cross and rising to life again (where Christ now sits at the right hand of the Father), Jesus established his indisputable Lordship over both those who have died and those who still live.

Even now, he is making intercession for the believers as the author of Hebrews affirms: "*Consequently, he is able to save to the uttermost those who draw near to God through him, since he always lives to make intercession for them*" (Hebrews 7:25).

236. Judge Not!

Why do you pass judgment on your brother? Or you, why do you despise your brother? For we will all stand before the judgment seat of God . . . —*Romans 14:10*

PAUL EXHORTS BOTH PARTIES TO CEASE THEIR UNSEEMLY behavior towards one another. His use of *brother* here implies that there exists, by virtue of a shared salvation in Christ, not only a fraternal bond but an equal station in the family of God.

One who *passes judgment* on the other in such matters of days and diets takes upon himself the office of a judge, an office that does not belong to him. And the one who *despises* his brother in such matters of days and diets similarly acts outside of and beyond his capacity to judge his brother's conscience.

And Paul is not alone in his exhortation. James, the brother of our Lord, preached the same in his letter to the saints: "*There is only one lawgiver and judge, he who is able to save and to destroy. But who are you to judge your neighbor?*" (James 4:12).

Let us beware! For we do not possess the authority or the ability to judge such matters. They are reserved for God alone to judge. We will, however, stand on the other side of the bench, before the judgment seat of God, as those who will be judged. Moreover, let us carefully heed the words of our Lord Jesus in this matter of judging another's conscience and motive:

> Judge not, that you be not judged. For with the judgment you pronounce you will be judged, and with the measure you use it will be measured to you. Why do you see the speck that is in your brother's eye, but do not notice the log that is in your own eye? Or how can you say to your brother, 'Let me take the speck out of your eye,' when there is the log in your own eye? You hypocrite, first take the log out of your own eye, and then you will see clearly to take the speck out of your brother's eye. (Matthew 7:1–5)

237. Each of Us Will Give an Account

. . . for it is written,

> *"As I live, says the Lord, every knee shall bow to me,*
> *and every tongue shall confess to God."*

So then each of us will give an account of himself to God. —*Romans 14:11–12*

CITING ISAIAH 45:23, PAUL NOW DEMONSTRATES THAT ATTItude which ought to possess the hearts of every believer, humility and reverence. As was established in verse 10, he further confirms: we are not lords, but will answer to the Lord. We are not judges but are to be judged. Each of us will bow the knee, give praise to God, confess his grace and glory, and give an account to him of our own choices in life.

That without exception, each and every one of us is to personally stand before God at the judgment seat and give account is without dispute. And meditating on the numerous references and allusions in Scripture to our judgment day ought to forever change our disposition toward our brothers and sisters in Christ in matters of indifference.

> For God will bring every deed into judgment, with every secret thing, whether good or evil. (Ecclesiastes 12:14)
>
> For the Son of Man is going to come with his angels in the glory of his Father, and then he will repay each person according to what he has done. (Matthew 16:27)
>
> For we must all appear before the judgment seat of Christ, so that each one may receive what is due for what he has done in the body, whether good or evil. (2 Corinthians 5:10)
>
> . . . knowing that whatever good anyone does, this he will receive back from the Lord, whether he is a bondservant or is free. (Ephesians 6:8)
>
> Then I saw a great white throne and him who was seated on it. From his presence earth and sky fled away, and no place was found for them.

And I saw the dead, great and small, standing before the throne, and books were opened. Then another book was opened, which is the book of life. And the dead were judged by what was written in the books, according to what they had done. And the sea gave up the dead who were in it, Death and Hades gave up the dead who were in them, and they were judged, each one of them, according to what they had done. Then Death and Hades were thrown into the lake of fire. This is the second death, the lake of fire. And if anyone's name was not found written in the book of life, he was thrown into the lake of fire. (Revelation 20:11–15)

238. Never Lay a Stumbling Block

Therefore let us not pass judgment on one another any longer, but rather decide never to put a stumbling block or hindrance in the way of a brother. —*Romans 14:13*

WE'RE ALL PROBABLY FAMILIAR WITH THE SAYING THAT whenever you see a "wherefore" or a "therefore" you must go back and see what it's there for. In other words, Paul's "therefore" means what he is now exhorting conclusively is based on what he has been arguing. This is the culmination, the resulting praxis, of what a right view of our relationship to judgment and one another should look like in the body of Christ.

We are not to expend our energy passing judgment on others; rather, we are to judge ourselves in whether or not we are putting a stumbling block or hindrance before the path of our brother or sister in Christ.

The two words Paul uses here are instructive: *πρόσκομμα* (*proskomma*) and *σκάνδαλον* (*skandalon*). *Proskomma* is a word that means a loosely laid stone, something for someone to get their foot tangled on where they may twist their ankle or stumble and fall. The word *skandalon* is the Greek word from which we derive our English word *scandal.* It means an action that entices another to sin. Another way to say it is *to lay a temptation trap for another.*

Our work as Christians is not that of judging but of hospitality. We are to clear the way of obstacles for others to fellowship and grow in Christ. And, above all things, it should never be said of us that we participated in causing our brother or sister in Christ to stumble and sin. God forbid we should ever be responsible for a scandal in their lives.

239. Nothing Is Unclean in Itself

I know and am persuaded in the Lord Jesus that nothing is unclean in itself, but it is unclean for anyone who thinks it unclean. —Romans 14:14

AT THIS POINT, PAUL FINDS IT HELPFUL TO LAY OUT THE truth of the matter concerning meats in light of the new creation in Christ. But prior to doing so, it was necessary to establish the priority of charitably tolerating personal convictions of the weak brother on the matter. Ultimately, it is a matter of conscience that is under consideration, not the meats themselves.

Paul establishes that "everything created by God is good, and nothing is to be rejected if it is received with thanksgiving" (1 Timothy 4:4). He has taught this in other places, and it is based not merely on opinion but on the teachings of the Lord Jesus himself (cf. Mark 7:14–23). Nothing is unclean in itself.

However, for the one who thinks it is unclean, it is unclean for him. This is not to suggest matters of conviction are subjective and relegated to personal opinion. Rather, it means that for a weak brother to eat something that is truly clean while he is not convinced of it in his conscience, then he is sinning against his conscience. He is not sinning in the matter of eating the clean thing. He is sinning in the matter of violating his conscience which believes it is unclean (cf. Romans 14:23).

Two implications should be noted in light of all that has been said here (though Paul still has more to say on the matter). First, Paul takes the position of the stronger while tactfully and lovingly accommodating for the weaker. Second, the weaker should not remain weak for the sake of remaining weak but view the gracious tolerance of his fellows as room to build up his conscience according to the truth of Scripture.

240. Do Not Destroy The One for Whom Christ Died

For if your brother is grieved by what you eat, you are no longer walking in love. By what you eat, do not destroy the one for whom Christ died. —*Romans 14:15*

THE STRENGTH OF PAUL'S ADMONITION—"DO NOT DESTROY the one for whom Christ died"—indicates that he is speaking of matters here more profound than simply the displeasure or disapproval of the weaker brother. The Greek word translated "grieved" is *λυπέω* (*lypeo*) and means to cause severe mental or emotional distress. Recall, the issue under consideration is the Mosaic Law regarding diets and days.

Paul is writing to the church during a period of transition—after the resurrection of Christ but before the destruction of the Temple which effectively ended Judaism—in which not all believers were convinced that the new humanity in Christ meant the end of the ceremonial precepts of the Mosaic Law. (This is what the entire book of Hebrews is about, convincing Jewish Christians to not return to their Jewish observations because they were coming to an end. They were merely a shadow of the reality that came—Jesus, cf. Hebrews 10:1)

The principle can be lifted from this situation and be applied in modern circumstances where new believers may come to Christ with some religiously influenced background (i.e., Paganism, occult, false religions) that has malformed their conscience to be troubled by someone's Christian liberty. Where we have opportunity to walk in love, let us be charitable and not grieve our brother or sister in Christ. God forbid we are ever responsible for destroying one for whom Christ died.

241. Good, Evil Spoken Of

So do not let what you regard as good be spoken of as evil. —Romans 14:16

THE EXHORTATION HERE IS SIMPLE. PAUL ADMONISHES THE strong to not allow what is a blessing to be turned into its opposite (i.e., spoken of as evil). It was Christ who has attained this liberty for us and it was Christ who welcomed both weak and strong.

Since the liberty regarding diets and days attained for us by Christ is truly a blessing, the stronger ought, therefore, to regard the needs of the weaker and refrain from any unseasonable use of his liberty. To cause a brother to stumble or to create scandal in the community that in turn overshadowed the matter itself would be self-defeating and unwise. "Scoffers set a city aflame, but the wise turn away wrath" (Proverbs 29:8).

242. Righteousness, Peace, and Joy in the Holy Ghost

For the kingdom of God is not a matter of eating and drinking but of righteousness and peace and joy in the Holy Spirit. —Romans 14:17

WHAT A PROFOUND OBSERVATION PAUL MAKES ABOUT THE priorities of the Kingdom in light of his exhortations to both weak and strong believers in their approach to diets and days.

What is most important about the kingdom of God are those inward virtues of righteousness, peace, and joy in the Holy Spirit. What does eating and drinking have to do with the kingdom? It is not that they are sinful; rather they are non-essential in the grand scheme of things. To prioritize them is to miss the point of the kingdom of God.

> Better is a dinner of herbs where love is than a fattened ox and hatred with it. (Proverbs 15:17)

> Better is a dry morsel with quiet than a house full of feasting with strife. (Proverbs 17:1)

243. Acceptable to God and Approved by Men

For the kingdom of God is not a matter of eating and drinking but of righteousness and peace and joy in the Holy Spirit. Whoever thus serves Christ is acceptable to God and approved by men. So then let us pursue what makes for peace and for mutual upbuilding. —*Romans 14:17–19*

WHOEVER THUS SERVES CHRIST MEANS WHOEVER APPREHENDS what the kingdom of God is and what it is not, and then approximates his life and actions to that knowledge which is acceptable to God and approved by men. In other words, those who have a real consciousness of having been justified by faith in Christ and therefore are at peace with God and filled with a joy that could have only been imparted by God's Holy Spirit (cf. Philippians 4:7) is acceptable, yea, pleasing to God. He will also, because of his disposition of peace and joy, naturally appeal to his fellow man's expectations and receive his approval.

Calvin's comments on this passage are most instructive:

> Wherever then there is righteousness and peace and spiritual joy, there the kingdom of God is complete in all its parts: it does not then consist of material things. But he says, that man is acceptable to God, because he obeys his will; he testifies that he is approved by men, because they cannot do otherwise than bear testimony to that excellency which they see with their eyes: not that the ungodly always favour the children of God; nay, when there is no cause, they often pour forth against them many reproaches, and with forged calumnies defame the innocent, and in a word, turn into vices things rightly done, by putting on them a malignant construction. But Paul speaks here of honest judgment, blended with no moroseness, no hatred, no superstition.[91]

So then, says Paul, armed with this knowledge, let us pursue what makes for peace and mutual edification rather than pursuing our differences of opinions regarding days and diets.

91. John Calvin and John Owen, *Commentary on the Epistle of Paul the Apostle to the Romans* (Bellingham, WA: Logos Bible Software, 2010), 508.

244. Do Not Destroy the Work of God

Do not, for the sake of food, destroy the work of God. Everything is indeed clean, but it is wrong for anyone to make another stumble by what he eats. It is good not to eat meat or drink wine or do anything that causes your brother to stumble.
—Romans 14:20–21

IN TRUE PAULINE FASHION, THE APOSTLE SUMMARIZES WHAT he has been arguing. He makes a generic declaration that all things—diets and days—are clean; but what is not clean is to make another stumble by our liberty and destroy the work of God. Just as it is good to eat or drink freely; it is also equally good to keep one's brother from stumbling. We have liberty and privilege to do both. And if these two goods happen to cross ways, then we should choose our brother's welfare over food.

One question that might raise a question is how a mere mortal could "destroy the work of God." Jesus explained to his disciples that in this life "Temptations to sin are sure to come, but woe to the one through whom they come!" (Luke 17:1).

245. The Faith That You Have

The faith that you have, keep between yourself and God. Blessed is the one who has no reason to pass judgment on himself for what he approves. But whoever has doubts is condemned if he eats, because the eating is not from faith. For whatever does not proceed from faith is sin. —Romans 14:22–23

BY THE PHRASE *THE FAITH THAT YOU HAVE*, PAUL MEANS THE conviction by which the stronger is fully persuaded concerning diets and days. Paul is not diminishing the legitimacy of the stronger believers' liberty in Christ. But out of deference to his weaker brother, it is best to keep that conviction between himself and God.

There is a blessing, a certain joyful benefit, that comes to the one who refrains from putting himself in the position to condemn himself for violating his conscience. Ultimately, the believer needs to build his conscience according to the word of God; this can take time. In the meantime, it would be a sin to partake in a liberty one is not fully convinced is available to him. It is a sin to do anything that is contrary to faith (that of which one is fully convinced), even if that faith is immature or misguided.

But it is equally sinful to neglect growing up unto Christ, which is the building up of one's conscience by continually examining it in light of the word of God (cf. Ephesians 4:15, 1 Peter 2:2, 2 Peter 3:18).

246. Obligation to Bear the Weak

We who are strong have an obligation to bear with the failings of the weak, and not to please ourselves. —Romans 15:1

THOSE WHO HAVE ADVANCED FURTHER IN THE GOSPEL HAVE no place to be proud or puffed up; rather, the grace of growth comes with responsibility. In the same way the master must take the apprentice under his wing and mentor him, so must the stronger carry the heavier end of the load.

In his commentary on this passage, John Calvin rightly posits this principle is true of all of God's good gifts:

> For as God has destined those to whom he has granted superior knowledge to convey instruction to the ignorant, so to those whom he makes strong he commits the duty of supporting the weak by their strength; thus ought all gifts to be communicated among all the members of Christ. The stronger then any one is in Christ, the more bound he is to bear with the weak.[92]

As a concluding thought, it's notable that Paul is not preaching something he doesn't practice himself. He explains in his first letter to the Corinthians:

> For though I am free from all, I have made myself a servant to all, that I might win more of them. To the Jews I became as a Jew, in order to win Jews. To those under the law I became as one under the law (though not being myself under the law) that I might win those under the law. To those outside the law I became as one outside the law (not being outside the law of God but under the law of Christ) that I might win those outside the law. To the weak I became weak, that I might win the weak. I have become all things to all people, that by all means I might save some. I do it all for the sake of the gospel, that I may share with them in its blessings. (1 Corinthians 9:19–23)

92. John Calvin and John Owen, *Commentary on the Epistle of Paul the Apostle to the Romans* (Bellingham, WA: Logos Bible Software, 2010), 514.

247. For Our Neighbors' Good

Let each of us please his neighbor for his good, to build him up. For Christ did not please himself, but as it is written, "The reproaches of those who reproached you fell on me." —Romans 15:2–3

THE ROLE EACH OF US PLAYS IN THE COMMUNITY OF SAINTS is that of edifier. Though we are each endowed with different and varying gifts, we are to seek the good of our neighbor over pleasing our own selves—especially if one is in a leadership role. Paul exhorted the Ephesians in the same way when he wrote,

> And he gave the apostles, the prophets, the evangelists, the shepherds and teachers, to equip the saints for the work of ministry, for building up the body of Christ, until we all attain to the unity of the faith and of the knowledge of the Son of God, to mature manhood, to the measure of the stature of the fullness of Christ, so that we may no longer be children, tossed to and fro by the waves and carried about by every wind of doctrine, by human cunning, by craftiness in deceitful schemes. (Ephesians 4:11–14)

Previously it was noted that Paul practiced what he preached by submitting to others (i.e., pleasing his neighbors) for their good. But our ultimate example is Christ, who did not come to please himself but to humble himself for our sakes (1 Peter 2:24). He bore our reproach; as his followers, we too must bear our brothers' reproach. This attitude of bearing with and building up our neighbor can be variously applied as it's the true piety of a Christian.

> Whoever humbles himself like this child is the greatest in the kingdom of heaven. Whoever receives one such child in my name receives me, but whoever causes one of these little ones who believe in me to sin, it would be better for him to have a great millstone fastened around his neck and to be drowned in the depth of the sea. (Matthew 18:4–6)

Brothers, if anyone is caught in any transgression, you who are spiritual should restore him in a spirit of gentleness. Keep watch on yourself, lest you too be tempted. (Galatians 6:1)

Religion that is pure and undefiled before God the Father is this: to visit orphans and widows in their affliction, and to keep oneself unstained from the world. (James 1:27)

248. Written for Our Instruction

For Christ did not please himself, but as it is written, "The reproaches of those who reproached you fell on me." For whatever was written in former days was written for our instruction, that through endurance and through the encouragement of the Scriptures we might have hope. —Romans 15:3–4

AS WE HAVE SEEN PREVIOUSLY, CHRIST IS OUR EXAMPLE IN pleasing others before pleasing ourselves and in bearing with the weaker. After all, it is only by his grace that we are as strong as we are in our faith. But from where does Paul draw this example? From Scripture, of course. He cites Psalm 69, applying the truth of the passage to Christ who did indeed lay down his own life for us.

> Let not those who hope in you be put to shame through me, O Lord God of hosts; let not those who seek you be brought to dishonor through me, O God of Israel. For it is for your sake that I have borne reproach, that dishonor has covered my face. I have become a stranger to my brothers, an alien to my mother's sons. For zeal for your house has consumed me, and the reproaches of those who reproach you have fallen on me. (Psalm 69:6–9)

Paul is not finished. He doesn't leave his audience with this lesson alone. Like a good teacher, he shows off the *universal* truth which has been employed to teach his audience this *particular* truth about Christ's example.

It is as if Paul says to his readers, "Do you see what I just did there? I used Scripture to teach you this lesson. 'All Scripture is breathed out by God and profitable for teaching, for reproof, for correction, and for training in righteousness'" (cf. 2 Timothy 3:16).

Charles Hodge explains what Paul was doing in verses 3–4: "The object of this verse is not so much to show the propriety of applying the passage quoted from the Psalms to Christ, as to show that the facts recorded in the Scriptures are designed for our instruction."[93]

93. Charles Hodge, A Commentary on the Epistle to the Romans, New Edition (Grand Rapids, MI: Louis Kregel, 1882), 682.

Paul uses his example of employing Scripture to make his primary point to also show us that there is nothing in the Scripture that is vain or unprofitable. We should learn the Scriptures so that we might apply the universal truths lifted from the particular occasions for which they were written to give us wisdom in this generation. This is true both of the Old Testament (shame on those who opine it is of no relevance to us in the church age) and of the writings of the apostles. He is the same Spirit who authored both, never unlike himself from one generation to another.

It is through the endurance and encouragement of the Scriptures that believers in all ages find their hope!

249. In Harmony with One Another

May the God of endurance and encouragement grant you to live in such harmony with one another, in accord with Christ Jesus, that together you may with one voice glorify the God and Father of our Lord Jesus Christ. Therefore welcome one another as Christ has welcomed you, for the glory of God. —Romans 15:5–7

HERE PAUL CLOSES HIS EXHORTATION BY OFFERING A BENEdiction. He prays for those he has just instructed, knowing that unless the God of endurance and encouragement grant them his blessing, his words will have been offered in vain. His prayer is that they would live in harmony with each other as each seeks to live in harmony (accord) with Christ. It is the harmony of God's people that allows for their praise to be of one voice.

And because he trusts that God will hear his prayer and grant them to live in such harmony with one another, he follows his benediction with a charge animated by Christ's example.

May God grant you the grace to live in harmony with one another. And because God will grant you the grace to do this being of the company of the redeemed, being members of the new humanity, go and live in harmony. Just as Christ has welcomed you to the family of God, warts and all, welcome each other for the glory of God!

250. To Confirm the Promises

For I tell you that Christ became a servant to the circumcised to show God's truthfulness, in order to confirm the promises given to the patriarchs, and in order that the Gentiles might glorify God for his mercy. As it is written,

> *"Therefore I will praise you among the Gentiles,*
> *and sing to your name."*

—Romans 15:8–9

THE GREEK WORK FOR "GENTILES" IN PAUL'S WRITING IS ἔθνεσι (*ethnesi*) from which we get our English word ethnicity. The Hebrew word for "nations" in Psalm 18:49 is *goyhim* translated ἔθνεσι (*ethnesi*) in the LXX, the translation of Old Testament Paul would have been using.

Following the benediction and charge of verses 5–7, Paul further affirms by way of explanation and by way of scriptural witness that Christ became a servant to both Jew and Gentile alike. He has torn down the middle wall of partition between them so that both will praise God and sing his name together. The order of their salvation was merely strategic.

First, Christ became a servant to the Jews to fulfill the promises God made to the Jews by way of Abraham, Isaac, and Jacob. And Christ's ministry to the Jews was in fact a witness to the Gentiles (the various ethnicities) that the God of Abraham, Isaac, and Jacob is faithful to keep his promises to them. In other words, his prioritizing the Jews was not because they were somehow more faithful or righteous. He saved them first so they would be a priestly witness to the rest of the tribes.

To support his proposition, he then quotes from Psalm 18: "For this I will praise you, O Lord, among the nations, and sing to your name" (v. 49).

251. Rejoice, O Gentiles!

And again it is said,

> *"Rejoice, O Gentiles, with his people."*

And again,

> *"Praise the Lord, all you Gentiles,*
> *and let all the peoples extol him."*

And again Isaiah says,

> *"The root of Jesse will come,*
> *even he who arises to rule the Gentiles;*
> *in him will the Gentiles hope."*

—Romans 15:10–12

ADDING TO HIS QUOTATION OF PSALM 18:49 FROM VSS. 8–9, Paul then pulls a number of additional examples from the Old Testament Scriptures (Deuteronomy 32:43, Psalm 117:1, and Isaiah 11:10) to establish conclusively that the Gentile inclusion in the kingdom of God was not a Christian innovation. Matthew quotes the same passage from Isaiah to demonstrate a similar point in Matthew 12:15–21.

> Jesus, aware of this, withdrew from there. And many followed him, and he healed them all and ordered them not to make him known. This was to fulfill what was spoken by the prophet Isaiah: "Behold, my servant whom I have chosen, my beloved with whom my soul is well pleased. I will put my Spirit upon him, and he will proclaim justice to the Gentiles. He will not quarrel or cry aloud, nor will anyone hear his voice in the streets; a bruised reed he will not break, and a smoldering wick he will not quench, until he brings justice to victory; and in his name the Gentiles will hope." (Matthew 12:15–21)

The inclusion of the Gentiles in the kingdom of God was part of God's plan all along; and it is through Jesus Christ that this part of his plan is fulfilled. God started with the Jews, made them a priestly nation, and through them sent the world a Messiah, Jesus.

252. Joy and Peace in Believing

May the God of hope fill you with all joy and peace in believing, so that by the power of the Holy Spirit you may abound in hope. —Romans 15:13

BEFORE TURNING HIS ATTENTION TO SPEAKING OF HIS OWN ministry, Paul offers a final prayer on their behalf to the end that they will achieve the joy and peace in believing of which he just spoke. By living with each other's best interest in mind and doing so by the power of the Holy Spirit, all believers—Jews and Gentiles—may abound in the hope that comes through the patience and comfort of the Scriptures.

The world is a troubling place because of sin. But God has given us hope in Christ. When we live out the new lives given to us by Christ through faith in the gospel, and seek the welfare of our neighbors before ourselves, we emulate Christ who laid down his life for us. The product of this way of living is joy and peace and hope. When we emulate the world who seeks its own pleasures before the welfare of others, we harvest the same fruit as they—sorrow, discord, and despair.

253. Satisfied That You Are Full of Goodness

I myself am satisfied about you, my brothers, that you yourselves are full of goodness, filled with all knowledge and able to instruct one another. But on some points I have written to you very boldly by way of reminder, because of the grace given me by God to be a minister of Christ Jesus to the Gentiles in the priestly service of the gospel of God, so that the offering of the Gentiles may be acceptable, sanctified by the Holy Spirit. —Romans 15:14–16

PAUL BEGINS TO TRANSITION HIS LETTER FROM STRONG exhortation and teaching to mollifying the Roman church just before offering his salutation in which he appeals to their generosity for support to go to Spain. However, he is not attempting to lessen the exhortations by concession of his message but by assuring them of his faith in their goodness and ability to instruct one another is what is right.

Calvin says Paul made this statement, "with the view of pacifying the Romans, in case they thought themselves reproved by so many and so urgent admonitions, and thus unjustly treated," and suggests,

> There was much pride in the Romans; the name even of their city made the lowest of the people proud; so that they could hardly bear a teacher of another nation, much less a barbarian and a Jew. With this haughtiness Paul would not contend in his own private name: he however subdued it, as it were, by soothing means; for he testified that he undertook to address them on account of his Apostolic office.[94]

Nevertheless, Paul does soften his strong exhortations by appealing to his office as a minister to the Gentiles and saying he was, in a word, only preaching to the choir. But he needed to do this, not because he didn't think well of the church, but because his office demanded it of him. His role as a minister of the gospel was to ensure the full harmonious inclusion of the Gentiles into the church by means of the gospel of Christ and the sanctification of the Holy Spirit.

94. John Calvin and John Owen, *Commentary on the Epistle of Paul the Apostle to the Romans* (Bellingham, WA: Logos Bible Software, 2010), 525–526.

254. Proud of My Work for God

In Christ Jesus, then, I have reason to be proud of my work for God. For I will not venture to speak of anything except what Christ has accomplished through me to bring the Gentiles to obedience—by word and deed . . . —Romans 15:17–18

HAVING PREVIOUSLY COMMENDED HIS OFFICE AS "A MINISTER of Christ Jesus to the Gentiles," he now glories in the work he has accomplished in that office for the glory of God. The word translated proud here is the Greek word, *καύχησιν* (*kauchesin*), which means "to boast or take pride in."

Perhaps this is worrisome for some who see all boasting as sinful. Let us, however, take his statement in its proper context. Paul could have genuinely boasted of many great things; but he doesn't. As R.C. Sproul points out in his commentary on this passage,

> He penned more of the New Testament than any other writer; he did more, according to Acts, than any other apostle; he unquestionably had the keenest theological mind of any in the early church, and probably all of church history. We can only speculate how many were converted through his ministry in his own day, far less through the ages because of his writings.[95]

But Paul's exultation is not self glorification; it is an exultation in which he glories in "what Christ has accomplished through him to bring the Gentiles to obedience."

Further, it would be irresponsible to take what a person writes in one place and not consider their thoughts on the same issue in other places in order to gain a full perspective of their view. It might benefit us then to consider what Paul says of his ability and right to boast when writing to the Philippian Christians:

95. R. C. Sproul, *The Gospel of God: An Exposition of Romans* (Great Britain: Christian Focus Publications, 1994), 244–245.

For we are the circumcision, who worship by the Spirit of God and glory in Christ Jesus and put no confidence in the flesh— though I myself have reason for confidence in the flesh also. If anyone else thinks he has reason for confidence in the flesh, I have more: circumcised on the eighth day, of the people of Israel, of the tribe of Benjamin, a Hebrew of Hebrews; as to the law, a Pharisee; as to zeal, a persecutor of the church; as to righteousness under the law, blameless. But whatever gain I had, I counted as loss for the sake of Christ. Indeed, I count everything as loss because of the surpassing worth of knowing Christ Jesus my Lord. For his sake I have suffered the loss of all things and count them as rubbish, in order that I may gain Christ and be found in him, not having a righteousness of my own that comes from the law, but that which comes through faith in Christ, the righteousness from God that depends on faith— that I may know him and the power of his resurrection, and may share his sufferings, becoming like him in his death, that by any means possible I may attain the resurrection from the dead." (Philippians 3:3–11)

255. Fulfilled the Ministry

In Christ Jesus, then, I have reason to be proud of my work for God. For I will not venture to speak of anything except what Christ has accomplished through me to bring the Gentiles to obedience—by word and deed, by the power of signs and wonders, by the power of the Spirit of God—so that from Jerusalem and all the way around to Illyricum I have fulfilled the ministry of the gospel of Christ . . .
—Romans 15:17–19

AS PAUL GLORIES IN THE WORK HE HAS ACCOMPLISHED AS "A minister of Christ Jesus to the Gentiles," he establishes his office as an apostle by sharing what that work looks like in object, in effect, and in scope.

First, the object of his work was *to bring the Gentiles to obedience.*

Second, the effectiveness of his work could be seen in the effectiveness of the word when he preached, the effectiveness of the deeds he accomplished, and the power of the miracles God did in his midst and on his behalf. These are all evidence of the Holy Spirit of God working through him. Paul points to this supernatural effectiveness to demonstrate that he had been appointed by the Lord for this work.

Third, the scope of his work, which extended from Jerusalem to what is modern day Bosnia and Croatia is further proof that God's Spirit was upon him. The idea that he has *fulfilled* the ministry of the gospel of Christ means he has both supplied the region with the truth of the gospel and perfected the work (as much as was humanly possible) in the churches that were established. His ministry, in effect, supplied what was spiritually lacking.

Perhaps we can take away from this Paul's example who answered the call God had placed upon him (Acts 9) and fulfilled his vocation successfully by the power of God alone. In other words, the success in one's calling may be seen as validation of God's blessing when it is achieved without the tricks and schemes of men and accomplished in the power of God alone.

256. Ambition to Preach the Gospel

... and thus I make it my ambition to preach the gospel, not where Christ has already been named, lest I build on someone else's foundation, but as it is written,

> *"Those who have never been told of him will see,*
> *and those who have never heard will understand."*

—Romans 15:20–21

HERE WE GET A GLIMPSE OF PAUL'S MISSIONARY HEART. HE IS a church planter, a trailblazer, a pioneer. It is not out of arrogance that Paul makes this claim; rather, it is from a promise that he draws from Isaiah 52, a messianic passage that speaks of what the Jews called the Suffering Servant (Isaiah 52:13–53:12). Paul identifies Christ as the Suffering Servant and the source of the missionary impulse. God through his prophet Isaiah has made a promise that there will be people who have never heard of Christ who will be saved if someone preaches the gospel to them.

Though two millennia later, most of the world has heard the name of Jesus, there are still pockets of people around the world who don't know the name of Christ, people who have never heard the name by which we must be saved. "And there is salvation in no one else, for there is no other name under heaven given among men by which we must be saved" (Acts 4:12).

257. I Hope to See You

This is the reason why I have so often been hindered from coming to you. But now, since I no longer have any room for work in these regions, and since I have longed for many years to come to you, I hope to see you in passing as I go to Spain, and to be helped on my journey there by you, once I have enjoyed your company for a while. —Romans 15:22–24

HIS APOSTLESHIP AND CALLING TO TAKE THE GOSPEL WHERE it has not been heard is the reason Paul gives for having not visited the church at Rome sooner. However, since the gospel seed has been so planted in those regions that there remains no more fields to seed, and since he has desired to see them for many years, he is hopeful the opportunity to come to them has finally presented itself.

As a matter of fact, Paul adds, he can visit them on his way to Spain, a mission field he hopes to open up. And after he has enjoyed their company for a while, he is hopeful they will be able to help him get to Spain by means of prayer and financial support. After all, this is the primary purpose for his writing to the Church at Rome—his reason behind the reason for expounding the gospel so thoroughly.

It seems there are at least two noteworthy observations one can draw from this passage. First, Paul operates not only by faith but also by hope (Romans 8:25, cf. 1 Corinthians 13:13). These are connected but not exactly the same. It is true he is hopeful by faith, but it is hope that motivates his ministry. He is hopeful regarding eternity; he is hopeful regarding the power of the gospel; he is hopeful about the faith and generosity of God's people; he is hopeful he will be able to go to Spain.

Second, there is no real evidence of Paul having made the journey to Spain. It seems the early church fathers and historians (i.e., Origin and Eusebius) have no knowledge of Paul making the journey to Spain and there are only much later historians that appear to have speculated or even invented stories about Paul's journey.

In any event, while Christians have every reason to remain hopeful—"He who calls you is faithful; he will surely do it" (1 Thessalonians 5:24)—we must also learn to manage our own expectations by trusting the Lord when our earthly desires don't manifest in the ways we hoped.

258. The Fullness of the Blessing of Christ

At present, however, I am going to Jerusalem bringing aid to the saints. For Macedonia and Achaia have been pleased to make some contribution for the poor among the saints at Jerusalem. For they were pleased to do it, and indeed they owe it to them. For if the Gentiles have come to share in their spiritual blessings, they ought also to be of service to them in material blessings. When therefore I have completed this and have delivered to them what has been collected, I will leave for Spain by way of you. I know that when I come to you I will come in the fullness of the blessing of Christ. —Romans 15:25–29

IN THIS PERICOPE, PAUL ACCOMPLISHES TWO THINGS IN HIS relationship with the Roman church. In the first place, he explains to them his travel plans as a way of helping them manage their expectations. Lest they feel themselves deceived by what they might perceive to be his lingering, he lets them know about the ministry project that is currently occupying his attention.

It seems the Grecian churches (Macedonia and Achaia) had learned of the dire needs among the Jewish saints in Jerusalem and had taken up a love offering to relieve their brothers and sisters across the Mediterranean. The reasoning that motivated this kind of unusual generosity was the Grecian believers saw themselves as spiritually indebted to the Jewish believers for sharing the gospel with them when they were impoverished spiritually. Meeting the need of the fiscally impoverished saints at Jerusalem was an opportunity to pay a debt as it were.

The second thing Paul accomplishes by telling this story is he enlightens their imaginations. He teaches them by way of illustration about the kind of unity he has been preaching to them in his letter. The Gentile Christians in Greece were generous to the Jewish Christians in Jerusalem because they saw themselves as unified, as equally part of the body of Christ. They believed, as Paul taught elsewhere, "For he himself is our peace, who has made us both one and has broken down in his flesh the dividing wall of hostility" (Ephesians 2:14).

Further, by encouraging their unity and generosity by way of example, Paul is also preparing the church at Rome to receive him and his goal of taking the gospel to Spain with the same spirit, with "the fullness of the blessing of Christ."

259. Strive Together with Me

I appeal to you, brothers, by our Lord Jesus Christ and by the love of the Spirit, to strive together with me in your prayers to God on my behalf, that I may be delivered from the unbelievers in Judea, and that my service for Jerusalem may be acceptable to the saints, so that by God's will I may come to you with joy and be refreshed in your company. May the God of peace be with you all. Amen. —Romans 15:30–33

PAUL CONCLUDES THE HEART OF HIS LETTER WITH A STRONG appeal. Referring to the church at Rome as his brothers, he makes the affectionate appeal in the name of their mutual redeemer, the Lord Jesus, and by the love of the Spirit by whom he also appealed for the church's own affectionate unity earlier in the letter (Romans 14:17; 15:13,16).

It was a heavy burden Paul carried, knowing that the Jews, particularly those in Judea, had it in for him. He was even warned by the Spirit of God that he would be in danger if he went: "except that the Holy Spirit testifies to me in every city that imprisonment and afflictions await me" (Acts 20:23). As he indicated early in his letter, there were slanders who believed Paul taught false doctrine (i.e., doing evil so good will come, cf. Romans 3:8) but there were also the Jews who believed he taught departure from the Mosaic Law (cf. Acts 21:20–21).

His appeal is that they would strive together with him in prayer about his situation. By strive together, Paul means to be of one mind with him concerning Christ and concerning his three-fold petition (cf. Philippians 2:1–8, Colossians 1:7–8; 4:12; 2:1–2; 2 Corinthians 1:11).

His threefold petition is that he would be delivered from the zealous Jews, that his ministry of taking financial means from the Grecian churches to the church at Jerusalem would be an acceptable blessing, and that he might finally make it to Rome to see them and be refreshed by their fellowship.

As he concludes his appeal with a benediction—*May the God of peace be with you all. Amen*—we are able to see the heart of the apostle, a man of God who not only risked his life for the gospel but carried with him everyday, the burden of caring for the churches (2 Corinthians 11:28).

260. Our Sister Phoebe

I commend to you our sister Phoebe, a servant of the church at Cenchreae, that you may welcome her in the Lord in a way worthy of the saints, and help her in whatever she may need from you, for she has been a patron of many and of myself as well. —Romans 16:1–2

THE REMAINDER OF PAUL'S LETTER CONSISTS OF SALUTATIONS, commending those saints who have served the church and helped him in the ministry. He begins with Phoebe, whom he calls διάκονος (*dikonos*, translated "servant" in regard to activity or "deacon/deaconess" when it regards a church office).

It is clear from this passage that Paul had no issue with deaconesses. Many of the church fathers concurred (Origen, Chrysostom, Theodoret, etc.). Given the anachronistic nature of modern controversies surrounding women holding office in the church, it is best for us to simply take passages like this one at face value.

The Scripture says Phoebe was διάκονον τῆς ἐκκλησίας (*diakonon tēs ekklesias*). Since *ekklesias* is in the genitive case, the context means we translate it as a preposition, "of the church." Phoebe was a *diakonon* of the church at Cenchreae (a port city near Corinth). The next question is whether or not that means she held an office or just served the church like everyone else. Given the fact she was being commended to the church at Rome and Paul was asking them to receive her with hospitality, meant she would be carrying his letter to them. All indicators point to her carrying out duties in an official capacity.

One theory is that a female deacon (i.e, deaconess) in Paul's day might possibly refer to those widows he describes in his letter to Timothy (his son in the ministry) who are above sixty years old who committed to living out their days serving the church. Consider this excerpt in which he instructs Timothy in how to minister to widows:

> Let a widow be enrolled if she is not less than sixty years of age, having been the wife of one husband, and having a reputation for good works:

> if she has brought up children, has shown hospitality, has washed the feet of the saints, has cared for the afflicted, and has devoted herself to every good work. But refuse to enroll younger widows, for when their passions draw them away from Christ, they desire to marry and so incur condemnation for having abandoned their former faith. Besides that, they learn to be idlers, going about from house to house, and not only idlers, but also gossips and busybodies, saying what they should not. So I would have younger widows marry, bear children, manage their households, and give the adversary no occasion for slander. For some have already strayed after Satan. If any believing woman has relatives who are widows, let her care for them. Let the church not be burdened, so that it may care for those who are truly widows. (1 Timothy 5:9–16)

The word translated 'enrolled' in verse 9 of this excerpt is καταλέγω (*katalego*), which means to enumerate or to make a selection for membership in a group. It is often used for soldiers who are counted members of the rank and file.

Phoebe appears to also be a wealthy woman, or at least a woman of means, for Paul calls her a patron (*προστάτις / prostatis*), which is synonymous with *benefactor* (NIV) or *succorer* (KJV).

This relationship suggested by the term *prostatis* should not be confused with the Roman patron-client system, which was of a different order and alien to Greek tradition. Phoebe was a woman who had generously and faithfully supported the church with her life and her resources (i.e., time and money). Because she was carrying out the duties of a courier to the church at Rome, Paul urges them to receive her as a faithful servant of the church, one who was worthy of the saints, as his own sister in Christ. To this, the Greek father Chrysostom remarks, "Note how many ways Paul dignifies Phoebe. He mentions her before all the rest and even calls her his sister. It is no small thing to be called the sister of Paul! Moreover, he has mentioned her rank of deaconess as well.[96]

96. *Homilies on Romans* 30.3 (NPNF) 1 11:549–50 cited in Gerald Bray, ed., Romans (Revised), Ancient Christian Commentary on Scripture (Downers Grove, IL: InterVarsity Press, 1998), 355–356.

In the modern commercialized world of church hopping and church shopping, one can see, by contrast, how valuable a faithful testimony is, especially in the days when the church was yet to be widely recognized. Perhaps this is worth further contemplation as we see the Church's influence and recognition in remarkable decline in the modern world.

261. Fellow Workers and First Fruits

Greet Prisca and Aquila, my fellow workers in Christ Jesus, who risked their necks for my life, to whom not only I give thanks but all the churches of the Gentiles give thanks as well. Greet also the church in their house. Greet my beloved Epaenetus, who was the first convert to Christ in Asia. —Romans 16:3–5

IN A CULTURE THAT FAIRLY OFTEN TENDED TO DISMISS women as being insignificant, Paul is not ashamed to identify the faithful women who served Christ as his fellow laborer. First, he commends Phoebe, now Paul commends Pricilla (Prisca) and her husband Aquila, whom he calls "fellow workers in Christ Jesus."

The most we find in Scripture about this couple comes from Paul's historian, Luke, in his Acts of the Apostles:

> After this Paul left Athens and went to Corinth. And he found a Jew named Aquila, a native of Pontus, recently come from Italy with his wife Priscilla, because Claudius had commanded all the Jews to leave Rome. And he went to see them, and because he was of the same trade he stayed with them and worked, for they were tentmakers by trade. And he reasoned in the synagogue every Sabbath, and tried to persuade Jews and Greeks. (Acts 18:1–4)

The Roman Historian, Tacitus, tells us the Jews were put out of Rome because they were causing a stir in the city over someone named *Chrestus.* Many scholars suspect it was a variant spelling of *Christos,* and he meant Christ Jesus. In any case, Paul commends this couple as having risked their lives to save his. For this he gives thanks, and then further acknowledges that all the churches give thanks for this couple as well. Likely, Paul was not the only Christian they helped.

Finally, Paul greets the church that is meeting in Priscilla and Aquila's house and also, Epaenetus who was a firstfruit in his Asiatic ministry. The English word *convert* here is the Greek word, *ἀπαρχὴ* (*apache*), which literally means firstfruit. Paul seems to give honor for the firstfruits of his ministry in the various regions where he preached. See also 1 Corinthians 16:15: "Now I urge you, brothers—you know that the household of Stephanas were the first converts in Achaia, and that they have devoted themselves to the service of the saints . . ."

262. Terms of Endearment

Greet Mary, who has worked hard for you. Greet Andronicus and Junia, my kinsmen and my fellow prisoners. They are well known to the apostles, and they were in Christ before me. Greet Ampliatus, my beloved in the Lord. Greet Urbanus, our fellow worker in Christ, and my beloved Stachys. Greet Apelles, who is approved in Christ. Greet those who belong to the family of Aristobulus. Greet my kinsman Herodion. Greet those in the Lord who belong to the family of Narcissus. Greet those workers in the Lord, Tryphaena and Tryphosa. Greet the beloved Persis, who has worked hard in the Lord. Greet Rufus, chosen in the Lord; also his mother, who has been a mother to me as well. Greet Asyncritus, Phlegon, Hermes, Patrobas, Hermas, and the brothers who are with them. Greet Philologus, Julia, Nereus and his sister, and Olympas, and all the saints who are with them. Greet one another with a holy kiss. All the churches of Christ greet you. —Romans 16:6–16

PAUL CONTINUES TO WRAP UP THE LETTER WITH A LENGTHY passage of greetings to his friends and fellows in Christ who are residing in Rome. Though there is some speculation, and not a few educated theories about the various people listed here, what is most important is that Paul viewed these as dear saints, as fellows with him in the new humanity, the redeemed of Christ.

He refers to Andronicus and Junia not only as kinsman, either Jews or some blood relation, but also fellow prisoners. There is some special bond that develops between those who suffer together for the sake of righteousness and Paul counts these among that special rank. He also says that they were well-known to the apostles. The Greek word is the same as that used for the twelve disciples of Jesus, but most translators translate ἀποστόλοις (apostolois) here in minuscule because Paul seems here to be using the word to refer to those who are sent out of the church to plant churches rather than the Twelve, the original disciples of Jesus.

Other descriptive expressions Paul uses in his list are beloved, fellow worker, approved in Christ, family, kinsman, those in the Lord, those who have worked hard, chosen in the Lord, mother to me, brothers, sister, and saints. Each of this descriptions says something about their gifts and ministries for the cause of Christ but most importantly all of them are terms of endearment.

In conclusion, Paul exhorts the entire church to greet one another with a holy kiss, an intimate, familial expression of affection. In return, he greets them on behalf of all the churches of Christ, reminding them they are part of an even larger family of believers, the new tribe of the redeemed.

263. Brothers, Watch Out!

I appeal to you, brothers, to watch out for those who cause divisions and create obstacles contrary to the doctrine that you have been taught; avoid them. For such persons do not serve our Lord Christ, but their own appetites, and by smooth talk and flattery they deceive the hearts of the naive. —Romans 16:17–18

TWENTY TIMES IN THIS LETTER, PAUL APPEALS TO THE church as his brothers. This is a term that is as much endearing as it is an acknowledgement of their identity in the family of God. He warns his brothers to watch for those who would hinder the gospel work and injure the flock.

Paul warns them how to identify a wolf: it is one who causes divisions and creates a scandal over the instructions of the apostles. The ESV renders the English as saying 'create obstacles contrary to the doctrine that you have been taught.' It is a fine translation but seeing the word Paul actually uses can be helpful in seeing the critical nuance: σκάνδαλα (scandala)

In the New Testament, *σκάνδαλα* (scandala) is used four times in this form and is translated "causes of sin," "temptations," and "temptations to sin," in addition to this translation of "obstacles." The translation here seems fairly tame compared to the other translations of the word that gives us the English word scandal or to scandalize.

Those who divide the church and create temptations for those in the body of Christ to contend against the established teachings of the church are to be avoided. They are insincere no matter how believable they seem. They serve their own appetites and not the Lord Jesus Christ. The reason they sound so compelling and believable is because they are sophists: they flatter, and they use smooth speech to deceive the naive.

An interesting note is the single Greek word translated "smooth talk" is *χρηστολογία* (*chrestologia*). In classical Greek culture, a *χρηστολόγος* (*chrestologos*) is a bad person who makes a fine speech.[97]

97. William Arndt et al., *A Greek-English Lexicon of the New Testament and Other Early Christian Literature* (Chicago: University of Chicago Press, 2000), 1089–1090.

Beware brothers! Watch out for the sophists, those smooth-talking, scandal-making, schismatics.

264. Be Wise and Innocent

For your obedience is known to all, so that I rejoice over you, but I want you to be wise as to what is good and innocent as to what is evil. —Romans 16:19

IMMEDIATELY UPON WARNING THEM OF THE SCANDAL MAKers, the wolves so to speak, he commends them for their obedience lest they assume he thought unfavorably of them. Not so. Rather, he rejoices over them for their renowned obedience to the Lord.

He exhorts them to be wise concerning those things that are good and innocent toward those things that are evil. Given the context of both the larger exhortation to foster peace between Jew and Gentile and the more immediate context to beware of those who scandalize by causing division and undermining the teaching of the apostles, good and evil here seem to be benevolence toward one another and sophistry (i.e., smooth talk and flattery), respectively.

In other words, Paul is saying I know you have a renowned testimony for your obedience to Christ but beware of those who cause division by smooth talking and flattery. Make sure you're committing yourselves to welcoming one another and avoiding cunning and duplicitous speech.

265. Peace and Grace

The God of peace will soon crush Satan under your feet. The grace of our Lord Jesus Christ be with you. —*Romans 16:20*

PAUL CONCLUDES HIS EXHORTATION CONCERNING THEIR unity—to be wise concerning those things that are good and innocent toward those things that are evil—with a promise and a prayer.

He reassures them with the promise that the God of peace would soon make them victorious. Paul refers to God as *the God of peace* because unity and division seems to be, by all accounts, the biggest challenge the church at Rome was needing to overcome.

Satan, who is the author of confusion, and a liar and murderer from the beginning, would soon be crushed by their obedience to the gospel (Genesis 3:15, cf. Luke 10:17–19; Rev. 12:11). The God who saves lawless, contentious sinners is a God of peace. To be saved from lawlessness is to be made peaceful. And by living out the gospel that saved them, God would soon crush Satan *under their feet.*

Further, those who dwelt in Rome would be utterly familiar with the *Pax Romana* (peace of Rome) mantra. Rome, violent as it was, brought peace in a way never before seen in the ancient world, albeit through force. But there was a peace more glorious than what Rome could achieve. God, through Christ, had established a new humanity whose chief attribute was peace, just as Jesus had told his disciples: "By this all people will know that you are my disciples, if you have love for one another" (John 13:35).

But they would need the unmerited assistance of the Holy Spirit, the gift (or grace) of our Lord Jesus. To this end, Paul prays for his friends and fellow believers in Rome.

266. Particular Greetings

Timothy, my fellow worker, greets you; so do Lucius and Jason and Sosipater, my kinsmen.

I Tertius, who wrote this letter, greet you in the Lord.

Gaius, who is host to me and to the whole church, greets you. Erastus, the city treasurer, and our brother Quartus, greet you. —*Romans 16:21–23*

BY INCLUDING THE GREETINGS OF THE FELLOW LABORERS with him, Paul is fostering unity amongst the believers throughout the world, ratifying his epistle by showing others had consented to its content, and lifting up models of faithful Christians to whose character and service the Roman Christians can also aspire.

Among those present with Paul is Timothy, the younger pastor to whom Paul wrote two epistles that were recorded in canon. Paul's commendations of Timothy throughout Scripture testify to his remarkable character. In his second letter to Timothy, Paul refers to him as his "beloved child" (2 Timothy 1:2). In his letter to the Philippians, he writes,

> I hope in the Lord Jesus to send Timothy to you soon, so that I too may be cheered by news of you. For I have no one like him, who will be genuinely concerned for your welfare. For they all seek their own interests, not those of Jesus Christ. But you know Timothy's proven worth, how as a son with a father he has served with me in the gospel. (Philippians 2:19–22)

Some have speculated that Lucius was Luke the physician (Colossians 4:14) who traveled with Paul to document his missionary journeys and wrote the Gospel of Luke and The Acts of the Apostles. However, this is probably not the case, as Paul says of Lucius and Jason and Sosipater, that they are his kinsman, fellow Jews in Christ. Luke (*Loukas*) is Greek.

Jason and Sosipater are likely Paul's fellow Jews mentioned in Acts 17:5–9 and Acts 20:4, respectively.

Paul often used a scribe to write his letters, perhaps because of his poor eyesight (Galatians 4:15 cf. 6:11), though it was not uncommon to do so; he did occasionally write letters or portions of letters with his own hands, however (Cf Galatians 6:11; 2 Thessalonians 3:17; 1 Cor. 16:21; Col. 4:1). Here Tertius is serving as Paul's scribe.

There is much speculation about the identities of Gaius, Erastus, and Quartus but it is nearly impossible to conclusively determine any more about them. What is most important to know is that they were hospitable and committed to Paul's ministry and Paul's gospel.

In sum, let us be encouraged by the numerous individuals who, at a time when it was dangerous to do so, were following Jesus by following Paul (1 Corinthians 11:1). Christianity was born and blossomed in a particular region of the world, at a particular time in history, and there were particular individuals who lived, preached, served, suffered, and died for Christ.

These, like Paul, were not ashamed of the gospel of Christ for it was and is the power of God unto salvation (Romans 1:16–17).

267. To the Only Wise God Be Glory Forever

Now to him who is able to strengthen you according to my gospel and the preaching of Jesus Christ, according to the revelation of the mystery that was kept secret for long ages but has now been disclosed and through the prophetic writings has been made known to all nations, according to the command of the eternal God, to bring about the obedience of faith— to the only wise God be glory forevermore through Jesus Christ! Amen. —Romans 16:25–27[98]

PAUL CLOSES HIS LETTER WITH A DOXOLOGY, A SHORT EXPRESsion of praise to God; thus, *doxa* (glory) and *logos* (speaking) = *doxologia.* Doxologies are short formulaic expressions that enumerate the particular actions of God which ascribe greatness to him. It is notable that it was a study of the book of Romans that gave birth to the Protestant Reformation; and one of the major themes of the Reformation was *Soli Deo Gloria* (Glory to God alone).

Paul's doxology gives glory to God for strengthening the believers according to "my gospel and the preaching of Jesus Christ." Paul's possessive language is not a claim to the authorship of the gospel. Paul means the good news of righteousness through faith in Jesus Christ that he is preaching.

And although the gospel was proclaimed through the Law and the Prophets of the Old Testament, it was preached with much obscurity compared to the full revelation of God in the person of Jesus Christ. As Calvin notes, it was "indeed to no purpose that Malachi declared that the Sun of righteousness would arise, (Mal. 4:2;) or that Isaiah had beforehand so highly eulogized the embassy of the Messiah."[99]

98. An observant reader will notice we skipped verse 24. Some later manuscripts insert *η χαρις του κυριου ημων ιησου χριστου μετα παντων υμων αμην* (*The grace of our Lord Jesus Christ be with you all. Amen)* but in the earliest manuscripts the expression is not present, suggesting it was a later addition, perhaps a gloss or annotation accidentally inserted into the text when it was copied at a later date. The ESV translators have opted to follow the critical scholarship in their translation. *Stephen's 1550 Textus Receptus: With Morphology* (Bellingham, WA: Logos Bible Software, 2002), Ro 16:24. *The Holy Bible: English Standard Version* (Wheaton, IL: Crossway Bibles, 2016).

99. John Calvin and John Owen, *Commentary on the Epistle of Paul the Apostle to the Romans* (Bellingham, WA: Logos Bible Software, 2010), 555.

But now, as Paul notes elsewhere, "*. . . the fullness of time had come, God sent forth his Son, born of woman, born under the law*" (Galatians 4:4), and the gospel light has been made known to all nations. All nations everywhere are commanded to repent and believe this gospel.

He closes his doxology—and his letter—giving glory to God who is "only wise" and has now revealed the extent of that wisdom through Jesus Christ.

Paul further elaborates on the nature of this wisdom in his letter to the Corinthians:

> Where is the one who is wise? Where is the scribe? Where is the debater of this age? Has not God made foolish the wisdom of the world? For since, in the wisdom of God, the world did not know God through wisdom, it pleased God through the folly of what we preach to save those who believe. For Jews demand signs and Greeks seek wisdom, but we preach Christ crucified, a stumbling block to Jews and folly to Gentiles, but to those who are called, both Jews and Greeks, Christ the power of God and the wisdom of God. For the foolishness of God is wiser than men, and the weakness of God is stronger than men. For consider your calling, brothers: not many of you were wise according to worldly standards, not many were powerful, not many were of noble birth. But God chose what is foolish in the world to shame the wise; God chose what is weak in the world to shame the strong; God chose what is low and despised in the world, even things that are not, to bring to nothing things that are, so that no human being might boast in the presence of God. And because of him you are in Christ Jesus, who became to us wisdom from God, righteousness and sanctification and redemption, so that, as it is written, "Let the one who boasts, boast in the Lord." (1 Corinthians 1:20–31)

www.ingramcontent.com/pod-product-compliance
Lightning Source LLC
LaVergne TN
LVHW010630110826
845149LV00014B/2818